AGRARIAN CRISIS IN INDIA

AGRARIAN CRISIS IN INDIA

Edited by

DR. ANIL KUMAR THAKUR

and

DR. SURENDRA KUMAR

DEEP & DEEP PUBLICATIONS PVT. LTD.

F-159, Rajouri Garden, New Delhi-110027

AGRARIAN CRISIS IN INDIA

ISBN 978-81-8450-160-5

Typeset by S.S. COMPOSERS
3190, Mohindra Park, Shakur Basti, Delhi-110034.

Printed in India at NEW ELEGANT PRINTERS,
A-49/1, Maya Puri, Phase-I, New Delhi-110064.

Published by DEEP & DEEP PUBLICATIONS PVT. LTD.
F-159, Rajouri Garden, New Delhi-110027.
Phones: 25435369, 25440916
E-mail: ddpbooks@yahoo.co.in • ddpubs@gmail.com
Showroom:
2/13, Ansari Road, Daryaganj, New Delhi-110002 • Telefax: 23245122

Contents

Preface

Agriculture is the backbone of Indian economy. It is not only an occupation but also shapes our way of life. All Indian festivals are closely linked with agricultural crops from sowing to cutting. The past of Indian agriculture is glorious; the present is hoary and the future is challenging. Our agrarian economy is facing grave crisis, Some of the crises are natural and some are man-made. Our agriculture is still a gamble with monsoon even after completion of ten Five Year Plans. Flood devastations, drought and fall in rainfall are natural calamities whereas absentee landlordism, defective tenurial system; arbitrary fixation of rent, disparity in the ownership of land; paucity of financial resources, illiteracy and ignorance among farmers, partial implementation of land reform measures, prevalence of semi-feudal system in the rural area, indifferent attitude of the state and union governments; burden of indebtedness; lack of marketing facilities and rampant corruption in the distribution of fertilisers; improved seeds and agricultural tools are some of the glaring causes on account of which the agrarian crisis is deepening day-by-day despite the tall talks of the Government and Planning Commission to achieve 4% agricultural growth during 11th plan period which is stagnating presently at 2% per annum. This anthology is an humble attempt to diagnose the causes of agrarian crisis and to prescribe remedial measures. All research papers selected are from the papers submitted to the Annual Conference of Economic Association of Bihar in which all contributors have analysed the causes of agrarian crisis and its remedies in their own way.

ANIL KUMAR THAKUR
SURENDRA KUMAR

List of Contributors

A.K. Choudhary, Assoc. Professor, Deptt. of Agril. Economics, RAU, Pusa, Samastipur (Bihar).

A.K. Jha, SRF, Deptt of Agril. Economics, RAU, Pusa, Samastipur (Bihar).

Amalendu Kumar, Tirhut College of Agriculture, R.A.U., Dholi, Muzaffarpur.

Anju Singh, Lecturer in Home Science, MAM College, Naugachia, Bhagalpur (Bihar).

Arvind Kumar, Research Fellow, B.R.A. Bihar University, Muzaffarpur.

Ashok Kumar Maji, H.O.D. Economics, K.B. College, Bermo.

Ashwini Kant Jha, Lecturer in IRPM, MAM College, Naugachia Bhagalpur, Bihar.

Bharat Singh, Manager (Projects), National Council of Applied Economic Research, New Delhi.

Bhavna Jha, Lecturer in IRPM, MAM College, Naugachia, Bhagalpur (Bihar).

Bhavna Jha, Professor and Head, P.G. Department of Economics, B.N.M. University (W.C.) Saharsa, Bihar.

Chandrika Prasad, S.P.G., Deptt. of Economics, Nalanda College, Biharsharif, Nalanda, Bihar.

Dalip Kumar, Manager (Projects), National Council of Applied Economic Research, New Delhi.

Dev Raj, Prof. (IB)-*cum*-Examinations Controller, EMPI Business School, New Delhi.

Dinesh Prasad, H.O.D. Commerce, S.G.G.S. College, Patna City, (Magadh University).

Hari Narayan Pd. Singh, Lecturer in Economics, Kisan College, Sohsarai, Nalanda (M.U.).

Indu Rani Kesharwani, Department of Economcs, A.S. Collge, Deoghar.

Jawahar Lal, Lecturers in the Deptt. of Commerce, B.D. Evening College, Patna (Magadh University).

K.K. Agrawal, Lecturer, Deptt. of Commerce, R.B. Jalan College, Darbhanga (Bihar).

Manoj Kumar, Research Scholar, Faculty of Commerce, Patna University, Patna.

Md. Imteyaz Hassan, Research Fellow, B.R.A. Bihar University, Muzaffarpur.

Md. Murshid Alam, Research Fellow, B.R.A. Bihar University, Muzaffarpur.

N.C. Jha, Reader and Head, Deptt. of Economics, Madhupur College, Madhupur, S.K.M.U., Dumka.

N.N. Mahto, Visthapit College, Balidih, Bokaro, Jharkhand.

Nagendra Kumar Jha, Senior Lecturer in Faculty of Commerce, Patna University, Patna.

Pankaj Pursottam,

Parshant Kumar Singh, Research Scholar, Faculty of Commerce, Patna University, Patna.

Pashupati Ray, Department of Political Science, A.S. College, Deoghar.

Pooja, H.O.D. Economics, K.B. College, Bermo.

Priyanka Sinha, Member of the Faculty, Department of Commerce, Patna Women's College, Bailey Road, Patna.

Punam Singh, Lecturer in Sociology, MAM College, Naugachia, Bhagalpur (Bihar).

R.K. Shah, Deputy Controller, Mid-Western Region, Nepalgunj, Nepal.

R.K.P. Singh, Retd. Univ. Professor and Advisor, Farmer Commission, Govt. of Bihar.

Rama Shankar Singh, Tirhut College of Agriculture, R.A.U., Dholi, Muzaffarpur.

Ranjana Sharma, Lecturers in the Deptt. of Commerce, B.D. Evening College, Patna (Magadh University).

S.P. Saha, Head, Deptt. of Commerce, JMDPL Mahila College. Madhubani (Bihar).

Shyam Chandra Gupta, Lecturer and Head, Department of Commerce, J.N. College, Nehra, Darbhanga.

Sofia Fatima, Coordinator, Department of Commerce, Patna Women's College, Bailey Road, Patna.

Syed Alay Mujataba,

Talat Jabeen, Research Fellow, B.R.A. Bihar University, Muzaffarpur.

Tarique A. Sultan, Research Fellow, B.R.A. Bihar University, Muzaffarpur.

Vijay Kumar Yadav, Lecturer in Economics, R.K. College, Madhubani, L.N.M.U., Darbhanga.

Vinay Kumar Singh, Department of Economics, S.M.D. Collge, Punpun.

Vinod Kumar, SRF, Deptt. of Agril. Economics, RAU, Pusa, Samastipur (Bihar).

Wishwanath Kumar, Sr. Lecturer in Economics, S.B.P.G. College, Baragaon.

Introduction

Agriculture is the backbone of our Economy since the ancient era. We find the reference of worshipping agricultural tools, ox and Indra (the God of water and rainfall) even in the *richas* of Rigveda. Agriculture has been not only an occupation but also shapes our way of life and pattern of living. All Indian festivals are linked with our crop pattern. Though the contribution of agriculture in our GDP is consistently declining in the era of planned economic development, still it contributes 19% in our GDP and 56% of our labour force is dependent upon agriculture. Directly or indirectly 68% of our population relies upon agricultural production. As such no plan of economic development can be successful without solving agrarian crisis from which our economy suffers.

Historically the root cause of agrarian crisis is colonial legacy bestowed upon by British imperialism. They implemented defective land relationship and tenurial system to serve their own interest by turning out agrarian economy to produce raw materials for the production of industrial goods in their own country reducing our country as the market of their machine-made goods. They created an intermediate class commonly called Zamindar class. This class remained faithful to the empire and exploited the peasant mercilessly in numerous ways. It was why our leaders of freedom movement took the issue of agrarian crisis in the Karachi session in 1931 held under the Presidentship of Sardar Ballabh Bhai Patel. Since then "land to the tiller" became a popular slogan of freedom movement itself.

In the early years after independence the Union Government asked all State governments to enact land reforms Acts as agriculture was under State subject in the Constitution of India. All states enacted such Acts but in Bihar on account of appeal by the biggest Zamindar of Asia, Darbangha Maharaj, Shri Kameshwar Narayan Singh, the implementation of Zamindari Abolition Act, 1949 was delayed for seven years and was implemented from 1.4.1956. However, it was high achievement because the presence of Zamindars or intermediaries was the highest hurdle in implementing progressive measures to improve agrarian situation.

Land reform measures include three Fs:

(i) Fixation of ownership,
(ii) Fixation of tenure, and
(iii) Fixation of rent.

Even after 56 years of enactment of land reform Acts, the second and third measures have not been implemented in true spirit in most of the States. Many loopholes were kept in the Land Ceiling Acts themselves through which the big landlords succeeded in saving big high plots of land. The reason was, the landlords elected as M.LA. enacted the law for land reforms; their sons as administrators had the responsibility to implement those laws. So, the very feudal characteristic of socio-political structure stood into the path of implementation of land reform measures in most of the states. Of course, West Bengal and Kerala are exceptions to great extent.

The green revolution of mid-sixties increased our food production and we became self-sufficient in food grains but the benefits of green revolution went in the pockets of landlords. The wage of agricultural labours did not increase. The inequality deepened and this led to rural violence culminating into Naxalite movement. The defective land relationship further deepened the crisis. The tragedy is that those who own land, they don't cultivate and those who cultivate land do not possess land. Sharecropping, *Hunda* and *patta* system are prevalent. Absentee landloardism has further accentuated the agrarian crisis. Almost 80% land is owned by upper castes and intermediary castes. Most of the agricultural labourers and marginal farmers belong to SCs, STs and backward sections of society.

In nutshell; our agrarian economy is passing through many sorts of crisis. Our agrarian growth rate is stagnating or a very slow growth of about 2% per annum while the target of 11th plan is 4% per annum growth in agricultural production. The cost of agricultural input is increasing rapidly beyond the reach of marginal and small farmers. Land reform measures have been half-heartedly implemented and that also partially. Minimum agricultural wage Act is not implemented fully. The gap between rich and poor is increasing in rural sector of the economy. The entry of MNCs in agrarian sector has further accentuated the problem. Banks are anti-liberal in granting credit facilities to marginal farmers. They are liberal only to big landlords. In the absence of developed and organised market at village level; the middlemen deprive the poor farmers from the real benefits of their production. To increase production another green revolution is urgently needed covering all crops and all regions, so that the threat on food security could be amicably settled.

In short, there are multi-dimensions of our agrarian crisis. This book is an humble attempt to throw light on all dimensions of agrarian crisis so that solutions of the crisis could be sought in right perspective. The Anthology consists of twenty-four articles covering agrarian problems of Bihar and Jharkhand.

Mr. **Dev Raj** in his article deals with Agrarian Crisis both in Bihar and Jharkhand. Mr. **Ashok Kumar Maji** and **Pooja** while dealing with Agrarian crisis in Jharkhand conclude that eradication of poverty will remain a dream unless heavy public investment is made in agricultural sector. **Ramashankar Singh** and **Amlendu Kumar** deal with crisis of Betal vine growers. It is a micro study and strongly argue for proper marketing facilities for betal vine. Mr. **Ashwani Kant Jha** and Mrs. **Bhavna Jha** give an alternative source of financing to formal credit institutions for sustainable Agricultural Development and observe that credit-marketing and processing could be for mainstream agro-processing such as for food grains, oilseeds, fibres, sugarcane, milk and other livestock products and fisheries.

In Agrarian Crisis: 'A Distress for Vulnerable Section of the Society' **Bhavna Jha, Anju Singh** and **Puran Singh** have concluded that present policies and programmes are not able to protect a sizable section of vulnerable agricultural population from natural and market induced uncertainties. Mr. **Chandriak Prasad** correlates 'Bihar Agrarian Crises through Land Reform' and suggests for consolidation of holdings the implementation of the slogan of 'land to the tiller in true spirit, security of tenancy and proper record of land. Mr. **Dalip Kumar** and **Bharat Singh** examine the relevancy of thoughts of Swami Sahajanand Saraswati involving the agrarian crisis and also trace the history and role of Naxal movements. **Dinesh Prasad, Jawahar Lal** and **Ranjana Sharma** critically analyse processing of food industry in Bihar and observes that in the era of economic liberalisation, a public-private ownership will help in the development of food processing sector in Bihar.

In 'New Strategy of Agriculture in Bihar', Mr. **Hari Narayan Pd. Singh** emphasises the place of rural markets in the new strategies for agricultural development. **Md. Imteyaz Hassan** in his article studies the innovations in Rural Marketing. **Syed Alay Mujataba** and **Pankaj Pursottam** in 'Strategy of Agrarian Crisis in Bihar: Special Reference to Land Reform' deals with exemption of judiciary from the implementation of land reforms and organisation of poor peasantry into a militant race and various measures have been suggested. While dealing with 'Agricultural crises in Bihar and Jharkhand' **Nagendra Kumar Jha, Manoj Kumar** and **Parshant Kumar Singh** conclude that the slogan of development in the State should be now put as agricultural development. In 'Agrarian Crisis of Bihar' it has rightly been observed that a serious crisis has broken out in the field of Bihar agriculture. The crisis is most glaringly manifested in the growing incidence of starvation, deaths and low productivity, heavy indebtedness, cropfailure and no organised market for produce leading to agrarian unrest.

In 'Problems of Agriculture in Bihar and its Remedial Measures', Mr. **Murshid Alam** and **Talat Jabeen** highlight the problems of increase in pressure of population; defective land tenurial system, uneconomic holdings; joint family system, fragmentation and sub-division of holdings poor techniques of productions, inadequate irrigation facilities, flood devastations, lack of marketing facilities, lack of credit and financing facilities, problems of infrastructure, seeds and non-development of agro-based industries and suggest pragmatic measures to solve those problems. Mr. **N.C. Jha** deals with 'Impact of Agricultural Price Policy in Jharkhand's Eco-Development' and suggests that the agricultural price policy in Jharkhand will prove fruitful in the production and starts to yield nearer to all India average.

N.N. Mahto examines agrarian crisis in relation to industrialisation with reference to Bokaro Steel Plant and concludes that the conditions of small and marginal farmers wheresoever and leading to Naxlite movement is Jharkhand. Mr. **Pashupati Ray, Vinay Kumar Singh** and **Indu Rani Kesharwani** have dealt with Economic Reforms and Agriculture and observed that the recent law passed of Rural Employment Guarantee Scheme and the Food for Work Programme, if sincerely implemented and intensified, would not only lead to gradual diversification of labour force but also help in better food distribution and creation of durable rural assets. **R.K. Shah** has analysed Agrarian Crisis in Indian context historically and suggests second green revolution covering all crops and all regions.

Mr. **Shyamchandra Gupta** examines the Role of Commercial Bank in Agricultural Development of Bihar and observes that role of commercial bank in providing agriculture finance is satisfactory. 'Land Reforms: A Dismal Picture in Bihar', **Sofia Fatima** and **Priyanka Sinha** have concluded that the constitution has already been amended 13 times to erase the legal obstacles in the way of land reforms. Even then, a lot has to be done to make the incorporation of land reform, a grand success. In 'Commodity Derivatives Markets and Prospects for Cotton Futures in India', **S.P. Saha** and **K.K. Agrawal** observe that private initiative for the cotton economy can set-up cotton futures. However, a proactive government can hasten things. Mr. **Tarique A. Sultan** and **Arvind Kumar** in 'Land Reform Policy in Bihar: An Overview' have examined land reform measures in historical perspective and observe that effective implementation of tenancy reforms would go a long way in helping implementation of tenancy legislation also.

Vijay Kumar Yadav deals with 'Agrarian Crises in Bihar' and deals with both the problems and measures to solve them. In techno-economic appraisal of 'Winter Maize Revaluation in Bihar', **Vinod Kumar, A.K. Jha, A.K. Choudhary** and **R.K.P. Singh** reveal that winter maize is generating net cash inflow of Rs. 3575 million annually. Besides it creates employment and the condition of agricultural labour improves. It also improves food security along with farmer's exposure to market and helps in reducing labour migration from Bihar. **Wishwanath Kumar** deals with 'A Critical Analysis on Suicides of Farmers and Farm Loan Waivers' observes that loan waiver is the best temporary decision to the problems facing rural India. Significant and sustained improvement in the welfare of the rural people is not possible without a faster pace of growth in the rural economy and improvement in education and other important awareness about health services.

We hope this anthology will be useful to students, teachers, planners and to one who wishes to understand the reasons of agrarian crisis and steps to solve them in India in general and in Bihar in particular.

ANIL KUMAR THAKUR
SURENDER KUMAR

1

Agrarian Crisis in Bihar and Jharkhand

DEV RAJ

INTRODUCTION

Being aware that the widespread poverty in the country, remarked on the mid-night of August 14-15, 1947, Jawaharlal Nehru said that, " everything else can wait, but not agriculture" is even more relevant today for the Bihar and Jharkhand state as there is an urgent need to look into the following points at the earliest, such as: (i) Enlarging the area under assured irrigation; (ii) producing the inputs needed by farmers such as seeds, fertilizers, pesticides; and farm implements. Above all, strengthening of infrastructure in the field of Agricultural research and education are most important. Bihar was reorganised on 15th November, 2000. The total area of Bihar is 94,163 sq. km. and as per 2001 Census the population is 82.88 million. However, the present population of the state is about 90 million of which 37 million are below the poverty line. The population of Bihar to the total population of India works out to 8.07 per cent and

86.86 per cent of the population is living in rural areas prior to reorganization. After the reorganization of Bihar, the rural population has increased to 89.53 per cent to the total population of the state. Bihar is a backward state.

Main Objective of Planning for Agriculture Sector are as under:

- Strengthening of Transfer of Technology;
- Thrust on the Seed development;
- Assurance of Standard Quality of Agricultural Products;
- Natural Resource Management; and
- Special Area Programme.

ANNUAL PLAN: 2008-09: BIHAR STATE

Table 1 gives the details of schemes proposed during the annual plan for Agricultures and Allied activities.

Table 2 gives in details of the draft 11th Five Year Plan for Sector of the Bihar state as under.

From Table 2 under reference, it may be observed that the actual/anticipated expenditure was more that planned outlay. The total outlay was put at Rs. 49,096.87 lakhs, while the actual/anticipated expenditure works out Rs. 59,679 lakhs in the 10th Five Year Plan. When, we look at the outlay of new schemes the allocations works out to 27.10 per cent of the total outlay, while the actual/anticipated expenditures came down only 16.09 per cent of the total expenditure own to lesser efficiency in the state concerned.

In the 11th Five Year Plan the total outlay for agriculture and allied activities has been provided to Rs. 1,69,771, which shows an increase of 35.15 per cent increase over the 10th Five Year Plans' actual expenditure. While, on the new schemes the allocated amount over the actual expenditure in the 10th Plan increased from 16.09 per cent to 51.34 per cent of the total outlay. This seems to be good point to cover the other areas to ensure that the rate of growth of GDP will increase substantial.

The 11th Plan, i.e. 2007-12 for the Bihar State envisages a growth rate of:

TABLE I

Schemes Proposed in during 2008-09: Annual Plan

S. No.	*Scheme Proposed*	*Outlay in 2007-08 (Rs. Lakhs)*	*Proposed in Annual Plan 2008-09 (Rs. Lakhs)*
1	*2*	*3*	*4*
1.	Macro Management Mode of Agriculture Development		1190
2.	Integrated Scheme for Oilseed, pulses, palm oil and Maize (ISOPOM)	15	50
3.	Jute Technology Mission Programme	15	50
4.	Seeds = @BRBN, and State Forms	1247.17 (of which 372 @)	3500 @
5.	Integrated Nutrient Management	1296.50	1000.00
6.	Agriculture Extension	1829.45	1600.00
7.	National Horticulture Mission	975.00	1000.00
8.	Micro Irrigation	Nil	500.00
9.	National Resources and Management	300.00	300.00
10.	Transportation and Handling: changes for N&P Fertilizers	325.00	400.00
11.	Kisan Aayog	23.80	75.00
12.	Tal and Diara Development	109.00	250.00
13.	Strengthening of Training Infrastructure (farmers/extension workers training) incl. Kisan Salahkar Yojna	177.63	700.00
14.	Strengthening and training infrastructure through establishment and strengthening of office building, etc.	177.63	700.00
15.	Agricultural Research and Education	2230.17	2700.00
16.	Rashtriya Krishi Vikas Yojna		10,000.00

Source: Annual Plans: 2007-08 and 2008-09, Planning and Development Department, Govt. of Bihar, pp. 68-74.

TABLE 2

Draft 11th Five Year Plan for Agriculture Sector

(Rs. Lakhs)

S. No.	*Plan*	*Continuing Schemes*	*New Schemes*	*Total Outlay*
1.	10th Plan: 2002-07	36792.28	13304.59	49096.87
	(at 2001-02 prices)	(40177.00)	(19602.00)	(59679)
2.	11th Five Year Plan			
	(2007-12)	102785.00	86986.50	169771.00
	Of which:			
	Annual Plan: 2007-08	17780.33	1766.92	26207.26
		(17760.33)	(7456.92)	(26207.26)
	Annual Plan: 2008-09	41170.14	2393.00	43563.16

Note: Figures in brackets are actual/anticipated expenditure.
Source: 10th and 11th Draft Plans: 2002-07 and 2007-12, respectively Annual Plans: 2007-08 and 2008-09, Planning and Development Department, Govt. of Bihar.

- Agriculture = 5 per cent;
- Industries = 11 per cent; and
- Services = 10 per cent.

Besides, a rate of growth of 5 per cent envisaged for agriculture in the 11th Plan calls for an increased Public Expenditure in Irrigated Flood Control measures. In order to

TABLE 3

Bihar's Annual Outlay for Agriculture: 2008-09

(Rs. Lakhs)

1.	Agriculture	25800
2.	Animal Husbandry	1282.90
3.	Dairy	4407
4.	Fisheries	550
5.	Sugarcane Development	2523.25
6.	Cooperation	9000.00
	Total	23,563.15

attract the private investment, Public Sector investments in infrastructure like: Roads' Power, and Education, etc. have to be increased. In the Annual Plan for the year 2008-09, the Bihar government has provided the outlay for agriculture sector as under:

Agriculture and Allied Sectors

In the states of Bihar and Jharkhand there is an urgent need to take the effective steps in the following areas, such as: (i) Scientific progress represented by the on-going digital, (ii) Biotechnology upgradation; (iii) Space and other technological revolutions; and (iv) the social revolution represented by the 11th Schedule of the Constitution, 73rd Amendment Act to Panchayati Raj. This in turn will call for new revamping and reinforcing of vast National Agricultural Research System, comprising of the Indian Council of Agricultural Research (ICAR), fostering strategic partnerships with relevant advanced research institutions in the States, India and abroad.

Following steps have been taken the State/Central Governments during the recent years for the improvement of Agriculture and Allied sector as under:

- Under the Kishan Sammman Yojna—the best farmer of the state was awarded with "Kisan Ratna" award.
- The Agriculture input subsidy is being given up to 50 per cent at the rate of Rs. 4,000 per hectare.
- Further, for Agriculture—implements/machines, the state government had decided to provide additional 25 per cent subsidy to the existing Central Government rate of 25 per cent subsidy.
- The food grains production increased from 79.60 lakh MT in 2004-05 to 123.97 lakh MT during the year 2006-07. About 1.95 lakhs quintal of seed were processed in the Rabi 2007-08.
- To encourage the agri. Education and research in the state, Bharti Mandan Argiculture College, Saharsa and Horticulture College in Noor-sarai, Nalanda district have been established.

TABLE 4

Physical Targets and Achievements in Agriculture in Bihar State

(Rs. Crores)

Items/Units Cooperatives	*Tenth Plan (2002-07)*		*11th Plan (2007-12)*		*Annual Plan*	
	Target	*Actual*	*Target*	*Actual*	*2007-08 (Outlay)*	*2008-09 (Outlay)*
1. Short-term Credit	2679.00	745.89	3000		223.94	600
2. Long-term Credit	145.18	27.41	0		0	0
3. A: ICDP opening in 7 districts (Godown)	837	341	266		125	141
4. B. ICDP proposed in 21 districts (Godown)	–	–	1680		–	100
FISHERIES						
1. Fish Production (000 Tons)	350	261	600		340	350
2. Fish seed Production (millions)						
(a) Fry/Finger (Nos.)	600	400	550		450	450
PHED						
1. Rural piped water supply						
(a) Continuing (Nos.)	100	69	185		15	70
(b) New and Recognised (Nos.)	150	57	200		10	25
(c) Piped water supply (Nos.)	30	10	0		3	10
2. Piped Water Supply—Semi-urban areas (Nos.)	0	0	50		0	0

- Bihar State Fruit and Vegetable Corporation is being revived.
- To promote horticultural crops in the state, massive orchard expansion programmes called "Naya Bag Lagao Abhiyan" was started in 2007-08.
- Work on Mega project of 4 lakh litres of milk processing was established. Tetra packing of milk project commenced in Bihar Sharif in Nalanda district at a cost of Rs. 12,100 crores.

- More than 700 fish farmers were sent to Andhra Pradesh for 10 days' training at government cost.
- Further, decision was also taken to revive 121 closed hatchery through public-private partnership mode.
- Production of low input breed has been started in Bhagalpur poultry farm.

Bihar is a Crucible in India's Battle against Poverty

I. Bihar with a population of about 90 million, of which 37 million are below the poverty line. While the Bihar accounts for 8.07 per cent of India's population, it contribute only 1.6 per cent of the country's GDP. Its per capita income has averaged a mere 1.5 per cent growth per annum, the lowest among the major Indian states. Bihar has planned for an average of 4.5 per cent to 8.5 per cent in the next Five Year Plan, i.e. 2007-12. Public investment is expected to be around Rs. 600 billion and private sector investment Rs. 1070 billion in the 11th Five Year Plan. At present there are 13,800 Secondary Schools in the state.

II. By 2020—Bihar would require 12-15 thousand of megawatts of electricity. All proposed investment till date would create 7000 megawatt leaving a gap of 5-8 thousand megawatt of electricity. Bihar have to reach 1000 units per capita norm by 2012.

III. Bihar needs 5.40 lakh metric tons of foodgrains per month for Public Distribution System. Owing to inadequate storage capacity only 1.50 to 1.75 lakh metric tons of foodgrains are available for PDS.

World Bank's Initiatives: Bihar and Jharkhand States

In the year 2004-05 when the World Bank reviewed its Country Strategy for India and decided to focus its efforts in the poorest states of the country, the Bank identified Bihar, Jharkhand, Orissa and Uttar Pradesh and initiated the support to these states as a development agenda.

The following initiatives were taken by the World Bank as a projects active in Bihar as under:

1. Reproductive and Child Health II
2. Third National HIV/AIDS Control Project
3. Tuberculosis Control Project II
4. Vocational Training India
5. National Agriculture Innovation Project
6. Disease Surveillance
7. Food and Drugs Capacity Building
8. Lucknow-Muzaffarpur National Highway
9. Grand Trunk Road Improvement
10. National Highways III.

The World Bank has already given lending support to Bihar with a US $ 63 million under Bihar Livelihood Project, named Jeevika to improve the livelihoods of the rural poor in 4,000 villages in the poorest districts of Nalanda, Gaya, Muzzafarpur, Madhubani, Khagaria, and Purnea. It is expected to directly benefit about 2.9 million people belonging to 590,000 households.

MANAGING FLOODS IN BIHAR

Bihar being as flood-prone state, with 76 per cent of the population in north Bihar living under the recurring threat of devastation by floods, the Government of Bihar has identified improvement of flood control as a priority area where they would like the World Bank to help. The World Bank along with the department for International Development (DFID) is providing technical support to the Government of Bihar for flood forecasting and management. A number of initiatives are already been underway to improve the technical and institutional capacity of the state for flood management by developing and implementing a comprehensive Flood Management Information System (FMIS) to support flood control and management through early warning and emergency response systems, a comprehensive flood website, upgrading of hydraulic measurements and telemetry, training and building the capacity of officials and looking at new technological approaches to improve the decision-making process before, during and after a flood takes place. It is expected that to help the state to move from merely responding to a disaster to improved disaster preparedness. Further the World Bank also received a request for a development Policy Loan that will enable the state government to implement its broad development agenda.

Further, it may be mentioned that the Asian Development Bank (ADB), the Department for International Development (DFID), and the World Bank are jointly working to support Bihar's development agenda. Moreover, it is expected that if projects are implemented well they will show immediate results and create much bigger impact in reducing the poverty in the state.

TABLE 5

Per Capita Net State Domestic Product at Current Prices

(Rs. Crores)

S.No.	*Year*	*Bihar*	*Jharkhand*	*INDIA*	*% share to India*	
					Bihar	*Jharkhand*
1.	1999-00	5766	12747	1589672	0.36	0.80
2.	2000-01	6396 (10.9)	10294 (-19.2)	1700467	0.38	0.56
3.	2001-02	6197 (-3.1)	10972 (6.6)	1849360	0.34	0.59
4.	2002-03	6928 (11.8)	11865 (8.1)	1994248	0.35	0.59
5.	2003-04	6913 (-0.12)	12941 (9.1)	2239939	0.31	0.58
6.	2004-05	7467 (8.0)	17493 (35.2)	2526408	0.30	0.69
7.	2005-06	7875 (5.5)	19066 (9.0)	2870750(P)	0.27	0.66
8.	2006-07	—	—	3325817(Q)	—	—
9.	2007-08	NA	NA	NA	NA	NA

Source: Draft Plans: Bihar and Jharkhand States for 10th and 11th Five Year Plans and Govt. of India: Economic Survey: 2007-08.

Fifteenth years into India's economic reforms, the country's poorest state Bihar, is finally gearing itself to catch up with the rest of India. A slew of fiscal and legislative reforms implemented in the recent past stand testimony to this silent transformation taking place in a state that has, for long been stereotyped as a "failed state" in popular public imagination. Bihar is the first state to abolish the Agriculture Product Marketing Control (APMC) Act, thus providing additional avenues to farmers from sale of produce, to repealing the Urban Land Ceiling Act and adopting the Model Municipal Act which is expected to attract organised construction and real estate firms to Bihar, to providing a Single Window Clearance Act, 2006 and a State Investment Promotion Board (SIPB) to facilitate industrial investments, Bihar has indeed come a long way.

What is more, to make a positive impact on the state's financial health, it has also undertaken a number of measures to eliminate the revenue deficit and contain the fiscal deficit in a time-bound manner. Further, financial powers have been decentralized to line departments, and outdated financial rules, particularly with regard to public procurement, have been replaced with those that provide efficiency, transparency and accountability.

Agriculture and Allied Activities in Jharkhand

Total land area under Jharkhand is 79,710 sq. km. with a population of 2.69 crores. There are 28 districts in the Jharkhand state. Projection of the 11th Five Year Plan under the Agriculture are as under:

PROBLEMS OWING TO THE BIFURCATION OF BIHAR

1. Owing to the bifurcation of the Bihar State: Two Projects under education namely North Koel Reservoir Scheme and Batane Reservoir: the head-works are located in Jharkhand, while the area irrigated is mostly in the new state of Bihar. As a result, submergence areas are in Jharkhand and a question arises as to which state will give land for compensatory.

2. The BSCB has brought down the NPAs from 51.56 per cent to 28.67 per cent for availment of Refinance, the NPA s are required to be brought down to 20 per cent, as a eligibility criteria for refinance.
3. To Provide Infrastructure for support: Teachers and Education: the following points are to be taken on an urgent basis for improving the education in the Jharkhand State.
4. Limit of Innovation Project of 50 lacs;
5. For next 5 year plan the state's share should remain 25 per cent instead of 50 per cent.
6. Limit of support for IED children be enhanced.
7. The equally important aspect is balanced regional opportunities as most of the institutions are

TABLE 6

Projection 11th Five Year Plan Under Agriculture and Allied Activities: Jharkhand State

(Rs. Lakhs)

S. No.	*Agriculture and Allied activities*	*Outlay*	*TSP*	*SCSP*
1.	Crop Husbandy	51263	18400	11630
2.	Horticulture	9104	5630	660
3.	Social Conservation	16107	8352	25204.
4.	Animal Husbandry	14972	5345	1545
5.	Dairy Development	29559	17277	3480
6.	Fisheries	6495	3516	800
7.	Cooperation	95704	56600	15060
8.	Agri. Research and Education	17998	15420	–
9.	Other Agriculture Programme			
	(a) Agriculture Programme	1645	810	–
	(b) Capital formation	4272	1860	–
	© State share to CSS	3606	1710	–
10.	TOTAL AGRICULTURE:	251775	135820	35953
11.	TOTAL PLAN EXPENDITURE:	4024000	1740602	411155
12.	AGRCULTURE TO TOTAL PLANNING'S EXPENDITURE:	6.26%	7.80%	8.74%

Source: Draft Annual Plan, 2008-09, Planning and Development Department, Government of Jharkhand.

TABLE 7

Proposed Outlay on the 11th Five Year Plan: Jharkhand on Education

(Rs. Lakhs)

Parameter	Total Outlay, 2007-12			Approved outlay for 2007-08		
	Total Outlay	TSP	SCSP	Total Outlay	TSP	SCSP
1. General Education of which:						
(a) Primary Education	324850	125428	40136	43935	23049	7030
(b) Secondary Education	49430	19085	6107	6870	2369	1099
(c) Higher Education	19683	7725	2081	3040	887	488
Total Education:	4024000	1740602	411155	667600	353624	72996

Source: Draft Annual Plan, 2008-09, Planning and Development Department, Government of Jharkhand.

TABLE 8

Proposed Anuual Plan: 2008-09 Outlay: Jharkhand

(Rs, Lakhs)

Parameter	TotalOutlay (2008-09)	TSP	SCSP
(a) Primary Education	59620	19629	9333
(b) Secondary Education	8470	3639	1325
(c) Higher Education	1910	896	364
TOTAL EDUCATION	70000	24164	11022
Total Planning Outlay:	800000	408239	100535
% Share of Education to Total Plan's Outlay	8.75%	5.92%	10.96%

Source: Draft Annual Plan, 2008-09, Planning and Development Department, Government of Jharkhand.

located on metro/Urban and developed states. A poor and tribal dominated state like Jharkhand lags far behind on account of the colonial higher education policy still persisting in one way or another.

8. Hence, improving access to all and ensuring access to weaker sections and tribals in particular, raising the budgetary allocation for higher education, increase in grants and scholarships for students, building and sustaining quality and finally the regulation of the higher educational institutions in general and those in the private sector in particular, are some of the pressing issues before the Jharkhand state, which need to be urgently addressed at the earliest.
9. Jharkhand is a newly created state infected with many weak features of development, there is an urgent need for a special package to be spelt out in the field of higher education. For this, a continued and well thoughtout policy is urgently needed before allowing the free entry of FDI in the higher education to enable the state to achieve the objective of equity with social justice. For this, a viable and appropriate policy and regulated higher education system to support the objective have to be worked out in brain storming sessions keeping in view the changing global scenario.

CONCLUSION

It has been observed that Bihar and Jharkhand state, both the states could not utilize the amount allocated under the 10th Five Year Plan, i.e. 2002-07 in the expenditure made actually/anticipated there are huge gaps. In the 11th Five Year Plan, 2007-12 seeks to substantially empower and will use the Panchayati Raj Institutions as a delivery mechanisms of the services that are critical to inclusive growth in the plan outlay on Agriculture and Allied Activities. With the Amendments to the Constitution in the 73rd and 74th will led to the establishment of elected institutions of local self-government to ensure efficiency and utilization of allocated amount in the rural areas and the rest in the urban areas. With this the concept of Mahatma Gandhi, i.e. "Local products of the local use" and not only "mass-production but also by the mass-population" will put these states to ensure higher rate of growth in the Agriculture and Allied Activities during the 11th Five Year Plan. It will further increase the Gross Domestic Products of these states, higher rate of growth in the state/s economies, poverty will come down and per capita income and good health will elevate the growth rate of Bihar and Jharkhand. A key feature of the inclusive growth strategy in the 11th Plan is that growth of GDP should not be treated as and end in itself, but only as a means to an end. This can done well by adopting monitor able targets which would reflect the multi-dimensional economic and social objectives of inclusive growth in the states.

2

Agrarian Crisis in Jharkhand

ASHOK KUMAR MAJI AND POOJA

Agriculture provides livelihood support to about two-third of the country's population and continues to be the backbone of the economy. The contours of Indian agriculture started showing improvement gradually after the mid 1960s with the introduction of high yielding varieties, and the growing emphasis on the development of agro-infrastructure like irrigation, input supply, storage, marketing and distribution of food-grains. The revolution, however, was biased towards irrigated regions and the benefits from this were not shared equally amongst all stakeholders across the country. In spite of India's process of economic reforms since July 1991, lack of availability of quality inputs coupled with less vibrant and deficient institutional reforms have continued to plague the Indian agriculture. The time has come to map the existing agricultural infrastructure in the country and to find out the issues and challenges for their speedy resolution. This paper attempts to examine the growth performance of agricultural sector in the country in the post-reform era and tries to offer solution to the issues and challenges faced by agricultural development in India. Efforts have also been made to recommend some strategies which the government has to keep in mind while negotiating in WTO on agricultural issues so as to ensure livelihood security and employment opportunities to the large agrarian population of the country.

Despite a mere 22 percent contribution to the gross domestic product (GDP), agriculture still provides livelihood support to about two-third of the country's population. Agriculture, the single largest private sector occupation provides employment to 56.7 percent of country's work force. Keeping in view the significance of the primary sector in export earning, food security and adequate input supply to the feeder industries like textiles, sugar, rice and flour mills, milk industries, etc. any policy change in this sector, positive or negative, would pose a multiplier effect on the entire economy.

India has taken notable strides in the agricultural sector during the last four decades of economic planning. After remaining a food-deficit country for about two decades since independence, India's effort in self-sufficiency has produced positive results as the food-grain situation in the country changed dramatically. The contours of Indian agriculture started showing improvement gradually after the mid-1960s with the introduction of high yielding varieties (HYV) of crops. The subsequent emphasis was laid on the development of agricultural infrastructure for supply of agro-inputs like irrigation, power, water, seed and fertilizers, creation of storage and marketing facilities and provision of adequate and fair distribution of food-grains.

Innovation in the agricultural technologies and production strategies enhanced public investment in infrastructure, research and development. The green revolution strategies followed much vigor and on a wide scale, especially in those areas which are endowed with irrigation and other agro-infrastructure. However, studies confirm that the spread of green revolution of 1960s and 1990s. In the 1980s new improved crop varieties, technologies and enterprises were developed for rain-fed, dry wet and waste lands which improved the agricultural productivity and income in such regions. In 1990s the deceleration in the agricultural growth was due to the decline in the total factor productivity in various cereals which caused concern amongst planners and researchers in the agricultural fields.

In this backdrop, this paper makes an attempt to examine the growth performance of the agricultural sector of the country, special reference to Jharkhand and tries to offer solutions to issues and challenges facing agricultural development in particular state.

The newly created Jharkhand state was carved out of Bihar and become a state on 15th November 2000. Having an area of 79714 Sq. K.M. Jharkhand has the potential to develop as the financially most viable to ate in the whole country owing to the mineral-based resources and the available industrial infrastructure. The state comprises the district of Ranchi, Gumla, Lohardagga, East Singhbhum, West Singhbhum, Hazaribag, Giridih, Koderma, Chatra, Dhanbad, Pakur, Sahebganj, Simdega, Latehar, Bokaro, Palamu, Garhwa, Dumka, Deoghar, Godda, Saraikela, Kharsawan and Jamtara.

The new state in bordered by Bihar, Madhya Pradesh, Orissa and West Bengal to its north, west, south and east respectively.

The states total geographical area is 79.7 lakh hectares. Out of this cultivable land is 38 lakh hectares and present net sown area is only 18.04 lakh hectares. The net irrigated area is only 1.57 lakh hectares, which is 8 percent of the net sown area. More than 24 percent land is covered by forest area. Jharkhand population is 26,909,428 according to provisional census 2001 figures.

Agriculture is the backbone of the economy of state, as majority of the population depends directly on it. Since many decades, it occupies a place of pride. People get their food from agriculture in various forms, i.e. cereals, fruits, vegetables, etc. Many large and small industries depend on agriculture for raw material. Foreign trade also depends on agriculture as it supplies more for exports. Thus the fact is the core of Indian economy not only Jharkhand.

Having high targets of state's economic growth, agriculture that contributes an important share of state's GDP and 75-80 percent of population depending on it for their livelihoods, its contribution to state's economic development is unmatchable. However, agriculture in our country is characterized by seasonality, perish ability and variability which makes it susceptible to variability which makes it susceptible to vagaries of climate and markets. Due to several of these uncontrollable factors of production, huge risks are recorded in the economic activity of agriculture. Today planners, agricultural scientists and agricultural economists are worried about the slow growth rate of agricultural production in the recent years.

AGRICULTURAL INPUTS: ISSUES CHALLENGES

The slogans like 'food for all', sustainability in agriculture, etc. can be turned into reality only when effective steps are taken to ensure agro-extension services and adequate and timely provision of quality inputs like irrigation, fertilizer, credit seed, power to needy small and marginal farmers. The need of the hour is to enhance productivity and to ensure livelihood security in both irrigated and rain-fed areas. This can be achieved if we ensure more and more public-private partnerships, empower women for their active involvement in agriculture, strengthen agriculture and horticulture through modern innovations and technology revolutions, sustain and expand trade in farm-commodities without neglecting sanitary and phyto-sanitary dimensions of the sector. The rate of quality inputs in the development of state agriculture in the coming periods can not be overemphasized. The following paragraphs describe emerging issues in the usage of agro-inputs and various problems in their effective management.

Irrigation

Growing population, unsustainable land use practices, extensive deforestation, increasing demand of water-intensive industries and agriculture are leading to the fast depletion of world's fresh-water reserves and becoming the basis for many water-related contaminated diseases. The exploitation of natural resources like water has a direct bearing on agricultural productivity, food security and public health. Since this has a direct linkage effect on the environment and society at large, the much anticipated and rapid agricultural progress in an agrarian country like India, requires effective management of this vital agricultural input. Since rainfall in Jharkhand is confined mainly to the southeast monsoon months of June to September and is usually quite erratic, the creation of potential irrigation facilities and achievement of the potential becomes the need of the hour.

Though Jharkhand experiences about 125-150 cm. rainfall annually, frequent. Besides of that it is estimated that in the summer months, nearly 60 percent of total tube wells do not function and most of the ponds, water tanks and other water resources dried up due to fast depletion of water table, less recharge of grand water aquifer. In states like Jharkhand, emergence of frequent erratic rainfall pattern and unsustainable water use in Jharkhand calls for effective management of rain and surface water to ensure sustainability in agricultural production.

Credit

The rural credit system, as we see today, has evolved over the last five and a half decades. During this course, the system witnessed many reforms mainly as the outcome of recommendations of various committees and expert groups appointed by Government of India and RBI from time to time. The agriculture credit system received its first and significant policy directions from All India Rural Committee which recommended new initiatives. The committee recognized the existence of co-operative structure and recommended state financial support for its strengthening. It also recommended the establishment of large sized multipurpose credit societies and nationalization of the Imperial Bank of India (now known as State Bank of India) for extending banking services in rural areas.

Though these steps helped in augmenting the flow of agriculture credit to some extent, credit supply from the co-operatives did not march the demand for credit. It will not be free from bias if we say that the objective of ensuring timely and adequate institutional credit to the needy farmers in the state has been satisfied. Even today many of farmers in the state are still unable to liberate themselves from the clutches of the so-called moneylenders and exploiters. This is more predominant at the situation where a large part of the rural areas are un-banked or are suffering from severe staff-shortage in the existing bank branches.

Seeds

Quality seeds, the basic input for agriculture, accounts for 25 to 30 percent of increment in the crop-yield. In Jharkhand more than 80 percent of the farmers rely on farm-saved seed. The low seed replacement rates results in low productivity. The public sector continues to play a dominant role in production and distribution of low-value high-volume seeds like cereals, pulses and oilseeds whereas high value low volume segment like vegetable and horticulture crops have witnessed private sectors intervention in Jharkhand. The national seed policy of Government of India calls for a convergence between public and private sector. Since the country is one of the signatories of WTO and is regularly negotiating with the developed and developing world on agriculture trade, commerce and plant protection, etc. the time entails an enabling environment not only for promoting quality seed production in India but also to protect rights of farmers and plant breeders by promoting investment in development of new varieties. The farmers and other private players in the agriculture should take advantage of the liberalized and simplified seed export and import regime to facilitate availability of quality seed to the farmers of Jharkhand and help Jharkhand to become a national and global hub for quality seed production.

Fertilizers

There is huge variation in the consumption of fertilizers across states. In the plains, per hectare consumption was high but low in state like Jharkhand. This shows that the poorer the region, the lower the purchasing power and thus the lower the fertilizer use in the agriculture.

CONCLUDING REMARKS

Agriculture, even today, is considered to be a viable

source of livelihood and rural job sector. Food and livelihood security is not only of great economic significance, but also a very important social-political concern in agrarian state, Jharkhand.

In a sense agricultural sector in Jharkhand has been subjected to countless problems. The following are some of the basic problems responsible for this poor state of affairs:

- Low public investment in irrigation and poor maintenance.
- Poor maintenance of rural infrastructure, specially canals and roads.
- Decline in investments in rural electrification and in its availability. This has greatly affected production in eastern India, whereas huge groundwater potential remains untapped.
- Rising level of subsidies for power, water, fertilizers and food are eating into public sector investments in agriculture, besides encouraging inefficient use of scarce resources such as water. This further aggravates environmental problem leading to loss of soil fertility and decline in groundwater, which reduces return of capital.
- Inadequate credit support.
- Stringent controls on movement, marketing, credit, stock and export of agri products that effect their profitability. In the face of pressure from WTO, there is apprehension that without speedy domestic market reforms, an opportunity to capture world markets would be converted into a threat to the future growth of agriculture of Jharkhand.
- Demand constraints (slow growth of the urban economy, restriction on exports) lack of land reforms, failure of poverty alleviation schemes, slow growth in rural wages).
- Controls of the agro-processing industry.
- Poor extensive service.

For the agricultural system to be sustainable, the

productivity of soil must be conserved and maintained. Organic farming is sometimes used as synonyms of sustainable agriculture that give due focus to the enhancement of soil quality. Sustainable agriculture (SA) can be defined as "Agriculture that is productive and profitable, conserve natural resources, protect the environment and enhance public health, food quality, and safety."

The ambition growth rate of 10 percent which is unattainable without bring forth the agrarian society of the country which is the backbone of our economy. So due to stress should be given first and foremost in which majority of the population is engaged, i.e. agriculture. In states particularly in Jharkhand any growth rate is farce without bringing up the agrarian society of which 63 percent live under BPL. Eradication of the poverty and enlistment of the living style of the people is a long distance dream unless new budgetary provision is provided for the all round development of the agrarian society of Jharkhand.

3

Marketing Crisis of Betel Vine Growers: Micro Study in Bihar

RAMA SHANKAR SINGH AND AMALENDU KUMAR

Betel vine (Piper betle L.), being one of the important commercial crops of Bihar and the one: least land, labour, capital intensive crop providing employment throughout the year to over 1.5 million people in the state, facing a lot of problems like lack of an organized market, involvement of middlemen, presence of commission agents, price fluctuation, finance problem, lack of packaging, preservation and storage facilities, inadequate transport infra-structures, etc. causing adverse impact on crop production and its trade and ultimately depriving the growers from their monetary benefits.

INTRODUCTION

Betel vine (Piper betle L.) is one of the important commercial crops of India, Bangladesh, Srilanka, Malaysia, Singapore, Thailand and Philippines. In India, it is extensively grown in the states of Bihar, Bengal, Assam, Karnataka, Tamil Nadu, Kerala, Orissa, Andhra Pradesh, Maharastra, etc. Bihar

(3200 ha) ranks fifth in acreage while Karnataka (8700 ha) remains on top (V.R. Balasubrahamanyam, 1994). It is grown over an area of 50,000 hectares. The annual turnover of betel vine is estimated at Rs. 10,000 million providing livelihood to several lakhs of families engaged in its cultivation and trade. This crop also earn foreign exchange of about Rs. 7000 millions every year in the country through export of its leaf. In Bihar, two major varieties of this crop is grown namely—'Deshi' and 'Magahi'. It is the least land intensive crop cultivated in bareja. Only about 15 desimals of land is considered as an economically viable unit that can provide a livelihood of five family members over 15 years. Cultivation of betel vine is highly labour and capital intensive (Meenakshi Sundaram, 1987) and it provides employment throughout the year both in the production and marketing. The average cost of cultivation in Bihar is about Rs. 96664.14 and the estimated net income (annual) is over Rs. 50,000.00 per hectare. The cost of production per hectare has been estimated at about Rs. 391.30 per 10,000 leaves (50 dholi) and gross and net income per hectare as Rs. 1,51,945.55 and Rs. 55281.41, respectively (Amalendu Kumar, 2007). In the state, the annual turn over from this crop is estimated to be about Rs. 100 crores and more than 1.5 million people are engaged as labourers and traders. It is a shade loving, evergreen, perennial leaf. It has been cultivated in India for centuries and has got social, cultural, religious as well as medicinal values over the years but it is mainly used for chewing purpose. In course of time, offering betel vine as "bida" has become a symbol of offering and acceptance of mutual love and friendship. It is good for respiratory system and also used for the treatment of bronchitis, cough and cold. Fresh crushed leaves are used as antiseptic for cuts and wounds. It's root is used to prevent child bearings. It is hot, acrid, bitter, astringent, aromatic, carminative, stimulant and aphrodisiac and it is also used for to relieve cerebral congestion and satyriasis (S.G. Joshi). Leaves contain good amount of vitamins (vit-B and vit-C), carotene, aminoacids, essential oils and asperagine. When betel vine leaf is taken with tobacco for chewing purpose; mouth cancer has been seen very common as serious health hazards.

As the growers of betel vine are facing a lot of problems regarding production as well as marketing of their produce, an study was conducted to identify the various constraints encountered by the growers in the state.

METHODOLOGY

This study is based on the primary data collected from the two districts namely: Bhagalpur and Vaishali in Bihar. The details of the sampling procedure and selection of sample growers are being presented below:

The reference year of the study was July 2003 to June 2004.

TABLE I

Sampling Procedure

Stage I		*District-I Bhagalpur*		*District-II Vaishali*
Stage II	Block-I Kahalgaon	Block-II Pirpaiti	Block-I Hazipur	Block-II Bidupur
Stage III	Village-I Bhawanipur	Village-II Tarwa	Village-I Chhoti Yusufpur	Village-II Daudnagar

TABLE 2

Selection of Sample Growers

Selected Villages	*Total number of Growers under the Villages*	*Number of Sample Growers*	*Percentage of Sample Growers to the total Growers*
Bhawanipur	126	19	15.07
Tarwa	134	20	14.92
Chhoti Yusufpur	109	17	15.59
Daudnagar	115	18	15.65
Total	484	74	15.28

RESULTS AND DISCUSSIONS

This section of the study analyses the constraints faced by the betel vine growers. The selected growers were asked to indicate the constraints through a suitably designed schedule. The information collected by interviewing the selected 74 growers was tabulated to identify the most important constraints of betel vine production in the sampled areas. These were categorized into two broad categories, i.e. Agro-biological constraints and economic constraints. The agro-biological constraints included severity of diseases, pests, rain, and winds, lack of improved vine cuttings technique of this highly perishable betel leaves. The economic constraints included inadequacy of capital, high cost of bareja, labour, irrigation, vine cutting, fertilizers and pesticides, inadequate market facilities and adverse price fluctuation.

The collected data were analyzed and average rank of all the identified constraints was determined and presented in Table 3 which clearly showed that under biological constrains, growers reported higher percentage in case of severity of diseases, the major problem in production of betel vine as reported by 77.02 per cent growers. In both the sampled areas, almost cent per cent growers were using their traditional planting material since long. Most of the growers were growing the crop with their indigenous knowledge, skill and their past experiences. They were unaware regarding the improved method of cultivation, etc.

The table further revealed that the second most important constraints faced by the growers were the severity of pests (48.65) but the majority of the growers were not knowing the specific pests and pesticides. They were using the pesticides on the recommendation of the local sellers. The third most important constraints reported by the growers was perishability of betel vine leaves (41.89). The other constraints were: severity of winds (40.54), rain (37.84), non-availability of good planting materials, etc.

Under economic constraints, inadequate marketing facilities (71.62%) to growers was reported as the most important constraint especially in Bhagalpur District where there was no organized market within 25 kilometers from the sampled areas allowing middlemen involvement causing low sales proceeds of betel vine growers due to price spread and increase in market margin. The second most important constraints reported by the growers was, lack of capital as the crop requires heavy capital investment.

It was found that not a single grower obtained crop loan from any institutional agencies in both the sampled areas forcing growers to go to non- institutional agencies for loan like middlemen, traders, neighbors, etc. who purveyed loan to the growers against the advance sale of their produce usually offering a price much below the prevalent market price or charging high interest rate.

The third most important constraints as reported by the betel vine growers was high cost of irrigation. As the crop requires sufficient moisture throughout the year especially during summer season and for newly planted crop in

TABLE 3

Constraints of Betel Vine Growers

Sl. No.	*Constraints*	*Number of Growers responded*	*Growers response (%)*
A.	**Agro-biological**		
	1. Disease severity	57	77.02
	2. Pest severity	36	48.85
	3. High perishability	31	41.89
	4. Wind severity	30	40.54
	5. Rain severity	28	37.84
	6. Non-availability of good Planting materials	19	25.67
B.	**Economic**		
	1. Inadequate marketing facilities	53	71.62
	2. Lack of capital	52	70.27
	3. High irrigation cost	47	63.51
	4. High cost of bareja construction	43	58.11
	5. High cost of labour	41	55.41
	6. Price fluctuation	36	48.65
	7. High fertilizer cost	32	43.24
	8. High pesticide cost	23	31.08

particular, which requires two to three times irrigation daily for three to four initial months. During summer also, irrigation is given at weekly interval. High construction cost of bareja was the fourth most important constraints as the cultivation of betel vine totally depends on bareja construction ensuring high humidity and moderate temperature throughout the year for the crop. High labour cost, fluctuations in prices, high cost of fertilizers and pesticides, etc. were the other prominent constraints reported by the growers in the sampled areas.

MARKETING CONSTRAINTS

It is known that the betel leaf is highly perishable commodity and it does not last long. It has very low endurance against adverse weather conditions. At the same time, even a little damage to the leaf makes it defective leading to reduction in its demand. Consequently, its price decline sharply and problems occur in its marketing. Different types of constraints encountered by the growers during the marketing of betel leaf has been presented in Table 4.

This table showed that the most serious constraint in marketing of betel vine was the price fluctuation as reported by cent per cent growers (100%) followed by lack of organized marketing (97.29%), lack of current market information (94.59%), lack of procurement centre at village level (90.84%), lack of transport infrastructure (85.13%), lack of financial assistance (83.76%), bumper harvest (82.43%) reduces market price, distantly located market (79.73%), lack of proper packaging facilities (78.83%) and lack of storage facilities (44.59%) in descending order of severity of constraints. Lack of unity amongst the growers, lack of Self-Help Groups of growers, lack of pharmaceutical industries, etc. were the other important marketing constraints affecting directly or indirectly.

The other reasons behind low remunerative prices received by the growers are the presence of other competitive products like gutka, tobacco, pan parag, etc. and poor advertisements highlighting the health benefits and medicinal

TABLE 4

Constraints Faced by the Growers in Marketing

S.. No.	*Constraints*	*Number of growers responded*	*Growers response (%)*
1.	Price fluctuation of betel vine	74	100
2.	Lack of organized marketing	72	97.29
3.	Lack of market information	70	94.59
4.	Lack of procurement centre at village level	67	90.54
5.	Lack of transport infrastructure	63	85.13
6.	Lack of institutional finance	62	83.76
7.	Bumper harvest of the crop	61	82.43
8.	Far away market	59	79.73
9.	Lack of technical know-how	58	78.38
10.	Lack of storage facilities	33	44.59

values of betel vine. It may also be noted that despite of being highly risk prone crop, there is no provision of insurance facility for the crop. In addition, there is no change/increase in the selling price of betel leaves since long whereas the cost of inputs involved in its cultivation and marketing has been increasing gradually over the years. It was also observed that the price variation between assembling and consuming in the market is very high and the prices tend to increase with the increase in distance.

CONCLUSION

On the basis of overall analysis it can be concluded that marketing is the most important constraints for the growers. Lack of organized market ensures entry of middlemen who fix the prices causing adverse and uneconomic low price realization by the growers. Lack of market information makes the growers dependent on the information supplied by the traders. Lack of improved packaging facilities and use of traditional materials and methods followed resulting in damage of betel leaves during transportation. During peak season or bumper harvest of the crop when supply exceeds the demand, decrease in prices arrests the benefits of better crop of the growers. Lack of modern storage and preservation facilities worsen the situation further. Commission agents without their any contribution on the production farm, in fact, control the market robbing the major share of benefits accrued to the growers.

References

Amalendu Kumar (2007). Economics of Production and Marketing of Betel vine in Bihar; Agro-Economic Research Centre for Bihar and Jharkhand (Ministry of Agriculture, Govt. of India); T.M. Bhagalpur University, Bhagalpur.

Meenakshi Sundaram (1987). An Economic Analysis of Production of Betel Vine in Tamil Nadu, *Agriculture Situation in India*, Vol. XII, No. 1, December.

S.C. Joshi, "Medicinal Plants" (Edited book). Oxford and IBH Publishing Co. Pvt. Ltd., New Delhi, p. 307.

V.R. Balasubrahamanyam (1994). "Betel vine" (Edited book). National Botanical Research Centre, Lucknow, pp. 6-7.

4

An Alternative Source of Financing to Formal Credit Institutions for Sustainable Agricultural Development

Ashwini Kant Jha and Bhavna Jha

INTRODUCTION

Concerns for rural 'credit' are age old and universal. But they seem to have emerged more from the empathy for agriculture and its people rather than better scientific temper to understand the role of 'credit'. Following Desai and Mellor 1993 this temper may be articulated somewhat as follows: The need for external financial services arises from three basic reasons. One, there is a lack of simultaneity between realisation of income and act of expenditure. In other words, these two do not arise at the same point in time. This gap for farmers results from their incomes being once or twice in a year though their expenditure is more continuous. But it also arises for other entrepreneurs such as agri-business firms. So the difference in the need for external finance between these two groups is more of degree rather than kind. Two there is a problem of indivisibility of fixed capital such as wells and pump sets, water harvesting structures, tractors, processing machinery or a storage godown all of which requires large expenditure that cannot be divided into smaller payments unless loan is available. And three, there are stochastic surges in capital needs and savings that accompany technological innovations for agriculture. Adoption of such innovations itself is facilitated by loan when there is cash deficit and/or lump sum large expenditure on productive inputs and assets. And when that results into cash surplus deposit service needs arise. To put it differently, credit service is needed when investment surge follows the savings surge, and deposit service is needed when latter follows the former.

Thus, while first of these three reasons implies that credit can fill in the cash deficit period, the other two imply that credit and deposit services must "follow or accompany" but "not precede" technical change. The external financial services cannot sustain for agriculture that is stagnant and under out-dated technology (Dantwala, 1966 and Dandekar 1993). In the language of project appraisal returns to these services being low and uncertain they cannot fructify nor can they sustain. In macroeconomics language the engine of agricultural growth is technology-embodied (working) capital. And in the operational language of RFIs this implies 'credit' be combined with new technological inputs and/or assets such as HYV seeds, fertilisers, water harvesting resources, etc. and also the new knowledge as an input to use them scientifically.

ROLE OF BANKERS IN AGRICULTURAL DEVELOPMENT

Bankers and technologists must collaborate and co-operate in promoting external financial service needs of agriculture. Just as the current emergence of hi-tech branches of the nationalised commercial banks is a step in the right direction, such a collaborative co-operation including through inducting adequate technical personnel in RFIs for the hard-core agriculture that centres around foodgrains, food and fibre enterprises is.

Another role of the bankers is to view rural sector that requires both credit and deposit services rather than one and the other. And in extending these services the sequence is that RFIs must "accompany or follow" rather than "precede" technology.

The third role, the bankers have, is to constantly keep balancing their goals of profitability, solvency and liquidity for their institutions rather than view each of these or even developmental objectives in isolation. It is this type of role that would assist them resolve the dilemmas that may arise in their pursuit of commercial and developmental objectives.

Lastly, conventionally RFIs have viewed rural 'credit' as "supervisory credit" which is perhaps induced by the perception that farmers are irrational and (hence) misuse loans. This must, however, change to "counselled-credit" (Padmanabhan, 1988). This is because irrationality hypothesis has now been widely refuted and misuse of loans is intractable given the fungibility of credit. Moreover, "supervisory-credit" implies a "holier than thou" attitude (Padmanabhan, 1988). But "counselled-credit" approach has a subtle recognition that illiteracy is not equivalent to lack of practical knowledge that the village folks have in ample measure. Such a recognition has also in turn a room for bottom-up and self-directed rather than top-down and exogenously induced rural credit model or manage.

Agriculture is the single largest private sector in which decision makers are rational, efficient and responsive to change under given agro climatic resources, and agrarian and technological structures. Most of the 109 million farm-households are owner-operators. Tenant farmers are more in Eastern India. But even this region has of late an accelerated growth in crop-yield and agricultural production in general (Saha and Swaminathan, 1994). Long-term agricultural production growth in post-Independence period was 3 per cent per annum, while it was less than 0.2 percent in 50 years prior to Independence (Blyn, 1966). Growth rate in post-Independence period was also higher than 2 per cent growth in population. Indeed, agricultural growth in 1970s and 1980s has become broad-based in terms of crops/enterprises, farms, and regions (Sawant and Achutan, 1995, Sawant, 1997 and Ray, 1998). Annual compound growth rate of crop-output during mid-1980s to mid-1990s was 3.58 per cent. Milk production growth was 4.5 per cent per annum, while annual meat production growth was 7.6 per cent and egg production growth was 5.68 per cent during the same period (Ranjhan, 1997). Fisheries sub-sector had also better growth during this period; it being 6.71 per cent for inland fisheries and 6.18 percent for marine fisheries (Dehadrai, 1997).

REACH OF THE POOR BY RFIS

The failure of co-operative credit institutions to meet the growing rural credit needs is revealed by the All India Debt and Investment Surveys. As per these surveys the share of institutional credit in total rural credit was merely 7.2 per cent for rural households in 1951-52 and it rose to 18.1 per cent in 1961-62. Lack of coverage of rural households by the co-operative institutions led to the nationalisation of commercial banks in 1969 so as to extend their credit to rural households. The increasing emphasis on *priority* sector lending and targeting poor and weaker sections lead to the emergence of Regional Rural Banks in 1975. These developments have no doubt helped in widening the access of rural households to institutional credit and increasing the total flow of formal credit to agriculture in particular. As of 1991-92 the share of informal institutions in rural credit has increased to 64 per cent. Yet the formal credit institutions shied away from loaning to poor because of high transaction costs, perceived risk due to absence of collateral securities, etc. In 1990-91 about 60 per cent of the rural poor households comprising marginal farmers, landless labourers and rural artisans are left out of the formal credit system. As of 1990-91 out of 63 million operational holdings below 1 hectare of land only less than 25 per cent of them had access to agricultural credit from the formal institutions. Therefore, they continued to depend on informal agencies by paying exorbitant rate of interest.

Micro-fianance Access and Outreach in Rural India

Micro-Finance: Coverage of Rural Household (1994)	
1. Total Rural Households (in lakhs)	1186.3
2. Total Number of Accounts of Credit Institutions (in lakhs)	465.9
a. Scheduled Commercial Banks and RRBs	323.1
b. Primary Agricultural Credit Societies	137.0
c. Primary and State Land Development Banks	5.8
Micro-Finance: Coverage of Operational Holdings (1990-91)	
1. Number of Operational Holdings below 2 hectare (in lakhs)	820.7
1.1 Number of Loan Accounts below 2 hectare (in lakhs) of which:	238.4
a. Term Loans	179.5
b. Term Loans	58.9
2. Number of Operational Holdings above 2 hectare (in lakhs)	232.1
2.1 Number of Loan Accounts above 2 hectare (in lakh) of which:	91.3
a. Short-Term Loans	72.0
b. Term Loans	19.3

Source: Kaladhar, K., Micro-finance in India: Design, Structure and Governance, *Economic and Political Weekly*, October 18, 1997.

EVOLUTION OF SHGs AS A RE-EMERGING CONCEPT

The rural households demand for credit has been growing due to their limited land resources and poor technology and hence small base of their economic activity on one hand and growing family size, increased consumption requirements, social obligations, etc. on the other. The institutional agencies lack the required mechanism to assess their credit needs and perceive that most of it is for non-productive purposes. Another reason is that Rural Financial Institutions (RFIs) hesitate to monitor large number of small accounts with potential risks that arise due to clients inability to provide collateral security. All these led to evolving supplementary credit delivery mechanism by lending at a group level—the Self Help Groups (SHGs) concept came into existence. And in so doing, NGOs in some areas played a very important role.

Some Basic Characteristics of SHGs Promoted by NGOs

1. Organisation	Homogeneity in terms of economic/socio-economic status, common identity of activities etc.
2. Nature of Target Groups	Generally poor and weaker section of the people in rural areas.
3. Management rotated.	Selected/elected leader and duly generally Holds meeting regularly.
4. Financial Instruments	
a. Common Fund	Created out of savings, interest earned on loan, bank loans, donations, etc.
b. Savings	While in certain cases no fixed rate of savings, in some cases mobilization regular and fixed rate of savings, and in some cases as per capacity of the members.
c. Loaning	Decided by the purpose, quantum and the resources available with the SHGs. Purpose of loans for individuals include consumption, clearing outside debt, social, medical, education, business,.agriculture, etc. and loans for common production activities.
d. Repayment Period	Shorter than those prescribed by banks.
e. Rate of Interest	Varies from 12 to 60 per cent. In few cases the interest rates are determined by the NGOs.
5. Linkage with Banks	Banks treat SHGs but not their individual members as borrowers.

PRELIMINARIES

In a national level committee though most members were impressed with the past experiences with the SHGs they were unanimous not to recommend target-oriented approach to this programme of linking SHGs with the formal RFIs. This is to avoid the pitfalls of being caught in the managerial approaches that are implied by this concept being either a "mode" or "strategy" when it is implemented. It is also to avoid disreputing the concept of informal self-help group which has a long and successful history in India with "Such potential advantages as scale economies, peer pressure, etc." despite potential demerits like collusion.

HISTORICAL BRIEF OF SHGs

Informal self-help groups oriented to saving and credit functions are not a new phenomenon. Some form of credit instruments were in operation even before 1904 when the Co-operative Credit Societies Act was passed. Credit instruments such as *Mdhisand Chit Funds* were popular especially in South India. While Nidhis are mutual loan associations, *Chit Funds* are voluntary associations for mobilising rural savings. *Nidhis began* in South India by the middle of 19th century. They had several distinguishing features such as encouraging thrift, mobilising small savings and inculcating in the members habit of punctuality and planning for future. *Chit Funds* also aimed at a system of building mutual help, confidence and strength among small groups of people. The *Madras Provincial Banking Enquiry Committee* (1930) as well as the Travancore Enquiry Committee (1930) referred the useful role played by Nidhis and Chit Funds in the rural areas of Kerala and Tamil Nadu as an important source of credit to people with moderate needs.

GENERAL FEATURES OF SHGs AND ROLE OF NGOs

SHGs are voluntary associations of people formed to attain certain collective goals, which could be economic, social or both. Since SHGs are informal groups their legal status has not been defined. What they initially intended was to bring together people particularly economically weaker sections and to undertake activities of mutual interest. However thrift, credit and income generating activities emerged as the major activities of the SHGs. In other words, the SHGs evolved a system for collective savings, group consumption credit, as well as integrating social and economic goals among small groups. The initial growth in SHGs has been in areas where they received support from NGOs. NGOs supported not only for the formation of SHGs but identifying economic activities, imparting training, and even financial support in the initial stage.

DIFFERENT MODELS OF SHGs LINKAGE ENVISAGED BY NABARD

Model I

The bank may provide credit in bulk directly to the groups irrespective of the group being formal or informal but mostly to the latter. The group in turn would undertake on lending to its members on terms agreed upon mutually among them. The quantum of credit given to the group should be in proportion to the saving mobilised by the group, saving credit ratio varying from 1:1 to 1:4 depending upon the assessment of capabilities of SHG by the bank.

Model II

In situation where local branch does not have adequate confidence in lending to the SHGs or where the latter for certain reasons is unwilling to be linked directly to the bank, the bank may finance such SHGs through an NGO that has promoted them, if the NGO is willing to borrow. In such cases, bulk financing of the NGO could be considered. Where this alternative is preferred, the local bank should closely observe the working of the SHG by attending its meetings and through other means, so that the branch may develop necessary confidence in the SHG and link up with it directly at the end of the period of bulk financing arrangement with the NGO.

Model III

In the event of some members requiring loans of larger size than would normally be feasible under the saving linked loaning to the SHG, the group could appraise the requirement of the individuals and recommend the proposal to the bank for direct lending to the respective individual members. The SHG shou ld however be willing to accept responsibility for ensuring proper end-use of credit and timely repayment. In such a case, as also in those where SHGs apply for loan for creating common service facilities or for certain collective activities, the bank loan as well as refinance assistance would be governed by usual terms and conditions (NABARD, 1995).

NABARD's PILOT PROJECT ON SHGs

National Bank for Agriculture and Rural Development (NABARD) supported and funded in 1986-87 Mysore Resettlement and Development Agency (MYRADA) sponsored action-research project on saving and credit management of SHGs. This experience yielded useful insight into aspects like dynamics of group organisation, saving potential, approach to use of financial resources including external funds, priorities of needs, repayment performance, etc. The insights from the action-research project lead to a wider survey on SHGs by NABARD. This survey was conducted in 1987 covering about 50 SHGs spread over different parts of the country. The basic objective of the survey was to study the composition of SHGs, nature of activities undertaken, nature of dealings with banks if any. A sizeable number of these SHGs was undertaking saving mobilisation and credit dispensation. These studies provided valuable insights and encouraged NABARD to explore the possibilities of establishing linkage between SHGs and banks. Since the saving and credit operations of these groups have considerable departure from the traditional banking norms, NABARD held extensive consultations with Reserve Bank of India, commercial banks, NGOs, etc. and launched a pilot project linking SHGs with commercial banks in 1991-92. Subsequently, the linkage project was extended to cover co-operative banks and regional rural banks.

The pilot project had the following major objectives. First, to evolve supplementary credit strategies for meeting the credit needs of the poor by combining informal credit system with the strength of the technical and administrative capabilities and financial resources of the RFIs. Second, to build mutual trust and confidence between the bankers and the rural poor; and finally to encourage banking activity both on the thrift as well as credit among those whom usually the RFIs found it difficult to cover. The project envisaged that the link between the two would be advantageous to both the banks and SHGs. The banks would benefit in terms of reduction in transaction cost, better loan recoveries, mobilisation of large savings, etc. SHGs would benefit in terms of large quantum of financial resources, better technology and skill upgradation through different schemes of the banking sector.

Highlights of the Progress of SHGs All India

1.	Number of SHGs linked during 1998-98	18678
2.	Cumulative number of SHGs linked up to March 1999	32995
3.	Percent of Women Groups	84
4.	Number of Familiar Covered: Cumulative	560000
5.	Number of Participating Banks	
	a. Commercial Banks	202
	b. Regional Rural Bank	129
	c. Co-operative Banks	35
6.	Number of States or UTs Covered	24
7.	Number of Districts where SHGs were linked	280
8.	Number of NGOs Participating	550
9.	Bank Loan released (Rs. Million)	570
10.	NABARD finance released (Rs. Million)	520
11.	Loan per family (Rs.)	1019

Source: Y.C. Nanda, Role of Banks in Rural Development in the New Millennium, National Bank for Agriculture and Rural Development, Mumbai, January 2000.

The criteria for selection of the SHGs proposed by the NABARD involved the following major considerations. The SHG should have been active at least for past six months and must have successfully undertaken saving and credit operations; groups should be functioning in a democratic manner; banks should be convinced of the genuineness of the group formation and its objectives; the members of the SHG should have a homogenous background and interest; the group strength should be between 10 and 20; the group should be maintaining proper accounts and records; and finally the interest of NGO which promoted the group must be evident in a sustained manner. In order to facilitate smooth implementation the banks were advised to launch the linkage project in clusters of blocks or districts rather than in isolated locations.

Some Recent Findings of Programme of SHGs and Bank Linkage

The following observations are based on a study on SHGs linkages conducted during 1997. The study covered macro data on SHGs as well as at the bank branch level data. These bank branches included five nationalised banks and three RRBs located in southern, eastern and central regions of the country. The findings are: (i) 69 per cent of SHGs linked as on March 31, 1996 were in southern states of Andhra Pradesh, Karnataka, Kerala and Tamil Nadu, (ii) commercial banks accounted for 64 per cent of the linked SHGs followed by 35 per cent by RRBs and barely 1 per cent by cooperative banks, (iii) Nearly 85 per cent of the SHGs linkage was achieved through intermediation of NGOs, (iv) most of the members joined SHGs to make savings with their safe custody, while availing personal credit such as for consumption, emergency, education and in some cases production purposes was more important reason, (v) sixty-seven per cent of the SHGs studied took loans, (vi) in all the nationalised banks more than 70 per cent of the SHGs were credit linked, while in RRBs it was around one-third. But majority of the SHGs had less than 25 per cent of the members availing loans, (vii) Seventy-eight per cent of the SHGs were women groups, (viii) most of the SHGs members were below poverty line, (ix) modal size of membership of SHGs was up to 10, (x) mode for SHGs with savings per member was more than Rs. 25, (xi) amount of loan per SHG varied from Rs. 463 to Rs. 15,980. The amount of loan per member varied from Rs. 4 to Rs. 360, (xii) modal interest rate for SHGs was 24 per cent with over 62 per cent of them paying this rate, while another 32 per cent of them paying 15 per cent, (xiii) loan recovery rate of SHGs was more than 75 per cent, though modal value for SHGs for which data are available it was 97 per cent, and (xiv) there was lack of unanimity about the interest in this programme in the top, middle and lower levels of management in the Commercial Bank.

Future opportunities for rural credit for farmers (i.e. APS) include production (i.e. working capital) loans for agriculture and allied sectors and investment loans just not for tractors and irrigation but also for water harvesting structures, land levelling, soil conservation, more efficient equipments for irrigation, and also for livestock and fisheries. Such credit for agri-input business sub-system (AIS) may not be just for farm input manufacturers of large size but also for those who are small sized and for those who are in input marketing business which is often located in district and thesil towns and sub-towns. And credit for agro-marketing and processing sub-system (AMPS) could be for main-stream agro-processing such as for foodgrains, oilseeds, fibres, sugarcane, milk and other livestock products, and fisheries. These industries need working capital as well as term loans for their modernisation.

References

Blyn George (1966). Agricultural trends in India: 1891-1947: Output Availability and Productivity. Philadelphia: University of Pennsylvania Press.

Dehadrai, R.V. (1997). Growth in Fisheries and Agriculture: Resources and Strategies. In *Agricultural Development Paradigm for the Ninth Plan Under New and Anomie Environment,* (ed.) Bhupat M. Desai. New Delhi: Oxford and IBH Publishing Company Private Limited.

Desai, Bhupat. M.A. Study of SHGs and Linkage Programme: A Review.

Indian Journal of Agricultural Economics, January-March, 2000. (forthcoming) Ghatak Subrata. *Rural Money Markets in India.* Mcmillan Company India Limited, New Delhi, 1976.

Institute of Financial Management and Research, *Chit Funds and Finance Corporations,* Madras, 1975 .

Gopal Karkal. *Unorganiscd Money Markets in India.* Lalvani Publishing House, Mumbai, 1967.

Karmakar, K.G. *Rural Credit and Self Help Groups: Micro-finance Needs and Concepts in India.* Sage Publication, New Delhi, 1999.

NABARD. Linking Self-Help Groups with Banks: An Indian Experience, Mumbai, 1995.

NABARD. Reserve Bank of India's Working Group on Non-Governmental Organizations and Self-Help Groups Report, Mumbai, 1995.

Nanda, Y.C. *Role of Banks in Rural Development in the New Millennium.* National Bank for Agriculture and Rural Development, Mumbai, 2000 .

Rao, Dinker K. and Rajaram Dasgupta. *A Study of SHGs and Linkage Programme,* National Institute of Bank Management, June 1999.

Ray, S.K. (1998). Sources of Change in Crop Output. New Delhi: Institute of Economic Growth, University Enclave. March (unpublished).

Sawant, S.D. (1997). Performance of Indian Agriculture with Special Reference to Regional Variations. *Indian Journal of Agricultural Economics,* 52:3, July-September.

Sawant, S.D. and C.V. Achutan (1995). Agricultural Growth Across Crops and Regions: Emerging Trends and Patterns. *EconomIc and Political Weekly;* 30:12, March 25.

5

Agrarian Crisis: A Distress for Vulnerable Section of the Society

Bhavna Jha, Anju Singh and Punam Singh

The latest official statistics on poverty (1999-2000) suggest that nearly 26 per cent of our population is below the poverty line. Non-official estimates generally suggest a much higher proportion. Practically all estimates of poverty, official or non-official, indicate that incidence of income poverty is more in rural areas than in the urban areas, and this difference has persisted over time. Translated into the number of people below the poverty line, even on the basis of official estimates, nearly 193 million of the rural people in our country are poor. According to another estimate, the figure could be as high as 209.4 million (Sen and Himansu, 2004). For a country which is aiming at poverty alleviation for the last fifty years or more, these are not, to say the least, comforting figures.

Apart from the relatively large population of households suffering from low incomes, rural households also suffer from deprivations in terms of education and health. The discrepancy is much wider when it comes to the girl child. The indicators such as life expectancy, infant and child mortality and child malnutrition are appallingly high. It can be safely presumed that the incidence of all such deprivations is more severe among the rural poor.

There is a large concentration of the chronically poor in certain regions. Over 70 per cent of India's poor are located in six states, i.e. undivided Uttar Pradesh, Bihar and Madhya Pradesh and Maharashtra, West Bengal and Orissa. While these states together account for roughly half of India's population. The first three states account for approximately 36 per cent of the country's population but 48 percent of the poor. Households depending on agricultural labour, and small and marginal farmers and rural artisans constitute the bulk of the rural poor. Slightly less than half (48 per cent) of the rural poor are agricultural labourers and more than a quarter (28 per cent) are self-employed in agriculture. Among the social groups, the scheduled castes and scheduled tribes, particularly the latter, account for a proportionately larger number of the poor. The same is true about women-headed households. Within the households, women and the elderly suffer greater deprivations.

Apart from the chronically poor, a large number of non-poor households are vulnerable. They can easily slip into the category of the poor due to different types of 'shocks'. The 'push' can come from-personal tragedy, e.g. disease and death of the earning member, loss of assets due to natural disasters, or loss of livelihood, or severe impact on the current income due to market-induced factors. If any of these factors persist for long, a household with a thin asset base and without the advantage of a safety net would join the ranks of the chronic poor. Too much should not therefore, be made of the distinction between chronic and transitory distress. Factors which cause transitory distress can aggravate the plight of the households already suffering from chronic distress. Similarly, if transitory distress persists over a period of time it can lead to a state of chronic distress.

It is important that while attention should be focussed on alleviating chronic poverty, measures should be taken to protect the vulnerable sections, in fact, to help them to have a more sustainable household economy. In this connection, it may be useful to distinguish between the risk an individual household faces, i.e. idiosyncratic risk, and the risk faced by a large number of households, i.e. systemic risk. The latter is mainly due to natural disasters or market-induced 'shocks'. It needs to be pointed out at the outset that shocks of various type may reinforce each other. Households prone to natural disasters may suffer from market shocks as well, which would worsen their plight. And, a household level disability may further sap the capacity to withstand a market induced or natural calamity. I shall, however, concentrate on the market induced systemic risks.

Indian agriculture has undergone some major structural changes in recent years and this has enhanced the market induced vulnerability of a section of the rural population. Over a period of time, Indian agriculture has been progressively acquiring the 'small farm' character. By 1995-96, nearly 36 per cent of the cultivated area was operated by small and marginal farmers an increase from the 29 per cent in 1985-86. (See Table 1) I have analysed the causes for changes in the agrarian structure elsewhere (Vyas, 2002). It can be safely assumed that over 40 per cent of the land is now operated by small and marginal farmers. Such a tilt towards small farms could be observed practically in all parts of the country. With a meagre asset base, a large part of our agriculture is unable to withstand even minor shocks.

TABLE I

Area Operated by Operational Holdings

(Area Million Hectares)

Category of Farmers	*1980-81*	*1985-86*	*1990-91*	*1995-96*
Marginal (Less than 1 Hectare)	19.73	22.04	24.89	28.12
Small (1.0 to 2.0 Hectares)	23.17	25.71	28.82	30.72
Semi-Medium (2.0 to 4.0 Hectares)	34.65	36.67	38.37	38.95
Medium (4.0 to 10.0 Hectares)	48.54	47.14	44.75	41.39
Large (10.0 hectares and above)	37.71	33.00	28.65	24.16
All Holdings	163.8	164.56	165.48	163.35

Source: Indian Agriculture in Brief Various Issues and Agricultural Statistics at a Glance, 2003.

There have been significant changes in the output mix in agriculture. These changes are reflected in a shift of area from food grains to non-food grains, and within food grains from coarse cereals to finer cereals. During the last quarter century, the area under food grains has declined by over 10 per cent. The move from non-food grains to food grains is witnessed in all major states of India with the exception of Punjab and Uttar Pradesh. (See Table 2). Decline in the area under coarse cereals is even more steep and is an ubiquitous phenomenon. The land vacated by cereals is occupied by oilseeds, cotton, tobacco and sugarcane. By their very nature, these crops are mainly for sale in the market. Whatever changes take place in prices of these crops affects the farmers very profoundly.

TABLE 2

Area under Foodgrains in Different States to Total Cropped Area

(Triennium Ending 1975-76 and Triennium Ending 2001-02)

	States	*T.E. 1976*	*T.E. 2002*	*Difference*
1.	Orissa	84.40	63.20	-21.20
2.	Kerala	30.90	12.20	-18.70
3.	Andhra Pradesh	72.60	55.60	-17.00
4.	West Bengal	85.60	70.00	-15.60
5.	Gujarat	46.40	32.10	-14.30
6.	Rajasthan	74.50	60.60	-13.90
7.	Maharashtra	70.30	59.40	-10.90
8.	Tamil Nadu	67.50	59.90	-7.60
9.	Haryana	76.30	70.90	-5.40
10.	Jammu and Kashmir	87.80	82.60	-5.20
11.	Assam	73.70	69.30	-4.40
12.	Himachal Pradesh	90.00	86.80	-3.20
13.	Karnataka	65.10	62.30	-2.80
14.	Punjab	68.20	77.00	8.80
15.	Uttar Pradesh	72.60	80.60	8.00
	All-India	74.40	64.30	-10.10

Sources: CMIE, Agriculture, February 2004.

A similar change, in fact a more far reaching change, has taken place in the input structure. It is mainly influenced by the spread of modern technology and the relative prices of different inputs. Inputs such as fertilizers, insecticides, mechanical power and improved seeds occupy a prominent place in the input structure. They have substituted organic manure, animal power and farm-retained seeds. Purchase of inputs claims a large share of farmers' cash expenditure. Wherever more 'progressive' agriculture is practiced, e.g. OM cotton, the proportion of input costs, and consequently the current outlay on inputs, goes up. The value of inputs, which was 55,401 crores in 1993-94, rose to 1,03,555 crores in 1999-2000, i.e. by two times. The farmers have to take resource to credit to a much large extent than in the past for the purchase of these inputs. (See Table 3).

TABLE 3

Value of Inputs, Output and Flow of Production Credit in Agriculture at Current Price

(Rs. Crore)

Year	*Value of Output Agriculture*	*Value of Input Agriculture*	*Flow of SAO Credit*
1993-94	204874	55401	9752
1994-95	236607	63654	11932
1995-96	256698	72026	15273
1996-97	302744	74415	16956
1997-98	319586	83125	18632
1998-99	387546	93005	20601
1999-00	405576	103555	23694

Source: Rural Credit and NABARD, 2003 (For Value of Output from Agriculture) and National Accounts Statistics, 2001 (For Value of Input from Agriculture).

These changes are taking place at a time when the rate of growth in agricultural production is decelerating. Careful analysis by scholars has shown that the productivity gains achieved during the Seventies and the Eighties could not be sustained in the last decade (Deshpande *et al.*, 2004). The process of deceleration in the growth of agriculture had started in the nineties, when the agricultural growth rate came down to less than 2.4 per cent, from 3.8 per cent per annum in the previous decade. Except for one year, 2003-04 the downward slide has continued. The average agricultural GDP growth in the first two years of the Tenth Plan was 1.8 per cent. It is likely to be 1.5 per cent in the third year. The declining trend in productivity, as signified by the yield per hectare, is more disturbing. The deceleration in yields has been witnessed in practically all crops and in a majority of regions. In fact, there was virtual stagnation in the yields of 'commercial crops during the Nineties with sugarcane registering less than 1 percent growth in yield per year, and cotton and tobacco witnessing negative growth. The serious drought years in the earlier part of this decade has had a part in accentuating the decline, but the factors causing distress to agriculture are more abiding.

Deceleration in productivity has to be viewed in the context of the rising share of purchased inputs, especially in 'commercial' crops. A number of studies at the state level, as well as the micro-level, have shown that once use of fertilizers cross the 'low utilization level', diminishing return starts. It is even more true in the case of pesticides (Venugopal, 2004, Birthal, 2004). The plight of the growers has been compounded flot only because of the declining trend in yield from inputs, but also because of output prices of agricultural commodities, especially of the commercial crops, remaining subdued in the last few years. As a result, the Terms of Trade (Index of Prices Received divided by Index of Prices Paid) remained stable during the last five years, hovering around J. 03-J. 08 in contrast to a rising trend in the previous decade. Recent years have also witnessed much larger fluctuations in the output prices around a mildly declining trend. The net result has been that Indian agriculturists face lower returns and larger uncertainty.

Obviously, not all growers in all regions faced a. similar situation. There were groups of producers who benefited from state policies on pricing and subsidies. There were also pockets where productivity growth could be sustained (Sen and Bhatia, 2004). But the fact that, on an average, the situation on both price and productivity levels was depressed suggests that in terms of loss of income, some groups have suffered more than what is reflected in the average decline in prices and output. These are the vulnerable groups mainly, farmers in dry land areas, agricultural labourers, marginal and small farmers all over the country and, commercial farmers who went in for heavy doses of purchased inputs to whom we should now pay larger attention.

During this difficult period, policy interventions and institutional support to agriculture proved to be grossly inadequate. Policy failure was reflected in much larger emphasis on prices and subsidies than on non-price productivity augmenting factors such as research, extension and investment in infrastructure. The way the administered price regime was unfolding in the last few years, it was clear that policy-makers were using prices as vehicles for transferring income rather than as signals for resource allocation. Indiscriminate use of subsidies, particularly input subsidies, crowded out the resources for public investment in infrastructure.

Measures to contain risks also proved ineffective and in certain cases, counterproductive. Basically, three types of measures were taken for mitigation risks. The Minimum Support Prices (MSP) were used to minimize market-induced risks, with a guarantee to purchase all the output at pre-announced prices. With the emphasis on covering all the costs of farming, actual as well as imputed and their operation largely restricted to a limited number of crops-mainly rice, wheat and sugarcane-MSP contributed to a greater distortion in the cropping patterns rather than proving itself an effective shield for the agriculturists. The second measure to mitigate risks was crop insurance. In actual practice, it has proved to be of marginal support only in some regions (for e.g. Gujarat) and for some crops (for e.g. groundnuts and paddy). A measure to insure income in the face of market-induced risks as well as decline in yield due to natural causes is being introduced as a pilot project in a few districts for a few crops. There is a National Fund, for Calamity Relief, with a limited objective of providing relief to victims of natural calamities. Its operations during the last five years could provide assistance to 10 percent of the requests made by the states. Though there is a renewed emphasis on Forward. Markets, they have yet to make a substantial presence. In sum, we do not have an effective policy for minimising uncertainty or providing strength to farmers to withstand natural and market-induced risks.

Institutional failures are even more glaring. In the present context, the two most relevant institutions are extension and credit institutions. With one of the world's largest extension system, one would have expected that all sections of farmers to receive timely and proper advice on and support for the adoption of an appropriate enterprise and technology mix. In fact, the role of the extension institutions in acting as a conduit between the scientists and users is practically non-existent. There are a few instances of private enterprises entering the field, of extension of technology in raising crops and animal husbandry. However, the main source of information on modern inputs are the inputs suppliers who have a field day in 'educating' farmers in the use of purchased inputs. They, naturally have a vested interested in increasing the use of inputs they might be dealing in irrespective of their impact on productivity. Studies at the ground level from all parts of the country, and more so from the regions where input use is increasing rapidly, suggest that there is a disproportionate use of all inputs on the farms, leading to increased liability of the farmers. The blame for the suicides of agriculturists in some parts of the country can be, at least partly, attributed to the failure of the extension agencies who could not check spurious inputs or guide the farmers in the proper use of inputs.

Another major handicaps faced by the farming community is in the functioning of the credit institutions in the formal sector, i.e. Rural Financial Institutions (RFI). It is quite clear that RFIs are not advancing credit to agriculture at the rate warranted by the increased requirement of credit with the larger use of purchased inputs. Some of the poorest parts of the country, e.g. the tribal belt extending from Jharkhand to Andhra Pradesh and encompassing tribal areas of Bihar, Orissa, Maharashtra and Chhattisgarh, are inadequately served by RFIs. Even in the other agriculturally advanced areas, the share of credit from RFIs in the total cost of the inputs is low and there is no indication of the gap being filled.

Rural Financial Institutions, particularly commercial banks, advance three reasons for, their unsatisfactory performance in rural areas. These are: (1) low absorptive capacity in rural areas, (2) high transaction costs, and (3) greater risks. Only recently as a member of two different committees, I have had the opportunity to examine the functioning of RFIs in detail (NABARD 2001, Reserve Bank of India 2004). I have more to say on these aspects a little later.

With the reluctance and or inability of RFIs, farmers have to take recourse to nonformula sources, i.e. input suppliers, traders and bigger landlords, to obtain credit. While it may be easy to get credit from these sources, it is also true that the terms they offer are onerous; their methods of recovery could also be more ruthless. Farmers who are heavily indebted to these sources, but unable to generate additional output and, therefore default in repayment, face severe consequences. It is no coincidence that the largest number of suicides are reported from areas where farmers get heavily indebted to non-formal sources of credit.

Declining growth rate in production, stagnant prices and high cost of production have hit the agricultural sector as a whole. There are certain sections of the agricultural population which have fared worse than others. The more important among them are the agricultural producers in dry areas. Large parts of Gujarat, Rajasthan, Maharashtra and Orissa fall in this category. With depleted land resources, low and uncertain rainfall and low prices of their produce, these farmers are worse off even in normal years. Long-term trends in the productivity of the crops grown in the dry areas, e.g. coarse cereals and pulses suggest a stagnation in their yields. Their plight is further aggravated as three out of four years of this decade have proved to be 'below normal' in rainfall in large parts of the dry region. Whatever savings they had were depleted during these prolonged dry years. Their capacity to withstand any shock, natural or market-induced, has been completely eroded.

The only saving feature in these regions is the fact that a larger proportion of the holdings are medium to large. But, there are a substantial number of small holdings as well. In these regions, those with marginal and small holdings are worse off. As producers, they get paltry returns from their farming which are further affected by adverse weather and market conditions. Generally, these groups also have a subsidiary source of income in dairy and animal husbandry enterprises which are sustained on open grazing. The depletion of commons as a result of prolonged drought in several areas has made the cattle and other animals more a liability than an asset. Another source of income for these households is farm and non-farm labour. From available evidence, it seems that the employment opportunities have dwindled and there is no commensurate increase in wages (Bhalla, 2003). Severe distress is evident among these groups of small farmers and agricultural labourers—and these categories overlap in dry areas.

The plight of the farmers who have gone the whole hog with diversification is equally distressful. While the former groups, i.e. small and marginal farmers in dry areas, suffer from acute malnutrition and starvation, more of the suicide cases are reported from the groups who have borrowed heavily to purchase inputs for what they thought were more remunerative crops. With the high input slow output scenario described earlier, the result has been the failure to repay the loans. As most of these loans were contracted through so called non-formal sources who could report to social pressures as much as coercive tactics, many self-respecting farmers have take the extreme step of suicide to save face.

I will like to suggest three pronged strategy to save the situation from further deterioration viz.,

- Instituting creditable risk mitigating measures.
- Investment for strengthening land and water resources.
- Strengthening supportive institutions, especially in the areas of extension and credit.

Support Measures for the Poor

We have an array of measures to support the poor and mitigate the risks faced by them; more general programmes such as poverty alleviation programmes, and programmes to strengthen backward regions, as well as specific programmes to mitigate risks, such as Minimum Support Prices, Crop Insurance, National Calamity Fund, Safety Nets for Indigent and Handicapped People, and so on. There is no better indication of their ineffectiveness than the sorry plight of a large section of the rural people. Several of us have commented on the lacunae in these programmes and have suggested measures to strengthen them.

The principal policy measures to mitigate risks are Minimum Support Prices (MSP) and crop insurance. It has offered limited safeguards to a section of producers, mainly wheat and rice growers in selected areas, and has distorted the all-locative function of prices and created a strong lobby of rent seekers. Suggestions have been offered to minimise the damage and improve upon the present policy On MSP. The Income Guarantee Scheme, tried in a few districts, is not a substitute for the ill-managed MSP. It has all the disadvantages of MSP with additional demands on scarce resources.

There is considerable scope in improving our programme of crop insurance. Its coverage has to extend much beyond the limited area and the limited number of crops. Eventually,. a more comprehensive insurance product has to be offered to the farmers, going beyond crops, and including insurance of animals and equipment, and covering life and health aspects of the rural population. Several of the operational lacunae have to be removed. It should however be clear that, even with all these reforms, we will not be able to recover premia from the rural poor at actuarial rates. An element of subsidy is inevitable. This is the type of subsidy for which there is full justification on grounds of both equity and efficiency.

As far as natural risks are concerned, the farmers in the risk-prone areas have devised their own coping mechanisms. These involve self-provisioning on the one hand and diversification to supplementary and complementary enterprises on the other. Generally, mixed crops, dominated by cereals (the major source of calories) and pulses (the major source of protein), characterise the cropping pattern in the dry regions, especially on small farms. And, animal husbandry—dairying mainly—is the major supplementary occupation. In our anxiety to introduce 'high value' agriculture, this pattern is being discouraged, without extending assured food supply through, say PDS, and without ensuring institutional support in marketing and credit for the new crops. In the absence of these supportive measures, we are exposing the vulnerable farmers of dry areas to a high risk environment. This may not apply to small farmers on the fringe of cities and towns for whom a ready market for fruits, vegetables and other high value crops exists. The uncertainty faced by them arises more due to sharp price fluctuations.

In this context, contract farming is suggested as a way out. Certainly, if properly implemented, contract farming arrangements can mitigate at least the market induced risks. Contract farming is not new to India. We have a long tradition of contract farming, particularly in sugar and to a large extent in milk. Experience has shown that in areas where contract farming is organised in the cooperative mode, with a major say of the producers at all the stages in the value chain, it has not only contributed in improving productivity on the growers' farms, but has also afforded them an assured income and a larger share of the consumer's rupee. Contract farming with the involvement of large private firms as collaborators has shown mixed results, with more failures than successes. Problems of moral hazard and adverse selection are rampant, and complaints about inadequate guidance in input use and farm practices as well as non-enforcement of contracts are voiced frequently.

In the present circumstances, the thrust of the policy should be on encouraging improvement in the productivity of the crops grown in the dry regions and on small farms,—mainly coarse cereals, pulses and kharif oilseeds. Measures to encourage productivity in the dairy sector is equally important for these groups. These regions can have a comparative advantage in dairying-based on open grazing due to large areas of cultivable wasteland and *goucher* land, provided a massive programme of land development is taken up in these regions. Only when the small farmers broadly reach their self-sufficiency level, and start generating surpluses from their traditional crops and enterprises, should diversification to input intensive high value crops and enterprises be encouraged. Our immediate task should be to encourage self-provisioning rather than market exposure as far as small and marginal farmers are concerned.

Finance for Land and Water Resources

Since the mid-Eighties public investment in agriculture has progressively declined. Nor has private investment been able to fill the gap. As a result, total capital formation in agriculture is decelerating. The bulk of the investment in both the public and the private sectors is accounted for by investment in augmenting irrigation resources; in the case of public investment, it is canal irrigation, and in case of private investment, it is in ground water exploitation. Because of lack of complementary investment in a bureaucratic handling of this resource use, the efficiency of canal water is seriously geopardised. On the other hand, concentration of private investment in ground water exploitation has resulted in over-exploitation of the resource leading to negative externalities in several regions of the country, especially in the arid and semi-arid areas where progressively larger areas are coming under the 'dark zone'.

In any strategy for protecting the vulnerable sections in agriculture, augmentation, conservation and efficient use of water should receive high priority. This would involve larger and more imaginatively planned investment, much greater collaboration between irrigation engineers and agricultural scientists, policy support to ensure equitable distribution and recovery of irrigation dues. In all these measures, the role of water users and the civil society institutions will be critical.

There is growing recognition of the inadequacies of our efforts in augmenting and rejuvenating land resources. However, it is yet to be translated in terms of investment and policy packages. The severity of the problem can be gauged by the fact that, according to the Ministry of Agriculture of the Government of India, more than 42 per cent of the geographical area of the country comprises degraded land. A substantial part of it is manmade. The extent of degraded land is, again, higher in the states with a larger share of rainfed agriculture. Remedial measures to rejuvenate these lands have not gone beyond tokenism. Investment in land development, by both public and private initiative, should receive serious attention. Failure to take credible action to stop the process of degradation and develop the degraded lands would mean that the natural resource base of our agriculture will be progressively weakened and the incidence will fall more seriously on the backward regions and the vulnerable sections of agricultural producers.

Schemes to be Supported

In any scheme for reducing the vulnerability of the poorer sections, especially small and marginal farmers, institutional support in research, extension, credit and marketing is of paramount importance. We have in this country a wide network of institutions working in these areas. However, there is such incongruence between the service delivery systems and the bulk of the poor in the rural areas, mostly accounted for by the small and marginal farmers, that the latter hardly get any support from them. For example, research and extension institutions bypass them as any improvement on their tiny holdings is not likely to make much difference at the macro level. In any case, because of the thin asset base, the capacity of these sections to face uncertainty is considered to be limited. Credit and marketing institutions find that the demands placed by these sections on the service providers are infrequent and in small bits. This makes the transaction costs heavy and uneconomical.

There are ways to cope with these difficulties and create a supportive institutional framework for the disadvantaged sections. Scaling up of their operations through cooperative effort has proved to be a viable solution, as the experience of Self Help Groups, now numbering nearly eight million, in dispersal and recovery of credit has convincingly demonstrated. An example of the successful interface between small producers and marketing institutions is provided by the dairy cooperative which have enabled an owner of one or two buffaloes to get the benefits of advanced and appropriate technology. The scope for institutional support can be further enhanced by making proper use of Information Technology. There are numerous models of institutional interventions to benefit marginalised groups. These models have to be adapted and extended to meet with specific requirements in different settings.

To provide immediate redress to the affected peasantry, measures to give relief to those heavily indebted to the private money lenders and traders are urgently needed. A proposal was made, long back, to restrict the total amount of interest due to the value of the sum initially borrowed, popularly known as the principal of *Dam Duppat*. This has to be enacted as a legislation and made applicable retrospectively. Similarly, the legislation prohibiting usurious money lending should be made effective in all the states. A measures of similar intent would be to encourage RFIs to take over the loans contracted by the farmers from private sources on their books. Waiving of interest or even the principal amount borrowed from RFIs will not help much unless steps are taken to lighten the burden of those who have contracted large amounts from non-formal sources.

We have a serious problem on hand because of the growing vulnerability of large sections of the rural population. It is possible, however, to turn the tide by:

- enhancing investment in strengthening the resource base of agriculture,
- by devising suitable instruments to protect, in any event to compensate small and marginal producers for losses from natural calamities,
- by designing organisational interventions to impart strength to their economy,
- by lightening the interest burden from the non-formal sources of credit, and
- by encouraging RFIs to take over the debts of the farmers from usurious sources.

A positive feature in our situation is that we have some

examples of success in all these directions. There is a need to extend and scale up these efforts.

Present policies and programmes are not able to protect a sizable section of agricultural population from natural and market induced uncertainties, nor to enable them to contribute meaningfully to the overall growth of the economy. We have a responsibility towards this section of agricultural population. Making them less vulnerable will not only contribute to social equity but will also accelerate economic growth. The choice seems clear.

References

Bhalla, G.S. (2004), "Globalisation and Indian Agriculture", *State of Indian Farmers*, A Millenium Study.

Bhalla, Sheila, Karan, Anup K., Shobah, T., "Rural Casual Labourers, Wages and Poverty 1983 to 1999-2000, *Working Paper IIPA*, 2004.

Deshpande, R.S., M.J. Bhende, P. Thipaiah, M. Vivekananda (2004), "Crops and Cultivation", *State of Indian Farmers*, A Millenium Study.

Mahendra Dev, S. (2004), "Is Rural India Shinning", *Working Paper No. 54*, Centre for Economic and Social Studies, Hyderabad.

Mehta, Aasha Kapur and Amita Shah, "Chronic Poverty in India: An Overview", Working Paper, IIPA, 2004.

National Bank for Agriculture and Rural Development, Expert Committee on Rural Credit (2002). (Chairman, V.S. Vyas).

Pingali, Venugopal (2004), "Input Management", *State of Indian Farmers*, A Millenium Study.

Pratap, S. Birthal, (2004), "Integrated Pest Management in Indian Agriculture", ICAR, Proceedings, National Centre for Agricultural Economics and Policy Research (NACP), New Delhi, India, National Centre for Integrated Pest Management (NCIPM), New Delhi, India.

Reserve Bank of India (2004), Report of the Advisory Committee on Flow of Credit to Agriculture and Related Activities from the Banking System, (Chairman, V.S. Vyas).

Sen, Abhijit and Himanshu (2003), "Poverty and Inequality in India: Getting Close to the Truth", Centre for Economics Studies and Planning, Jawaharlal Nehru University, New Delhi, Mimeo.

Sen, Abhijjit, Bhatia, M.S (2004), "Cost of Cultivation and Farm Income", State of Indian Farmers. A Millenium Study.

Sunderam, K. and S.D. Tendulkar (2003), "Poverty in India in the 1990s: Revised Estimates", *Economic and Political Weekly*, Vol. 38, No. 46, November 15.

Vyas, V.S. "Agriculture, Second Round of Economic Reforms", (2000), *EPW*, Vol. 36, No. 10, Year 2001.

Vyas, V.S. "Changing Contours of Indian Agriculture", *Facets of Indian Economy*, Ed. Rakesh Mohan, 2002.

Vyas, V.S., "Seven Lessons of Poverty Alleviation Programme", Mimeo.

6

Addressing the Bihar Agrarian Crises through Land Reform

CHANDRIKA PRASAD

Land reform is the most relevant weapon of agricultural development. But Bihar has been facing serious problems like subdivision and fragmentation of land holding, ceiling limits, crisis of tenancy right, unproductive Bhoodan Land, uneconomic holding, etc. The resulting figure shows that agriculture productivity of Bihar is the lowest in India. Land reforms ensure the social justice by changing tenurial relation in favour of the tiller. So, firstly, the consolidation of land holdings of 100 per cent is necessary by the government including community's participation through village land committee. There is need of good governance for this movement. Mere transfer of ownership is not enough in itself either to raise productivity. It should be supported by other going on rural development scheme.

The land reform is a very important programme to eliminate obstacles to economic and development arising out of defects in the agrarian structure. Land reforms are an effective weapon in a rural economy dominated by small and marginal farmers and agricultural workers. The term land reforms includes not nearly redistribution of land but also tenancy and other land management aspects including consolidation of holdings, measures to conserve land-use, prevention of its degradation, etc. Land reforms ensure social and economic justice by changing tenurial relations in favour of tillers. Changes occuring in the agrarian structure through direct intervention of government are characterised as land reforms. The consolidation of holding is a very important factor. These include changes in the land tenure and redistribution of land among the less privileged classes besides establishment of services related to agricultural credit, supply, marketing, extension and research. The policy of land reforms aims at increasing the output of agricultural commodities with given resources which is likely to help in generating additional income and employment for the majority of rural population since other source of economy have a little scope to absorb the burden of ever-increasing unemployment.

The defective land system is one of the cause of the low productivity of agriculture in Bihar. This state was the poineer in Bhoodan Movement but this movement failed to have any appreciable impact on the problem of landlessness and iniquitous distribution. Out of 21 lakh acres donated under Bhoodan scheme, only 7 lakh acres has been distributed. 17 lakh 85 thousand acres land was announced surplusland from land ceiling act but only 3 lakh 85 thousand acre land was redistributed in 1984. 1400 such big landlords was recognised whose had above land ceiling in 1983 in which above the one lakh sixteen thousand acre land was among ten landlords. According to the government lists among one hundred landlords had above the 500 acre land in 1990. It should be improve even after the Independence but it failed. It is a matter of access sorry that Bihar's politicians ever since Independence have let loose a reign of casteism and corruption, rapacity and exploitation, which has pushed the state several fathoms down the surface. All surplus land has not in fact, became available for redistribution. The actual process of land redistribution has been extremely slow. Dead lines have been repeatedly fixed for completing the implementation of the land ceiling but in vain. Attempt at co-operative farming have suffered from pro-landlord bias. Tenancy has neither worked towards an identification of real tenants nor towards promoting cost-sharing practices.

Today only in Panjab, Hariana and west side of U.P. this programmes has made substantial progress, are developed in grain production due to the solvation of consolidation of holding. Panjab solved the problem of security of tennure by simply eliminating tenants, converting most of them into agricultural labous. The success of 'Operation Barga' in West Bengal, under which heritage and cultivable land rights were provided to shareholders, should also encourage in Bihar to bring about tenancy reform which would generate greater employment and enhanced output, and thus reduce poverty. West Bengal and Keral shows rapid development in which 65.8 per cent and 48.1 per cent reduced the poverty during 1977-78 to 1987-88 33 per cent poverty reduced in Karnataka in the same period. Gujarat and Maharashtra shall the rapid development due to the consolidation of holdings.

Bihar has an extremely low resource-base. The net cultivated land area per head in the state comes to 0.37 acre. 64 per cent of its population has farm holding of less than one hectare. The small and marginal farmers constituting as they do 78 per cent of the total number of farm households, account for 30 per cent only of the total land area. The land holding pattern in Bihar is uneven 64.34 per cent of the land holding, are less than one hectare in size, and 14.64 per cent between one and two hectares. The economic base of Bihar is very weak and narrow. Only 26.0 per cent of the cropped area was irrigated in 1973-74. Bihar remains deficient in food supply. It remains a food deficit state. Sub-division and fragmentation of land are continuing unabated, leading to a phenomenal increase in the number of marginal and small holding since Independence. Small and scattered size of land holdings limit the adoption of new technology. It reflects serious imbalance in the man-land ratio. This imbalance in land-man ratio is the primary cause of setting in traditionalism in farming, misallocation of human resources, low marginal productivity of labour and other inputs and early operation of the Law of Diminishing Returns in agriculture, small output, small saving and the subsistence oriented character of farm organisation and management. The area under irrigation on small holdings being small, the intensive cultivation did not help in observing surplus labour substantially. They normally suffer from higher investment per hectare especially in form of houses. The farm practices are inferior.

Tenancy laws are highly restrictive. They were enacted in the context of exploitation of peasantry. The economic and political hold of large land owing classes has been considerably weakened. The deepening of democracy through successive elections and setting up of PRIS has strengthened the bargaining power of the rural poor.

The growth of net sown area slowed down considerably. This explains why, despite the accelerated increase in capital formation and the introduction of new technologies, the growth rate of agricultural output in the post-green revolution period as a whole was broadly the same as in pre-green revolution period in Bihar. Poverty removal rested on a series of expectation in regard to institutional changes such as land reforms. This reforms did not meet with success in certain part like North Bihar, Tall area of the Gangatic region where earstwhile zamindars continued to own large holdings and lease out land to the share croppers. The failure to redistribute land to the landless in any significant measure has been a major cause for persistence of rural poverty.

It is important, at the very outset, to understand the institutional, demographic and socio-political context within which agricultural growth has been taking place. The institutional framework itself has undergone some changes while it has shown rigidity in certain respect.

BIHAR—A PROFILE: AT A GLANCE

Bihar is second largest and one of the most populated states in India which lies wholly in the northern hemisphere stretching from latitude 24°20′10" to 27°12′15" north and from longitude 83°19′50" to 88°17′40" east. It has a geographical area of 94,163 sq km with a population density of about 880 per square km. The total population is 8.29 crore and out of that 188 lakhs are total main workers. Female Literacy Rate is 33.57 per cent, in Rural Area 30.03 per cent. Literacy rate in scheduled caste Women is 5.4 per cent in Rural Area. Sex Ratio in Rural Area 927, population density in Rural Area is 8.3 Average Annual Exponential growth rate 1991-2001 is 2.49 per cent. Decided population growth in 1991-2001 is 28.33 per cent. Total Rural Population is 74,199,596. Rural Area in sq. km 92358.40. It is observed that nearly 43 per cent of the total work force is engaged as Agricultural Labourer. Bihar was once the centre of learning and prosperity but now is in the morass of acute poverty, malnutrition, unemployment and under-employment. It is Octopus like semifeudal, caste-ridden social structure is the genesis of all problems.

OBJECTIVES OF LAND REFORMS

Without land reforms, the development of Bihar is not possible. It is well recognised that in the battle against hunger and poverty. The small and scattered holding should be consolidated necessarily and further fragmentation should be prevented. The maximum size of a holding should be fixed and that the surplus land over such a maximum, acquired and placed at the disposal of co-operatives.

The objectives have also restructure of land ownership, eliminate exploitation by providing security of tenure and regulation of rent for tenants and share-croppers, brings direct contact between the tiller and the state and give social and economic status to the landless by redistributive measures. It can provide a permanent asset base for a large number of rural landless poor by taking up land based and other supplementary income generating activities.

Bhoodan Movement

Through this movement, Vinoba Bhave impressed upon the landowners to demonstrate their compassion by donating 1/6th of their holdings and envisaged that the land so collected would then be suitably redistributed. The detail of a quired land and distributed was in this way. (Table 1).

TABLE I

Bhoodan Movement: Donation and Distribution of Land

(Till the 31 March 1956)

Sl. No.	State	Donated Land (in lakh acre)	Distributed	Surplus
1.	Andhra Pradesh	1.96	1.00	0.96
2.	Bihar	21.18	6.95	14.23
3.	Gujarat	0.34	0.27	0.07
4.	M.P.	4.10	2.43	1.67
5.	Maharashtra	1.10	0.83	0.27
6.	Orissa	6.39	5.80	0.59
7.	Rajsthan	6.02	1.41	4.61
8.	U.P.	4.37	4.21	0.16
9.	Aggregate including other State	45.90	23.23	22.67

Distribution of land is very bad condition in Bihar 12.52 lakh acre land was found unsuitable. Many difficulties came into existence.

Consolidation of Holdings

Land reform policy includes the consolidation of fragmented agriculture land holdings as its integral part. In order to have planned development of village and enhanced agricultural production, due emphasis has been laid in every Five Year Plan on the consolidation of fragmented landholdings. Accordingly the states have enacted legislation and initiate work towards consolidation of landholdings. States such as Uttar Pradesh and Haryana need to be mentioned due to their significant success. Consolidation of landholding in U.P. is in the process in about 9,000 to 10,000 villages. But Bihar is very backward in it. Only 96.05 lakh acres is consolidated in discontinued methods whereas in Haryana, U.P. and Punjab has been completed. According to views of E.H. Jacoby, "the smaller, the more fragmented and uneconomically shaped the farm is, the more expensive is production, since cultivation and harvesting are more complicated, the supervision of labour is either more expensive or insignificant, and proper drainage or irrigation is often impossible". The Table 2 below gives the state-wise consolidation of holdings in which Bihar is very poor.

TABLE 2

Consolidation of Land Holdings in the States of India

States/UT	*Area Consolidated (in lakh acres)*
Andhra Pradesh	8.18
Bihar	96.05
Delhi	2.33
Gujarat	69.98
Haryana	104.38
Himachal Pradesh	29.91
Jammu and Kashmir	1.37
Karnataka	26.76
M.P.	95.53
Maharashtra	226.50
Orissa	26.74
Punjab	121.81
Rajsthan	42.30
U.P.	481.63
Total	1633.47

Source: Annual Report (2005-06), Ministry of Rural Development, Govt. of India.

Imposition of land ceiling on agricultural holdings and distribution of surplus land.

Land ceiling laws were first enacted in the 50s and 60s. These were revised after national guidelines were issued in 1972. The declared surplus land is far less than the surplus estimated from agricultural census and other data. The declared surplus is less than 2 per cent of the cultivated area. The declared surplus land is not fully taken possession of due litigation. According to Ministry of Rural Development of India's Annual Report (2005-06) in Bihar, the area declared surplus land was 4,15,447 Acres in which 306964 Acres land distributed to individual among 3,79,528 beneficiaries.

Abolition of Intermediary Tenure

Intermediary tenures like Zamindars, Jagidars, in as, etc. which prevailed over 40 per cent of the total area were abolished. But Weste and follow land was distributed to landless. Bihar state has failed to record the tenancy and to provide security to the tenants and sub-tenants.

In Bihar, the Share-cropping is widely practised and it is customary to divide the total product 50-50 between the land owner and the tenant, when the former supplies only land and the latter all other inputs, the land owner must have a higher return, but if he is to supply ½ of the variable resources also either in the form of a greater share of the product or in the form of some lump-sum cash, rent for bring the additional costs.

The overall performance of agriculture is generally measured by per capital food grains production. Table 3 reveals that Bihar's positions absolutely and relatively very poor than other states. In terms of per-capita net-domestic product, Bihar's position is lowest among all other states in India

Shortcoming and Suggestions

Bihar is purely an agricultural state. Mostly population is based on agriculture. Marginal farmers and landless labourers are going on migration. Agriculture is not only means of subsistence life, profession or business but it is also a culture which is connected with soul. The geographical atmosphere is also favourable for agriculture but the development is not possible without land reform. There are following some shortcomings and suggestions.

Firstly, consolidation of hundred per cent of landholding is necessary. It can be seen that the number of fragmented land after land is increasing. Favourable time is up that all villagers' people want to improve it. The government have to do only as a catalystic agent. The Government have to give responsibility among villages to organise land reform committee. The Government should announce the consolidation of holding is essential anyhow. It increases production in rapid way. Water management, horticulture, plantation and allied activities like fisheries, poultry will be suitable. There is need to give a new direction to consolidation of land holdings measures and making it the foundation for poverty alleviation programme. The official,

TABLE 3

Production of Grains in Bihar

	Rice	*Wheat*	*Maize*	*Other grains*	*Pulse food*	*Total*	*Oil seeds*
Year-2000-01							
Land (Lakh Hect.)	36.56	20.68	6.21	0.56	7.17	71.18	1.54
Production Lakh Tone	54.44	44.36	14.97	0.58	6.22	120.59	1.31
Productivity Ktle/Hect.	14.89	21.46	24.11	10.37	8.67	16.94	8.51
National Productivity Ktle/Hect.	19.27	27.42	18.06	10.10	5.53	16.38	7.38
Year-2001-02							
Land (Lakh Hect)	35.52	21.23	5.94	0.53	6.94	70.19	1.39
Production (Lakh Tone)	52.52	43.91	14.88	0.53	5.47	116.82	1.17
Productivity (Ktle/Hect.)	14.65	20.65	25.04	10.00	7.88	16.64	8.41
Year-2002-03							
(Lakh Hect. Tone)	35.85	21.31	6.04	0.53	6.98	70.69	1.37
Production (Lakh Tone)	50.86	40.41	13.50	0.48	5.61	110.85	1.05
Productivity (Ktle/Hect.)	14.19	18.96	22.35	9.06	8.04	15.68	7.66
Year-2003-04							
Land (Lakh Hect. Tone)	35.89	20.30	05.97	0.47	6.72	69.37	1.40
Production (Lakh Tone)	54.29	36.32	14.09	0.45	5.19	110.34	1.19
Productivity (Ktle/Hect.)	15.13	17.89	23.52	9.57	7.12	15.91	8.50
Year-2004-05							
Land (Lakh Hect. Tone)	31.67	20.55	6.23	0.48	6.51	65.4	1.393
Production (Lakh Tone).	25.69	34.26	14.29	0.42	5.04	79.70	1.155
Productivity (Ktle/Hect.)	8.11	16.88	22.94	8.75	7.75	12.12	8.29

Source: Directory of Statistical and Evaluation, Bihar Govt. Patna.

particularly leaders of the Panchayati Raj bodies should be adequately motivated in the philosophy of integrated rural development.

Secondly, there is need for greater community participation. Effect of the new liberalisation economic policy in the rural areas has started. Big companies begin to give focus also in rural areas. If the land reform will not be effective in time, more complexity will arise. The policy of "land to the tiller" should be faithfully followed. The ownership rights in land should go to the persons who work on it. It is hoped that land reform will improve the economic and social status of the rural poor by greater participation of the community.

Thirdly, it is recognised that no significant success in implementation of land reforms can be achieve without seeking active help and co-operation from organisation of rural poor, voluntary agencies and other representative bodies. There is need of the effective and whole hearted implementation of land reform.

Fourthly, mere transfer of ownership or provision of security of tenancy is not enough in itself either to raise productivity or bring the marginal farmer/landless labourers above the poverty line. Therefore, the beneficiaries of land reforms most of whom belong to the poorest segments of the community, should be supported by other ongoing rural development schemes like institution credit ages, IRDP, DPAP, crope insurance, Kisan Credit Cards, infrastructural development programme, etc. to enable them to make productive use of the land.

Fifth, there is lack of land recorded. Land transfers among the members of the family and benami transfers is highly. The land records will have to be continuously updated so that the existing laws are strictly followed. So, there is need of good governance.

In this way even today about 70 per cent of the population is dependent on agriculture for livelihood, and in a rural economy dominated by small and marginal farmers and poor agricultural workers, land is a precious asset which has to be put to optimum use to get maximum benefit for the largest number. Ceiling limits on land holdings were imposed with the ostensible purpose to distribute the surplus land to landless. Even now there is facing a crisis of governance.

Reference

Bimal Jalan, The Indian Economy (Problems and Prospects), Penguin Books, 2004, pp. 128-29.

K.N. Prasad, Problems of Indian Economic Development (National and Regional Dimension), Sterling Publication Pvt., New Delhi, 1983, pp. 148-49.

Ugra Mohan Jha, Rural Development in India, (Problems and Prospectus), Annual Publication Pvt., New Delhi, 2000, p. 157.

Uma Kapila, Indian Economy since Independence, 16th Edition, 2004-05, Academic Foundation, p. 241.

Kurukshetra, December 1989, Publication Division, Patiala House, New Delhi.

7

Changing Agrarian Relations in Bihar in the Wake of Agrarian Crisis and Thoughts of Swami Sahajanand Saraswati

DALIP KUMAR AND BHARAT SINGH

I. INTRODUCTION

This paper analyses the changing agrarian relations and its impact on rural poor in the light of the thoughts of Swami Sahajanand. This paper has been divided into two parts:- firstly, it briefly discusses the changing agrarian relations in pre-independence period in Bihar and the role of Swami Sahajanand Saraswati therein. Secondly, the Post-independence agrarian relations and formation of some important private organisation (Caste Senas) and its impact on the wage structure of rural labourers in Bihar. The changing agrarian relation in pre-independence Bihar in terms of the different land tenure systems and their important features, land distribution, the relationship between the Zamindar and the peasants and its tenancy structure is discussed here. The rural labour if galvanised; can work as a major force for socio- economic change in the field of agrarian sector. High level of unemployment has been a concern for many decades in this state; especially, majority of the existing population is young and unemployed. "Unemployment bites deeply but bites especially the young" (Penneck-1980).

The experience of agrarian crisis is likely to have a serious and lasting impact not only on the rural poor but the society at large also. For rural labour it implies not only a current loss of income, but also a loss of chance to accumulate human capital, which will doubtlessly extend into the future.

NSSO Data (59th Round) also suggest that about 40 per cent of the farmer did not like to continue with agriculture. Out of which 27 per cent were reluctant to continue in this occupation precisely because of non-viability. About 36 per cent of the farmer of Bihar and West Bengal, 34 per cent of Orissa, 30 per cent of Haryana and Jharkhand, 29 per cent of Maharashtra and even 28 per cent of Punjab did not like farming as occupation. (NSSO, 59th Round, 2005).

The planner and policy-makers alike are, therefore, most anxious to evolve a rational, balanced, and effective solution to the agrarian problems. The critical and crucial factor affecting the employment situation and prospects of young people in India is due to spectacular growth of the population and the labour force recording during recent decades. The utilisation of the rural labour in the production framework of the society through appropriate human resources planning is the most challenging task for the state.

'The term 'agrarian relation' is a very complex in the historical, political and economic dimensions. The definition deals mostly with the problems and effects of tenancy on the agricultural production wage payment, class relations, class conflict, caste retaliation, general well beings of the tenants and so on. The production process, trends of employment and mode of wage rate of rural labour also affect changing agrarian relation.

Among various aspects of agrarian relations, the pattern of land distribution and land reforms occupies a prime place. The landlords in these agrarian regimes constitute a class in itself as also a class for itself. Highly conscious of their power and privileges, they are well organised to articulate the political and administrative decisions in their favour. The agrarian relations characterised by the above mentioned feature are technically designated as 'semi-feudal' production relations.

II. CHANGING AGRARIAN RELATION AND THE RURAL POOR IN TERMS OF THE DIFFERENCE IN PERSPECTIVES

The present agrarian structure in Bihar present a complex situation where one might observe a situation of simultaneous process of disintegration as well as the persistence of peasantry. An attempt has been made to explain the process in term of socio-economic differentiation largely based on Marxist and Chayanovian writings. According to the Marxist view, with increasing commoditisation and commercialisation a process is a set in Motion whereby rural producers are polarised into two distinct classes such as rural bourgeoisie and the rural proletariat and thus the peasants are differentiated into two antagonistic classes. (Chowdhury, 1998).

The Chayanovian view lays stress on homogeneous peasantry based on small-scale family labour farm. According to Chayanov, the peasant specific characteristics act to sustain the classless homogenous nature. If there is a differentiation amongst the peasantry, this is brought about by cyclical process. But there is no long-term developing trend of polarization of classes (Chayanov, 1977). Contrary to the Marxist view, Chayanovian view considers the differentiation of the peasantry as a demographic phenomenon. Since formulated, Chayanov's theory of peasant farm exerted profound influence on all subsequent works on peasant agriculture, including present day studies of the Third World.

In the prevailing socio-economic context of Bihar, any attempt to explain and analyses the question of peasantry, changing agrarian relations and rural poor by two mutually exclusive way (i.e. Marxist view and Chayanovian views) will be highly inadequate and outdated. The situation prevailing in Bihar at present is not exactly comparable and same with the situations prevailing in Russia. Bihar has her own peculiarity and funny agrarian relation. In view of these facts, it would not be worthwhile to isolate the issue of rural poverty from the process of differentiation that is taking place in rural Bihar. Bihar has been witnessing feudal exploitation and violence against the *Dalits* and other underprivileged section. There is close relation between the caste hierarchy and agrarian hierarchy in this state. The rural poor consisting of agricultural labourers and poor peasants are drawn from *Dalits* and lower section of backward casts. The landlord class organised themselves in a form of different *Senas* and armies, the most organised among them like as Ranveer Sena, People War Group, Bhumi Sena, etc.. The Naxlites, on the other hand, have three major outfits, namely, CPI (ML), Party Unity (PWG) and MCC. The caste base of most of the outfits is rooted in the rural proletariat but in terms of caste composition there is some divergence. If we try to analyse the situation of rural poor and pauperization in terms of differentiation perspective, we find the both neo-populist and Marxist views of differentiation have their limitations in the prevailing socio-economic context of Bihar.

III. AGRARIAN RELATIONS IN PRE-INDEPENDENT BIHAR, ROLE OF SAHAJANAND AND ITS IMPACT ON RURAL AGRICULTURAL POOR

Agrarian relations in pre-independent Bihar were of three main types: Zamindari, Ryatwari and Mahalwari tenures. Zamindars were the middlemen between farmers and ruler. The introduction of zamindari system, in the words of land revenue Commissioner, led to the process of sub-infeudation and *rack-renting* of the peasantry and the evils of absenteeism, unhappy relations between landlords and tenants and of multiplication of tenure holders of middlemen between the cultivators and the government (Mukherjee, 1952). The Ryotwari settlement and Mahalwari settlement, did not exist in State Bihar. These two were mainly functional in Madras, Agra, Awadh and Punjab Provinces. In 1929, the

'Bihar Provincial Kisan Sabha' was formed under the leadership of Swami Sahajanand Saraswati to fight against exploitation of farmers and Rural poor peasants. The aim was also to change the agrarian relations between Zamindar, Farmers and rural poor.

Swami Sahajanand Saraswati was, of course, a fascinating personality but what also added immense social significance to his struggle was the fact that he was able to found a massive organisation. The Bihar Provincial Kisan Sabha was formed in 1929 and a smaller Kisan Sabha had been formed even earlier in Patna district with a formal organisational structure, which was really institutionalised after a few years. Actually, it is correct to say that the Kisan Sabha never really became an 'organisation', but remained a movement (Hauser, 1961).

Civil Disobedience Movement and Involvement of Landlords

But if that is so for the whole of the history of the Kisan Sabha, in its first years it was even more nebulous: an idea, a forum, a propaganda platform, and a lobby. Almost immediately after the formation of the Sabha Bihar was plunged, with the rest of India, into the Civil Disobedience Movement, which, although helped in arousing the general consciousness of the masses, did not give the leaders of the Sabha the time to formalise its structure (Williams, 1933). In fact, the experiences of the Civil Disobedience Movement both outside and inside jails created the beginnings of the rift between the Kisan Sabhaites and some of the Congress leaders [BSCRO: 21/1933], and so disgusted was the supreme leader of the Sabha, Swami Sahajanand Saraswati, that for several years he cut himself off from politics altogether (Sahajanand, 1952).

But while, because of these problems, the Kisan Sabha remained disorganised, the landlords recognised its potentially dangerous character. In order to meet its challenge and to consolidate their position, they organised themselves and their supporters into three main bodies. The first was a clear-cut Bihar Landholders' Association, which included within it all the prominent zamindars. The second was a cleverer attempt to hide the organisation's basic class character; it was called the United Party and was supposed to represent the interests of various sections of the population. It even included a few Congressmen though its leadership was composed of the leading landlords, including the Maharajadhiraj of Darbhanga and the Raja of Surajpura. Having failed in their first attempt in 1928-29 to get the Tenancy Act amended, the landlords tried to do so through this United Party. Rai Bahadur Shyamnandan Sahay, one of the richest zamindars of Bihar, accordingly drew up a new tenancy bill with the obvious intention of strengthening the zamindars' position by giving them more powers. However, in order to achieve a semblance of zamindar-tenant unity in presenting the new legislation, the United Party conspired to develop a compromise measure by forming a 'Kisan Sabha' which held its meeting at Patna early in 1933 (Sankrityayana, 1943). Ironically, it was this effort of the landholders, which brought Sahajanand back into politics and vastly strengthened the Kisan Sabha (Sudhakar, 1973).

There was no unanimity among Congressmen about their approach to the Untied Party and its 'Kisan Sabha'. While leaders like Rajendra Prasad felt that as an election trick the United Party was doomed to failure, they also thought it might actually gain some concessions for the peasantry. Hence they felt, opposition to the United Party was 'unnecessary'. Some other Congress leaders thought otherwise:

My colleagues were agitated thinking that (an amended tenancy law) would increase the new party's influence among the peasants. They wanted the move to be opposed, but most of the Congressmen were in prison and the organisation was banned and could not do anything. They thought, therefore, of reviving the dormant Kisan Sabha. Word was passed on to Swami Sahajanand to activate the Kisan Sabha and expose the United Party's move. . . I felt that all this was unnecessary but, as I could not oppose it, kept quiet. (Prasad, 1957).

Sahajanand was apprised of the 'bogus Kisan Sabha' and its proposed session at Patna by Yadunandan Sharma and induced by him to attend the meeting. After much hesitation about re-entering politics, Sahajanand agreed and made a dramatic entry in the Patna meeting which was being conducted by such well-known zamindars and their henchmen as Dr Sachidanand Sinha (the 'Founder Modern Bihar') and Guru Sahay Lal (later President of the Bihar Chamber of Commerce). The Swami's unexpected presence caused considerable embarrassment to the sponsors of the meeting and his forthright stand there condemning such devious maneuverings marked the end of the effort by the zamindars to play politics through the use of the name of the Kisan Sabha. At the same time, this abortive attempt proved that even the zamindars had recognised the potential of an organisation like the Kisan Sabha even though until then it was no more than a name. Recognising that even the name spelled powerful magic for the Kisans, Sahajanand decided to organise the Sabha.

Despite of the efforts of Swami Sahajanand in the direction of giving the Kisan Sabha a life but formal organisational structure, it remained more a movement than an organisation. However, after 1934, the movement was, in a way, institutionalised though its primary instruments of operation continued by numerous meetings, rallies, 'struggles' and annual conventions rather than paper works. This was a reflection of the impatient leadership of Sahajanand, which, in spite of resolutions to the contrary, was not basically concerned, with the formal niceties of organisation. While the agitational character marked the movement as necessarily transitory in nature, it also provided it with an element of spontaneous strength. While the Congress relied on its organisational character for mobilising the people for its movements, the Kisan Sabha drew its organisational vitality from the different movements and struggles. And, for the time being at least, the Kisan Sabha's mode of working was more effective. Even the officials remarked that the 'Kisan Sabha touches the ryot more directly and its meetings are larger than the Congress' [BSCRO: 16/1935].

But Sahajanand also recognised and emphasised the need for organisation of the peasants, except that organisation to him meant organisation of mass action rather than a fossilised hierarchy of constitutional formalities.

You must speak in great numbers. Government officials are here and when you come in tens of thousands they will listen, otherwise they will think you need nothing because you are silent. In Gaya there were 50,000 Kisans and it caused a furore. We do not teach you to assault zamindars, only to get what is your right. We do not seek to create trouble between zamindars and tenants by The Government, zamindars and capitalists are strong.It was assumed that Zamindars would collect half the product from the farmers and pay two-third of the government. But the actual collections by the zamindar were very high and cultivator s share had been reduced from one-third to one fifth (Dharma Kumar, 1982).

The membership of the Bihar Provincial Kisan Sabha was estimated at 80,000 in 1935 and the figure for 1938 was placed at more than 250,000, which made it by far the largest such provincial body in India. However, these and all other membership figures can be taken as no more than approximations. Verification is extremely difficult in the absence of any other data as a basis of comparison. The one possible measure of activity and an indication of participation, if not of membership, is to be derived from the press and official estimates of local meetings and provincial rallies. At the height of the agitation, Sahajanand consistently addressed local village meetings of up to 5000 peasants, and the estimates of peasant rallies in Patna were commonly as high as or even higher than 100,000.

With the formation of the All-India Kisan Sabha at Lucknow in April 1936, the Bihar Kisan Sabha became one of the provincial units of that national body. The Congress Socialist Party pressed for the organisation of an all-India peasant association, and N.G. Ranga [1949: 1968) became a prime mover in the effort. While Sahajanand was named president of the first meeting at Lucknow, he had come to support the idea reluctantly, holding that a national organisation could function effectively cnly on the basis of a network of well-developed provincial bodies, which did not in fact exist (Sahajanand, 1952). While Sahajanand, once involved, extended total support, and to a large extent created and maintained the organisational framework by his own efforts, the A.I.K.S. suffered from the very shortcomings he had indicated There was insufficient local depth to sustain a national movement (Mitra, 1938).

IV. CHANGING AGRARIAN RELATIONS THROUGH THE KISAN MOVEMENTS

The Kisan Sabha may have faltered in finding its feet in other parts of India, but in Bihar, from its very inception, it was involved in strong movements both based on and in turn generating mass enthusiasm for it. The dropping of the proposed tenancy amendment marked its very foundation in 1929. This was construed by the peasants as a significant victory and proved to be a tremendous morale-booster for them. On the heels of this came the Civil Disobedience Movement; and the Great Depression; and Provincial Autonomy; and the Second World War; and the Quit India Movement, and, finally, Independence. The Kisan Sabha grew from strength to strength on the crest of these waves of stirring political and economic events.

No earlier political campaign in India had fired the imagination of the rural population and become inter-twined with agrarian issues, as the Civil Disobedience Movement of the first few years of the 1930s did. The simple and yet deep issues behind the agitation and the innovative methods of struggle—illegal manufacture of salt, boycott of government officials, non- payment of taxes, mass courting of arrests, campaign against foreign cloth, liquor and chowkidary levies, combined with boycott of courts, schools and colleges—mobilised the vast forces of the agrarian population in unison with the urban masses. The campaign became so intense as well as widespread that an official view was that 'The political history of 1930-31 is. . . a tale of constant agitation', and of the measures taken by the government to combat this dangerous movement. In the "war". . . which resulted, there were frequent and sometimes serious clashes between the forces of law and order and those of unrest. . . (Mansfield, 1932.) While the movement erupted most vigorously in the towns, the villages, too, were so seriously involved that the government and 'loyalists' has to set-up 'Aman Sabhas' (Peace Councils) in rural areas to utilise the traditional local hold of zamindars to keep the tenants away from rebelling against the State. These Aman Sabhas succeeded here and there in restraining the peasantry but in many part of rural

Bihar, 'police parties and other government officials were attacked by mobs of villagers who threatened to murder them'. 'In Bhagalpur, a regular camp (of peasant activists) had been started at Bihpur, where volunteers were lodged in barracks and were taught drill and lathi play, the whole routine being regulated by bugle call'. [*Ibid.*: 2-3]. Alarmed at this type of mass upsurge combined with the anger of people over the hanging of Bhagat Singh and his comrades, 'the Government of India attempted to secure the goodwill of Mr Gandhi and the Congress Party and their cooperation in the work of making a durable constitutional settlement' (Williams, 1933:12). However, even the Gandhi-Irwin Pact did not pacify the aroused people. In the urban areas it did have some effect because 'the cities and the middle classes were a bit tired of the *hartals* and processions' (Nehru, 1936:232). But for the villages 'the Delhi settlement instead of pacifying. . . stimulated the forces of disorder' (Williams, 1933: 3-4). These forces of disorder were taken by a section of the Congress leadership to be the factor which 'was needed to liven things up, a fresh infusion of blood . . . where could this come from except from the peasantry—and the reserve stocks there were enormous'. (Nehru, 1936). The peasants, the 'reserve stocks' of the nationalist movement, did not belie the expectations of the leaders. With tremendous enthusiasm they jumped into the fray and the Civil Disobedience Movement for a while became a 'festival of the masses':

> A sense of rivalry prevailed in the countryside. Every village wanted to have the honour of getting the largest number of people arrested. . . . None broke the law clandestinely because it was an open Satyagraha. During my tour of the countryside I often saw the villagers gather in open places decorated with buntings and plantain leaves and manufacture salt with great ceremony (Prasad, 1957: 312; Das, 1996).

From No Tax to No Rent Movement

The movement did not remain at the level of ceremonies: the peasants translated the movement into their own terms and that greatly disconcerted not only the government and the loyalist zamindars but even a section of the Congress leaders. Jawaharlal Nehru [*op. cit.*] had foreseen this. With the participation of the peasantry, the campaign, he said, 'would again become a mass movement touching the vital interests of the masses, and, what was to me very important, would raise social issues'. Transforming the no-tax campaign into a no-rent movement raised these social issues. The movement in Bihar did not reach the proportions of the extensive campaign in the United Provinces and, in fact, in Bihar it developed in such a manner that in practice the zamindars tried to camouflage its seriousness by paying their revenue in most cases while the tenantry desisted from the payment of rent. In fact neither the government nor the zamindars took any drastic action, except in isolated cases, to terrorise the recalcitrant tenantry for several months because:

They were not sure of their grounds, as they had the political struggle with civil disobedience on the one side, and the economic slump, resulting in agricultural distress on the other. The two merged into each other, and the Government was always afraid of an agrarian upheaval (Nehru, 1936:237).

Such, indeed, was the actual or potential threat of this no-rent movement in U.P. that rent was reduced there to the 1901 level although officials felt that this action was 'entirely contrary to the terms of the permanent settlement' and 'not in the least justifiable' [BSCRO:34/1931]. Nevertheless, the rent reduction conceded was substantial, varying between five to eight annas (Re. 0.31 to Re. 0.50) in the rupee in Benaras division and thus, while it did not fully come to grips with agrarian problem it did temper the prospect of a 'peasant rising' and 'agrarian upheaval'.

Despite this example of the 'victory' of the U.P. peasantry, however, Congress leaders in Bihar did not press for rent and revenue remissions, nor in fact did they show much enthusiasm for the radical declarations made at the Karachi session of the Congress. This was because, by and large, the Congress leaders in Bihar were 'Gandhians' rather than 'Nehru-ites'. Gandhi himself had much earlier made his position clear:

While we will not hesitate to advise the Kisans, when the movement comes, to suspend payment of taxes of the Government, it is not contemplated that at any stages of non-cooperation we would seek to deprive the zamindars of their rent. The Kisan movement must be confined to the improvement of the status of the Kisans and the betterment of the relations between the zamindars and them. (Gandhi, 1921).

Even Nehru recognised that there were different opinions among Congressmen on this issue and tried to work out a method in which both the zamindars and tenants could be involved in the movement:

If the tenants stopped paying their rents the landlords suffered immediately. A class issue was also thus raised. The Congress, as a whole, was a purely nationalist body, and included many middling zamindars and a few of the larger ones also. Its leaders were terribly afraid of doing anything, which might raise this class issue or irritate the zamindar elements. So, right through the first six months of civil disobedience, they avoided calling for a general no-tax campaign in the rural areas, although conditions for this seemed to me to be ripe. I was not afraid of raising the class issue in this way or any other way, but I recognised that the Congress, being what it was, could not then patronise class conflict. It could, however, call upon both parties, zamindars and tenants not to pay (Nehru, 1936:232).

The desire to avoid class conflict prevented Congress from taking a consistent line. While in U.P., under the leadership of Jawaharlal Nehru, it backed the no-rent campaign, in Bihar 'the landlord element in the Congress camp decided against a no-rent campaign; the "dictator": advised the tenants to cultivate good relations with their landlords, and Congress diverted its energies well-tried channels of agitation. Its chief objects pending Mr Gandhi's return from England was the collection of funds and the enrolling of volunteers' [Williams, 1933: 6-9]. The radical declarations were reduced to empty verbiage and the officials smugly remarked:

The revolutionary creed enunciated by the Congress at Karachi provoked little comment and less sympathy. Such a charges could not appeal to the class of petty landowners from which many of the provincial Congress leaders were recruited. Their self-interest recoiled from the prospect of conducting a campaign against the payment of rents which in most parts of the settled districts of Bihar amount to ten times the land revenue (Williams, 1933:5).

In spite of the wavering of the leaders, however, the peasants did agitate in their own manner and even the officials were constrained to record that 'the lawless spirit born of civil disobedience was always liable to drive dissatisfied tenants to violence when a dispute occurred between them and the landlords' (Williams, 1933:32). This also led the tenants to agitate militantly on agrarian issues and organise themselves into Kisan Sabhas. Kisan Sabhas were formed in Patna, Gaya, Monghyr (where three village officials were killed by irate tenants), Champaran (where the Bettiah estate, under the Court of Wards, tried to contain peasant anger by granting concessions) and Palamau where 'the genuine grievances of the raiyats gave new life to the local Kisan Sabha, but agitators used the opportunity to preach the non-payment of rent and *chaukidari* tax, the wholesale cutting down of the jungle, and physical resistance to the landlords' agents' [Williams, 1939:9-16]. In addition, 'orators toured Bihar making violent speeches. Large number of volunteers, mainly loafers and unemployed persons were collected in (rural) training camps in the Muzaffarpur, Champaran, Saran and Manbhum districts and gave displays to impress the public' [*Ibid*.: 10]. The 'public' may or may not have been impressed by this display of force by the lumpen proletariat and the peasantry but the Civil Disobedience movement did affect the Kisans themselves in terms of arousing their consciousness. Even Sahajanand, who had kept himself aloof from the movement for a large part (Hauser, 1961:61), observed:

> The Satyagraha . . . brought unprecedented awakening among the Kisans. The result was that their problems also came to the forefront. They had sacrificed their utmost at the behest of the Congress. . . However could these (Congress) leaders. . . neglect them when they had to utilise the Kisans in the coming struggle? [Sahajanand, 1952: 327-377].

In spite of their largely pro-landlord bias, even the provincial Congress leaders knew that they could not neglect the peasants. Besides, the peasants themselves by their repeated militant actions were drawing attention towards their plight and were giving indication that if nothing was done soon to ameliorate their condition, matters would go out of the hands of the Congress leaders. In order to control this peasant anger as well as to give an impression of doing things for the Kisans, the Bihar Provincial Congress Committee (BPCC) decided to investigate the conditions of peasants in Gaya district. This was in 1931. Up to this day (1997 no report has been prepared nor was any statement issued to the press after the investigation. The BPCC Enquiry Committee, under the chairmanship of Rajendra Prasad, toured extensively and took copious evidence from the villagers but 'its findings resulted in no recommendations for change, beyond seeking the reconciliation of landlord-tenant differences' (Hauser, 1961:51). In fact, some government officials saw in the activities of the Congress Enquiry Committee and the tours of prominent leaders, a specific effort to disabuse the peasants of the belief that Gandhi's Civil Disobedience Movement and the then economic dislocation (Great Depression) were somehow related (BSCRO:34/1931).

The very failure of the BPCC's Enquiry Committee to come up with a report, however, resulted in highlighting the plight of the Kisans of Gaya. For, in order to do the work the Congress had not done, in 1933 the Bihar Provincial Kisan Council appointed a Committee to inquire into the problems of the peasants and to publish a report. The five-member committee consisted of Sahajanand, Yamuna Karjee, Yadunandan Sharma, Yugal Kishore Singh and Badri Narain Singh. This committee also investigated the conditions by extensively interviewing peasants and published its findings in the form of a pamphlet prepared by Sahajanand.

Sahajanand's damning indictment of conditions in Gaya drew two sorts of reactions from the government. While one lot of officials felt that 'Kisan Sabhas established in Patna and Gaya districts were never a source of danger' (Williams, 1933:9), although Sahajanand was a dangerous individual engaged in a sinister conspiracy to set-up the cultivator against the landlord and initiate a 'Communist Revolt' on the Russian model '[Hauser, 1961:97], on the other hand there was more sober assessment in the admission by various administrators that Sahajanand's case was strong and based on a solid substratum of fact'. A member of the Bihar Executive Council admitted that the Swami was 'clever and (had) justification for a great deal of what he said' [BSCRO: 163/1934], while a local official observed that Sahajanand was 'genuine in his work for the ryots' and drew attention to facts which 'really need investigation' [BSCRO:16/1935]. The government launched such an investigation, and concluded that Sahajanand's charges were essentially true. It was admitted that in matters of receipts and rent reduction the law favored the zamindar and the courts, which in any case were out of reach of the tenant, also joined in opposing him; that Kisans were subjected to 'harassment and illegal exactions'; that the conditions of bhaoli (produce rent) tenants were worst 'as they cannot take a grain of crops without the zamindar's consent'; and that collected rents were excessive and squeezed the tenant in the case of fall in prices. Only on the questions of canal rates and upkeep of irrigation facilities did the investigating officer (the District Collector) differ with the Kisan Sabha report. He concluded significantly that the tenants knew their difficulties, 'only they do not know the remedy' (BSCRO:163/1934).

Not that the government knew the remedy. It 'felt that nothing could be done about any of these matters and that the legislative council in any event would not agree to strengthening the law to the detriment of the majority of its zamindar members. In apparent good faith the Governor periodically called together deputations of Zamindars urging on them the establishment of goodwill with their tenants' (Hauser 1961: 98). This was an oft-repeated and oft-neglected plea.

The land reform programme in Bihar has failed dismally. Though zamindari was statutorily abolished in 1952, the programme did not significantly undermine the traditional social base of land control, which remained in the grip of dominant caste.

Farmers' Suicides

Kisan Sabha estimates the more than 5000 farmers committed suicide in Andhra Pradesh since 1998, more than

3000 committed suicide in Maharashtra, about 1000 farmers committed suicide in Punjab from 1998 to the present, and about 5000 committed suicide in Karnataka over the same period. (People's Democracy, 2006). Unfortunately many of them specially farmers from smaller farm size could not sustain growing burden of loans from moneylenders, traders, dealers of inputs for many years. Because of loss of face before the community consequent upon mounting burden of debts, failures of credit, insurance and procurement delivery mechanisms and agencies they were forced to commit suicides. Various studies and reports have been conducted on this serious problem. (Indira Gandhi Institute of Development Research (IGIDR, Mumbai) has brought a comprehensive study on suicides of farmers (Mishra, 2006:41) for the government of Maharashtra. Study found various reasons for suicides. About 86.5 per cent suicides were because of indebtedness, 73.9 per cent for deteriorating economic status, and 40.5 per cent because of crop failures. Loss of face in community because of non-payment of loan, unable to marry their marriageable sisters and daughters, etc. About 91 per cent of suicides were committed by males. As per police record number of suicides in Maharashtra in 2004 alone was 4147. Study reported that number of suicides increased from 11,866 to 14,729 between 1995 to 2004. Study suggests that suicides in females registered decline after 1999.

V. POST-INDEPENDENCE AGRARIAN RELATIONS AND FORMATION OF MILITANT

Private Senas

Changing Agrarian Relations and Caste-Organisations in Bihar

The offshoot of Naxal menance is the main cause of the birth of Caste senas (private) like Sunlight Sena, Bhumi Sena, Kunwar Sena, Brahmarshi Sena, Ranvir Sena, etc. (Table 1). Caste is an important determining factor for the changing agrarian Relations. Just after the suppression of 1857 rebellion, many organisations came into existence like the Congress, the Landholders' Association, the Zamindar Association', etc. But in Bihar there started an era of forming

Caste Associations. The first Caste Association, The Kayastha Mahasabha was formed in 1887. It was followed by Bhumihar-Brahmin Association in 1889, Saryupary Brahmin Sabha in 1905, Rajput and Rawani Kahar Mahasabha in 1906, Marwari Young Men Association in 1907, Dusadh Sabha in 1911, Gope Mahasabha, Kewat Mahasabha, Kurmi Mahasabha and Nai Mahasabha (Barber) in 1912 (Dalip, 2001). The Triveni Sangh was combined organisation of Yadava, Koeris and Kurmi, in 1936. It was an attempt to form coalition of Castes to supersede other castes or caste groups.

But in early 70s two struggles emerged in rural Bihar. One was the struggle of the so-called backward castes for political dominance and the other of the marginal peasants and landless labourers for minimum wages and land reforms. It was directed both against the dominant forward and backwards.

TABLE I

The List of Some Upper and Lower Caste Organisations

Lower Caste Organisations		*Upper Castes Organisations*	
1. Lorik Sena	Yadavas	1. Sunlight Sena	Bhumihars/ Rajputs
2. Maoist Communist Centre	Dalits	2. Bhumi Sena	Kurmis
3. Peoples' War Groups	Dalits	3. Kuer Sena	Rajputs
4. CPI-ML	Dalits	4. Brahmarshi Sena	Bhumihars
5. Party Unity	Dalits	5. Ranvir Sena	Bhumihars
6. Lal Senas	Dalits	6. Savarna Liberation Front	Bhumihars

Source: Collected from the Different Reports, Articles and Newspapers.

Mandalisation of Economy

The 26 per cent reservation policy introduced by Karpuri-Thakur government in 1978 poured some oil in the burning fire of Caste-conflict and agrarian relations. The Mandal Commission reports-based politics played by politicians from Delhi to the remote villages added more fuel to the fire after 1989. Then came the Laloo-era after 1990. The picture became more enlarged and sharpened by Caste colours in every parts. This prompted the landholders mostly belonging to upper Castes (mainly Bhumihar and Rajputs) and lower Castes including Scheduled Castes to organise themselves in the name of Castes. Not only caste organisations but also caste-based 'private senas' were formed. Till date, more than 15 senas are operating in different pockets like Ranavir Sena, Kunwar Sena, Lawrik Sena, etc. (Table 1)

VI. NAXAL MOVEMENT AND CHANGING AGRARIAN RELATION IN BIHAR

Various causes of rural Naxal movement in Bihar are: (a) low rate of minimum wages, (b) ending the illegal encroachment of Government land *(Garmagarua Amm)* by landlord and its distribution among the land less, (c) Fishing right of the rural labourers in village based *ahar, pokhar and* rivers, (d) class retaliation, (e) non-economic demand like ending the sexual exploitation of women belonging to the rural poor, dalit, agricultural labourers households, and lastly (f) acquisition of the surplus land above ceiling and its redistribution among the Rural poor and actual management of wasteland. Various scholars have adequately demonstrated that one of the prime reason for the continuation of Naxal movement in Bihar is the weak implementation of land reforms policies and management of wasteland. In spite of the continued agrarian violence, implementation of land reforms continues to be weak in Bihar, mainly due to ineffective implementation of land ceiling programme and *Bataidari System. Another* important issue of land reforms in Bihar and particularly in central and north Bihar includes the distribution of Government land. Though the distribution of Government land to the weaker section is much more than that of land ceiling. Yet in central Bihar one of the important reason of the continued clashes between the landlords and the landless (agricultural rural poor) is the issue of forceful occupation of *Gair mazarua land* by the landlords immediately after Abolition of Zamindari System.

Land reforms have also benefited the agrarian rural poor with the effect of Naxal movement in Bihar. Naxal movement in Bihar is because of the weak implementation of land reform policies. Among the major issues of land reforms include the ineffective implementation of land ceiling and *Bataidari* issue. Till March 2000, 3.086-lakh acres land has been distributed to 3.80 lakh land less families. Of total beneficiaries, Scheduled Castes were 2.35 lakh, Scheduled Tribes 0.43 lakhs and other weaker section were 1.02 lakhs. Up to March 2000, 13.39 lakhs acres of Government lands have been distributed to 12.98 lakhs beneficiaries of different categories as shown on Table 2.

TABLE 2

Government Lands Distributed among the Different Category of Beneficiaries in Bihar

Sl. No.	*Category*	*No. of Families Benefited*	*Land Distributed (In Acres)*
1.	Schedule Caste	6.10 lakhs	5.48 lakhs
2.	Scheduled Tribes	2.39 lakhs	4.01 lakhs
3.	Backward Caste	2.83 lakhs	2.45 lakhs
4.	Others	–	0.58 lakhs
	Total	11.32 lakhs	12.52 lakhs

Source: K. Gopal Iyer, 2000.

Out of total 16.68 lakh acres of land donated under Bhoodan movement, an extent of 7.26 lakh acres were distributed unto March 2000 to 5.81 lakhs families. Home based lands have been distributed to 15.11 lakhs individuals covering 0.74 lakh acres. Every family has been given four decimal lands for residential purpose.

VII. MIS-MANAGEMENT OF WASTELANDS AND NAXAL MOVEMENT IN BIHAR

The mismanagement of a large chunk of wasteland (about 33.2 lakh hectare) in Bihar also adds fuel to the fire.

Which is an important cause of agrarian conflict. Traditionally, these lands have been used by dominant people in liaison with the local administration and *lathiats.* The government has failed to give possession of such lands to the landless. There is fight over grazing, pasture, fallow and other wastelands between those who has been using for long and those who make their claims.

Naxal leadership took this conflict as on opportunity to broad-base their movement. Under the banner of Naxal groups, such land has been grabed, some portion has been given to few rural landless poor also.

In spite of the several problems during the last few years, Government of Bihar has still not rendered justice to the rural poor in terms of proper distribution of Government land for cultivation and housing purposes.

The agrarian structure had been exploitative and detrimental to agriculture development and has led to violent clashes in rural areas in Bihar. The Walter Houser, expressed the reason of Naxal movement that the system of produce rent, share cropping, low agricultural wages, system of *begar,* etc. were the common features. Physical maltreatment, oppression, *Zulum* as forced labour called *begar* were clear indicators of the oppressive system. (Walter Houser, 1961, p. 24)

TABLE 3

Types of Wastelands in Bihar

(As on 1987-88)

S. No.	*Types of Wasteland*	*Area (in Hectares)*
1.	Barren and uncultivable lands	979223
2.	Permanent Pasture and other Grazing Lands	143373
3.	Land under Miscellaneous land	217055
4.	Cultivable wastelands	439338
5.	Current Fallow	1618885
6.	Other Fallow	923721
7.	Total Wastelands	4321595

Source: India Statistical Abastract, 1989.

Agriculture is the basic component of Bihar. Progressive and effective utilisation of long and broad aspect of agriculture has to be the main plank for tackling the problem of rural unemployment. But the agricultural sector of Bihar is unable to employ the available rural labour force. Seasonal unemployment is also one problem faced by rural youths. We know 'the empty mind is devil's workshop'. Rural youths are involved only in the peak time of agricultural activities, directly or indirectly, but in the seasonal gap that means lean period-unemployed rural workforce can think only some destructive ideas. So employment opportunities for the rural labour force varies from peak to lean seasons. In the slack seasons these rural youths move around caste leader, big landlord and political leaders. These leaders guide these rural youths and motivate them to join local senas. These landlords and political persons give protection to rural youths and also provide arms and ammunitions. Naturally, the land and political power passes into the hand of upper caste raiyats/under-raiyats and intermediate cultivating castes. Beside the upper caste landlords, there are landlords amongst backward castes like Yadavs, Koeries and Kurmis. At times, they join hands forgetting their caste- affiliations. The land controller of central Bihar retained the legacy of land control even after zamindari abolition. Beside, this zone had supremacy of Yadavs, Koeries, Kurmis along with Bhumihar, Brahmins and Rajputs, in the sphere of land control. Due to low level of wages and inadequate sources of employment, a large number of rural poor and labourers, change ideas and join local senas.

VIII. STATE SCENARIO OF RURAL NAXAL MOVEMENT

State of Bihar came to global notice in last few years for the activities of so many local rural Naxal violence. The violence in Bihar lend ample testimony to the fact that the naxalite movement has been very active throughout the decade both in central Bihar and Jharkhand State. Its reverberations were felt more loudly in central Bihar during last few years due to the rise of various landlords' armies.

The Government of Bihar has classified the area of influence of the naxalite movement into category A and category B districts. The category A districts include Patna, Gaya, Jahanabad, Aurangabad, Bhojpur, Palamu, Garhwa, Hazaribagh and Chatra. The category A districts have the naxalaite movements in a more volatile and intense form. The category B districts are less intense and include the districts of Rohtash, Bhabhua, Nawada, Lohardagga, Ranchi, Giridih, Dhanbad and Bokaro. Within Category A five districts are from Jharkhand state. It may be necessary to point out that the character of the naxalite movement has undergone a qualitative change after the emergence and aggressive participation of Ranvir Sena. Ranvir sena, the private militia of the upper caste Bhumihar, massacred over 35 backward caste Yadavas, and dalits. Among the victims, were 19 women, 12 men and four children on June 18, 2000 at Miapur under Aurangabad district. The BBC news team was told by sena spokes-person that their "operation will continue until we throw away the extremists in the Bay of Bengal where they come from." This team visited the state to report on the massacres in remote villages, in Bihar. The Miapur massacre, it may be recalled, is the latest in a series of attacks and counter attacks that were fuelled by caste conflicts. The Ranvir sena massacred 22 dalits and backward castes in Shankarbigha Village in Jahanabad district on 25 January 1999. They again struck on February 10 and killed 11 dalits in Narayanpur village in Jahanabad district. In retaliation, on March 18, 1999, the Maoist Communist Centre (MCC) massacred over 34 upper caste Bhumihars in Senari village in Jahanabad district. The cycle of caste-class violence goes on unabated in central Bihar.

Are Naxal Movement Class or Caste Wars?

The spokesperson of the Ranvir sena, said in a television "the communist start the trouble, calling it a class war. But what they actually started was a caste war. What choice have we got but to fight back against these extremists." The press releases that they have killed 34 people in retaliation to the murder of 34 upper caste men by communists in a nearby village in 1999. (K.K. Singh, 2000).

The killing on Senari on March 18, 1999 in Jahanabad district have shown the division of the Naxal group from their original path. Another killing at Latto village in Palamu on November 17, 1999. Confirming the aforesaid and posed question before us on the caste based rural violence. The *Times of India*, Patna, March 2, 1999 reported on the Senari killings that "there were no big landlords and was no conflict in those localities. The Bhumihars, who were killed, did not own more than the seven to eight acres of land. They had no links with Ranvir senas." So the Bihar violence are neither social nor economic rather it is based on caste antagonism. Next seven dalits mowed down at Mehandipur village under the Punpun police station in Patna district on 2nd October 2000. According to Deccan Herald News Service, Patna (October 3, 2000), the armed People's War Group men attacked three adjoining villages of Badepura, Shahbaazpur and Mehandipur late last night. When the villagers came out in protest, the armed men fired at them, in which six rural youths aged between 18 and 25 were killed and some others injured. All the deceased were dalits and members of the CPI (ML) Liberation. Bihar has for three decades been engaged in seemingly endless cycle of tit-for-tat caste murders.

Factors that various researchers conclude about masseurs are varied. Some see it as a caste struggle, the dalits trying to rise against the upper caste operation. Other try to read it as a natural consequence of naxalite movement. The state and the central government would project massacres as law and order problems. There are some people who would state that what ever is happening in central and south Bihar, is a social problem and there is no economic root to it.

The prime organisation representing the 'new naxalite', the CPI (ML) Liberation group, states unequivocally, "First of all, we do not subscribe to any theory of 'excitative violence' and still less to 'individual assassination'". On the issue of violence, its position is conditioned by the prevailing situation:

> "Everywhere in Bihar, it is the landlords who are armed, they derive a sadistic pleasure by beating and killing poor peasants, burning their houses and raping

their women. Secondly, by any human logic whatsoever, the rural poor cannot be denied their right to organise their own resistance forces to counter the attacks of landlord armies. Thirdly, if peasant struggle takes violent forms in Bihar, the root must be sought in the forms of oppression."

In fact, reports from Bihar indicate that wherever these 'new naxalite' have managed to acquire significant strength the incidence of day-to-day rural violence has gone down considerably. It is they rather than the established police machinery that are the best guarantee of law and order in the complete sense of the term.

Another feature attributed to 'extremists' is their lack of participation in the processes of electoral democracy. Again, this was true of the first phase of the movement, which was characterised by infantile adventurism. Emerging out of a long and sustained struggle among peasants in the Gangetic plains of Bihar, the 'new naxalite' appreciate the potency of the electoral processes, though they are not blinded by the stars of parliamentary practices in their eyes. (Das, 1997, Swami and Friends).

The qualitatively new aspect of the 'new Naxalite' movement as an important force in left politics has not had its significance properly noted by outside analysts. Political commentators on Bihar have got bogged down in the morass of the Congress-Janata syndrome and even as sociologists try to untangle the various strands of its complicated caste web, they have, by and large, ignored the broad correspondence of the caste and class structure. A refreshing aspect of the 'new Naxalite' movement has been that, unlike vulgar Marxists, it has neither ignored the caste question nor has it gone overboard on non-class understanding of caste, culture and ethnicity. The appeal to Kurmi and Yadava peasants as well as to dalit labourers, but the same time it recognises that caste is not an invariant absolute evidence its creative encounter with caste in Bihar. The non-dogmatic and non-sectarian approach is also reflected in discussion of other extra-economic matters like the position of women, issues of cultural heterogeneity, etc.

The new politics of the left in Bihar has been spreading not only in the areas of original Naxalite activity like Bhojpur but also to the tribal Jharkhand region and eastern U.P. Organisationally, there is a variety of bodies involved in the movement. They range from various factions of the CPI (ML), the most prominent being the Liberation and Party Unity groups, the MCC, mass organisations like the IPF and Mazdoor Kisan Sangram Samiti and agrarian trade unions like the Kisan Sabha. Although many of these groups have distinct organisational forms and there is even some rivalry between them on carving out 'spheres of influence'. There is similarity in their intent if not in their modes of operation.

In spite of the existence of several such organisations, fratricidal conflict, which was a marked feature of the earlier Naxalites, is much less today. There are occasions when these organisations criticize each other even severely, as for instance in the Liberation group's denunciation of the tactics of the MCC in utilising caste conflict which led to the Dalelchak-Baghaura and other massacres, but there have been instance of cooperation between these groups and indeed between them and other democratic elements even in parties like the Samajwadi Party and CPI. The re-enactment of Jallianwalla Bag or Arwal in April 1986 saw a broad movement arising with the participation of all that were horrified by the extent and nature of police atrocities. Today, the unfolding of the fodder scam has once again provided the opportunity for the Left and democratic groups to unite.

At the same time, the role of organisations like the Jan Sanskriti Mannish, All India Student Associations, Revolutionary Youth Organisation, Inquilabi Minorities Manch, Janwadi Mahila Morcha, etc. The struggle against religious fundamentalism, obscurantism ideology, rank Casteism and feudal oppression of women, in short, in a democratic awakening in semi-feudal Bihar, is increasing. And perhaps as logical outcome of the increasing presence of this 'New Left' in Bihar is its intervention in macro-issues.

Declining Naxalism

In the 1970s, the Naxalite movement in Bihar weakend on account of three major factors: its own adventurist stupidity, the developmentalist and computational intervention of Jaya Prakash Narain and repression by the state. But the movement did not collapse. Indeed, the grim agrarian situation and overall deterioration of the political scenario of the state created a new and more vital left. Its challenge cannot be met by old prescriptions. It embodies the emergence of a specific social democracy in the peculiar situation of Bihar.

It is difficult to delineate the formal organisations, which are involved in the peasant upsurge, and related political, social and cultural movements that are taking place in central Bihar. At most a general picture of the organisational networks can be drawn with only an approximation of the different complexities that hold the network together.

In fact, the conglomeration of organisations can trace its beginnings to the organised peasant movement in the area, which began in 1928 with the formation of the Patna District Kisan Sabha under the leadership of Swami Sahajanand Saraswati. Later it developed into the Bihar Provincial Kisan Sabha and became the core of the All India Kisan Sabha, which struggled against zamindari. After zamindari abolition in the 1950s, although the formal organisation remained extinct, largely under the control of the Communist Party of India (CPI), it lost its teeth. In the 1970s when the peasant movement grew up again in the region, albeit on different premises and demands, several rudimentary mass organisations of peasants came up here and there. In the early 1980s, the need was felt to consolidate them into one formation and the Bihar Pradesh Kisan Sabha was launched once again. It claimed continuity with the original Kisan Sabha of Sahajanand, even as it took up new issues related primarily to the demands of the small peasants and agricultural labourers.

IX. AGRARIAN CHANGE AND ITS IMPACT ON RURAL WAGE

Generally two types of labourers are found in Agricultural Sector: (a) Hired attached labourers, (b) Casual Labour.

(a) Hired Attached Labourers

They are normally employed for a year at a time and perform agricultural, non-agricultural, as well as domestic, work for the employer.

(b) Casual Labourers

They can be divided into those who are employed for a certain number of days and paid on a daily basis, and those who are employed to undertake a specific agricultural operation and remunerated according to the job done.

These two categories of agricultural labourers also differ in terms of their job mobility. The attached labourers are normally heavily dependent on one particular family for work. In contrast, the casual labourers are most independent. Increase in the wage of agricultural labourers in naxal affected areas in terms of kind/cash. The non-dogmatic approach and their record of not only ensuring economic gains for the rural poor through enforcing payment of minimum wages, prescribed by law but seldom actually paid by landowners, and even distribution of some ceiling-surplus lands in accordance with long-enacted but hardly ever implemented legislation, but also taking up 'constructive activities' like upgradation of community assets in the shape of irrigation works, wells pastures, etc. The naxalite movement in south-central Bihar have been playing a role of comprising both regulatory and promotional aspects in the field of rural wage. In short, their struggle has come to represent the very process of state formation in an otherwise anarchic situation.

In last few decades, there has been growing awareness among the rural poor and depressed people due to several factors like spread of literacy, the policy intervention by the government, increasing contact of rural labourers through migration with the scenario of Delhi, Haryana, Punjab and militant campaigns launched by leftist and ultra-leftist organisations. These situations create fertile soil for the Naxal movement in the context of rural wages. It has enabled to be more conscious of their fundamental rights of equality, freedom and right against exploitation. Now they cannot be fooled on the issue of labour related matters like minimum wages, labour relations and working hours. The social dynamics that has accelerated the process is both the causes and effect of the rising awareness among the rural poor. Now, they are not ignorant of the knowledge about the ceiling surplus land, about the fallow public land and other legislations related to the land ownership. From the fast ongoing socio-economic transformation, it can be inferred due to lack of proper and constructive direction, the state has plunged into the incessant violent incidents, which has the characteristics of the class war as well as the caste war.

X. CONCLUSIONS AND RECOMMENDATIONS

The history of changing agrarian relation in Bihar is the consummation of several factors like Unequal land-ownership, limited land availability, the fast growing population dubious political leadership, caste-class antagonism and spineless administration. A large chunk of unused land in rural areas is also the apple of discord between landlords and land-less peasants. In this situation the condition of rural poor has become very complex. The rural poor have become more poor in Bihar due to the burden of self-debt, burden of ancestral debt, food purchase, daughter's marriage, high dependency ratio, population growth, crop failure, litigation or case, unemployment, lack of institutional credit, low productivity, lack of subsidiary occupation, children education, etc.

In pre-independence era of Bihar, the sadistic Zamindars derived pleasure by beating and killing rural poor and small peasants, burning their houses and victimising their women. Now the rural poor are deriving strength by organising their own resistance forces to counter the offence zamindars. Therefore, the ugly-violent scene in Bihar can not be set right by old prescriptions.

In fact, situation of Bihar indicates that, wherever these 'new Naxalites' have managed to acquire significant strength the incidence of day-to-day rural violence has gone down considerably. It is they rather than the established police machinery that guarantees peaceful law and order situation in the complete sense of the term. Indeed, the grim agrarian situation and overall deterioration of the political scenario of the state created a new and more effective scene. Its challenge cannot be met by old prescriptions. It embodies the emergence of a specific social democracy in the peculiar situation of Bihar.

In essence, the entire Naxal movement revolves around involving the rural poor.

To stamp it out, needs of the hour are:

- to increase and ensure the wages of agrarian labourers, who account for 30-40 per cent of the total rural population,
- to seize the surplus land from big farmers, *mahanths,* and rich peasants; and to distribute of the same among landless and poor peasants,
- to accelerate the economic growth by promoting agriculture, building infrastructures, evolving proper water management to control floods and draughts and initiating industrilisation in rural areas,
- to protect the social dignity of dalits and backward castes and women by revitalising the low-enforcing agencies and by changing the feudal mind-sets of upper castes of *babusahebs, babhans* and *babajis,* and
- the centre must intervene with a special Bihar package with rational and strict guidelines for the effective and honest utilisation of money in the developmental works.

To sum up in a few words that the changing agrarian relation has glorious history in Bihar right from Gandhi's Champaran movement to Sahajanand's Kisan Movement. Naxal movement has also managed to acquire significant strength the incidence of day-to-day rural violence has gone down considerably but social awakens and dignity of dalits, backward castes and rural poor has risen. Budget 2008-09 presented by Finance Minister Mr. P. Chitamberam under the stewardship of Great economist PM Dr. Manmohan Singh. Proposed to waive off 60,000 crores loans of farmers. Such a drastic step has been taken in the wake of agrarian crisis leading to tragic suicides by a large number of farmers in the country. But it does not seems to be a pragmatic step to resolve the agrarian crisis. This huge amount could be spent on improving the irrigation facilities and other facilities related to improve the agricultural productivity. This policy of loan waiving will inculcate the habit of borrowing loans with the hope of getting it waived up in the future. In the state like Bihar, not a single farmer will get the benefit of the waiver of the loan because agricultural borrowing in Bihar is mainly non- institutional in nature.

References

BPKS (Bihar Provincial Kisan Sabha), (1936), Bihar Prantiya Kisan Sabha ka Vidhan—(Constitution of the Bihar Provincial Kisan Sabha), in Hindi, Patna.

BSCRO, File 34/1931, Letter of N.F. Peck, Shahabad District Magistrate dated 15 December 1931.

BSCRO, File 21/1933, Agrarian Affairs, Kisan Sabhas.

BSCRO, File 163/1934, Notes and Orders on Swami Sahajanand's Gaya Report, 12 November 1934.

BSCRO, File 16/1935, Extract from Fortnightly Report of the Commissioner of Bhagalpur, 4 April 1935.

BSCRO, File 16/1935, Fortnighly Report from J.R. Dain, Commissioner of Bhagalpur, 2 December 1935.

BSCRO, File 16/1935(I), report on Swami Sahajanand, Nasirganj, Shahabad district, 18 January 1935.

Chowdhury, A.M. (1998), Rural Landlessness and Institutional Reforms, Rawat Publication, New Delhi, p. 371.

Chayanov, A.V., (1997), Peasent Farm Organisation, quoted in Solomon, Susan Gross, The Soviet Debate, Colorado: Westview Press.

Das, Arvind N., (1981), Agrarian Unrest and Socio-economic Change in Bihar, 1900-1980, Delhi: Manohar.

Das, Arvind N., (1996), Changel: The Biography of a Village, New Delhi:

8

Processes Food Industry in Bihar: A Critical Analysis

Dinesh Prasad, Jawahar Lal and Ranjana Sharma

The desired growth of India's agriculture and allied sector in general and economic prosperity of rural farmers in particular are achievable only with an effective integration and synergy between agriculture and agro-based industries. Food processing transforms agriculture raw materials into safe, convenient, good tasting and nutritious products for consumers. It is a diverse industry that ranges from small and medium enterprises to major multi-national companies. It adds value, enhances shelf live of the perishable agro-food products, encourages crop diversification and ensures remunerative market price of the agricultural produce by making it more marketable. The use of appropriate processing technology for surplus production of cereals, fruits, vegetables, milk, fish, meat, poultry, etc. extensive research and development in innovative food technologies and aggressive marketing both inside and outside the country would ensure backward and forward linkage benefits to the Indian small and marginal farmers.

Food and agricultural subsidy has been increasing over

the years. Experts treat subsidy as a persistent malady affecting the fiscal health of the economy. The government's present policy is to declare minimum support price or central issue price of agricultural produce, whenever the market price is un-remunerative and to bear the shortfall of subsidy. The most practical remedy would be to ensure remunerative market price of the agricultural produce by making it more marketable. The question arises how? – By the simple device of processing it, packaging it and prolonging its durability.

For an agrarian economy like India, food processing has been found to be the key of economic growth. Food has one of the highest economic multipliers of any industry. It provides largest employment in the world, because for every job in the food sector, many additional jobs are created for retailers, suppliers and other business partners.

Globally, food is one of the first industries to develop scale and importance, whereas in Bihar, it is still negligible. Global experiences indicate that agriculture development in the country can be given a big boost by growth of agro and food processing industries. India currently produces about 9 per cent of the world's production of fruits and accounts for 11 per cent of the world's vegetable production. However, only about 2 per cent of the fruits and vegetables in India are processed. Lack of processing and inadequate storage of fruits and vegetables result in huge wastages. Currently Indian food processing sector employs about 13 million people directly and 35 million people indirectly. In 2004-05 food processing sector contributed about 14 per cent of manufacturing GDP with a share of Rs. 2,80,000 crores. Out of this, the unorganised sector accounted for more than 70 per cent of production in terms of volume and 50 per cent in terms of value.

FOOD PROCESSING IN BIHAR

There are several factors which favours agriculture sector in Bihar. The state is positioned to utilise its rich untapped natural resources such as fertile soils and abundant water. More importantly, it can avail of the benefits of increasing stress on the food processing sector at national level. Bihar is the 7th largest economy in India in terms of food production. The economy is primarily agrarian with agriculture, contributing to more than 38 per cent of the Gross State Domestic Products (GSDP). Bihar is eight largest producers of food grains in the country such as cereals, pulses, oilseeds and cash crops. The major cereals are rice, wheat and maize and major pulses are gram, arhar, moong and masoor. In addition, the major cash crops are potato, sugar cane, jute, tobacco and spices. Bihar is the third largest producer of vegetables and the sixth largest producer of fruits in India with a production of 8.3 million MT and 3.03 million MT respectively. Bihar is the only state producing *makhana* commercially. Bihar produces a large quantity of numbers of vegetable and it is largest producer of okra, second largest producer of potato and third largest producer of cabbage. Bihar produces large quantities of number of fruits. It is the largest producer of litchi, second largest producer of guava and third largest producer of pineapples. The major food producing district mostly overlaps with the vegetable producing district. Muzaffarpur and Vaishali districts lead litchi and banana production, Darbhanga, Champaran (East and West), Vaishali lead mango production and Rohtas and Bhojpur lead guava production.

Bihar ranks fourth in term of meat production in India. The production of eggs amounted to 789 million eggs (1.75% of the total egg production in India) in the state in 2004-05. Poultry meat is the fastest growing animal protein in India and estimated to increase but Bihar has negligible share in national poultry meat. Fish is one of the popularly consumed items in Bihar particularly in Mithila region and it is the fastest growing sub-sector indicating a growth rate of over 10 per cent per annum (NABARD, 2006). Fish production in Bihar is showing increasing trend. Bihar produced about 2.9 million tons of milk or 3.28 per cent of the total milk production in the country. A variety of spices are produced in Bihar. Chilli accounting for 39.5 per cent of production followed by turmeric which accounts 36.4 per cent of the production are the major spices which is produced in the state.

Food Consumption

As a consumer, Bihar, with a population of 83 million, (growing at about 2.43% per annum) is a large and growing market for food products. Food is the single largest component of private consumer expenditure, accounting for as much as 59 to 60 per cent of the total consumption expenditure. At a conservative estimate the current market for food in Bihar is whopping Rs. 40 thousand crores of which the processed food market including beverage is estimated at close to Rs. 18 thousand crores. At the estimated national growth rate of consumption of 7 per cent of food consumption market, Bihar is estimated to be Rs. 56 thousand crores in 2010 and Rs. 83 thousand crores in 2015.

The expenditure pattern indicates that the consumption of cereals continues to dominate the expenditure. There is a market trend in shift towards high protein and high nutrition foods such as dairy products, meat, vegetables and beverages. The expenditure increased by about 15 per cent of vegetables and that of eggs, meat and fish by about 40 per cent. The consumption pattern has not only changed in the urban sector but also in rural sector of Bihar.

Current Status of Processed Food Industries

In Bihar, the level of processing is negligible barring the dairy industry where the level of processing between 9 to 10 percent. The low levels of processing are a combination of complex issues including Bihar's investment climate, traditional demand for fresh produce, infrastructure constraints, weaknesses of local factor markets and institutional support.

The major food processing activities in the state are milling and milk processing. Currently, there are 58 roller flour mills, 4872 rice mills, 9 huller-*cum*-spellers and only 51 modernised mills. There are 45 licensed food and vegetable processing units.

The food processing in Bihar, today is mainly in the unorganised sector with over one thousand bakeries and confectioneries and even small scale grain processing continuing in the unorganised sector. The estimated growth rate of food processing sector in Bihar during the last two to three years is around 3.46 per cent as compared to approximately 7 per cent on all India basis.

The value addition happens mainly to primary processing. There is no raw or ripe mango processing unit in organised sector in the state. In vegetables, some processing of tomato into ketchup and juice happens in the organised sector and similarly for other vegetables including potato where chips and fries are produced in cottage industry and in unorganised form. For *makhana* the processing technology adopted is very rudimentary and labour intensive which is not matching with returns.

Most of the marketable surplus goes out of state either for table consumption or processing or value addition—mango and litchi are prime examples—thereby resulting in dual negative impact on the state economy, i.e., (a) loss in terms of value addition, and (b) revenue outflow in terms of importing it back in the state from outside.

Infrastructure for Food Processing

The state has inadequate infrastructure for food processing. A research by Rajendra Agriculture University, Pusa reveals that post-harvest losses in fruits and vegetables vary from 15-50 per cent in Bihar.

TABLE I

Post-harvest Losses in Fruits and Vegetables in Bihar

Fruits	*% loss*	*Vegetables*	*% loss*
Mango	25-30	Cabbage	17-27
Banana	15-25	Cauliflower	41-47
Papaya	30-50	Potato	15-29
Litchi	20-36	Tomato	19-31
		Onion	19-31

Source: Verma, V.S., 2002.

A study of Department of Marketing and inspection, GOI records that post-harvest losses of food grains in Bihar vary from 3 to 6 per cent. The study, however, does not account for farm level losses.

TABLE 2

Post-harvest Losses in Food Grains in Bihar

Crop	*% loss*	*Crop*	*% loss*
Paddy	4.88	Bengal Gram	3.66
Wheat	4.15	Moong	2.98
Maize	3.79	Urad	2.73
Pigeon pea	3.22	Masoor	5.66

Source: Department of Marketing and Inspection, GOI

Warehousing and Storing

Bihar has a total food grains storage capacity of 13.4 lakh tons, lowest in comparison to other states, which cater to only 12 per cent of the total food grain production in the state. Besides there are about only 120 to 130 rural godowns as against 7 thousand rural markets. So there is a urgent need to construct rural godowns for the benefit of small farmers. Bihar has 215 cold stores of which only 5.6 per cent are in cooperative sector and remaining in private sector. Most of the cold storage space is being used to store potatoes. The existing capacity in the state is extremely inadequate to cop up with production and hence there is urgent need to create warehousing infrastructure at vantage points.

Marketing Channels

There are more than 7000 rural markets and hats in addition to erstwhile 95 APMC *mandis* and 32 principal market yards. Out of these 7000 only about 855 rural hats have their own buildings and premises for providing rudimentary grading and sorting facilities. Vegetables mostly are not sold in agriculture market yards due to a number of reasons primarily being the distance from the production centres and the high cost entailed in transportation. There exists a large chain of intermediaries in the marketing system of cereals, fruits and vegetables from the farm gate to the ultimate user. There are primarily three channels through which the produce is marketed as on next page.

Marketing Channels

Potentials for Food Processing in Bihar

The value addition in FPI in India is estimated at about 20 per cent. The level of processing varies across segments and states. Given the current low level of processing in the state, there exists a tremendous potential if the right investment climate, operating environment and policy impetus are provided for the sector. The emerging retail boom provides another big opportunity for the state to establish food processing industries in the State of Bihar. Bihar already has a few agricultural commodities to cater to niche markets for a gainful utilisation of the existing potential, infrastructure creation and institutional development holds the key.

A decrease in post-harvest losses by just one percent will result in value addition of Rs. 80 crores to the GSDP by food grains and about Rs. 120 crores by the fruit and vegetable sectors. Thus, the total value addition to the state GSDP simply by minimising losses to 2 per cent in food grains and 15 per cent in fruits and vegetables would lead in value addition in GSDP by approximately Rs. 2000 crores.

The multiplier effect of investment in food processing industry on employment generation is 2.5 times than in other industrial sectors, higher than any other sector. The employment intensity is significantly higher in unorganised food processing sector as compared to organised sector for the same level of investment. For every Rs. 10 million investment, 1050 jobs are created in the unorganised sector against 140 jobs in the organised sector.

In spite of all the constraints in processed food industry in the state, there is a few successful stories which show the path for the food processing industry. COMFED is one example and *makhana* industry is another along with litchi. COMFED procures 5.7 lakhs litres of milk per day through milk unions—the milk procurement has increased by about eight times from 1991-92 to 2005-06. It processes about 9 per cent of the milk processed in the state. *Makhana* is unique to Bihar as it grown commercially only in Bihar. It contributes about 250 crores at farm gate prices and Rs. 550 crores at retail prices annually to the economy of Bihar.

Cereals and Pulses

There exists a large potential for scientific milling and processing of food grains like rice, wheat, maize and pulses. In case of rice and wheat, outdated technologies are used for milling resulting in lower recovery and lower value. There is no large scale processing unit for maize in the state but there is a huge scope for maize processing in the State. Looking into the large quantity of maize in food system, processing of maize for snack and other food items may also be planned. Feasibility for installing industrial units to process maize to get starch, ethanol and alcohol, etc. need to be studied. The interest has been shown by large private players such as M/s. India Gasohol Ltd., Tamilnadu to install four maize processing plants with an investment of Rs. 2500 crores in Begusarai, Muzaffarpur, Bhagalpur and Vaishali districts of Bihar. They plan to produce ethanol, alcohol, extra neutral alcohol and crucial oils, etc.

Fruits and Vegetable Processing

There are only 45 licensed fruit and vegetable processing units in the State, earning 20 to 30 times more foreign exchange per unit area than cereals due to higher yields and higher price available in international market (Planning Commission Study, 2003). Most of these units are engaged in the manufacture of fruit juices, fruit pulps, squashes, pickles, tomato ketchup/sauce, tomato juice, tomato paste, jam/jelly, squashes, fruit beverage, etc. However, the industry estimates that only about 2 to 3 per cent of the total produce is processed.

Farm level pre-processing facilities are absent—there are critical to preserve quality and prevent temperature shocks immediately after harvest. Warehousing and storage system for fruits and vegetables are absent except for potatoes and a few for onions. The fruit and vegetable processing segment is marketed by complete absence of cold chain along with the value chain resulting in quality deterioration and degradation of raw materials. Large numbers of these units are working on work order basis for larger chains.

Meat, Dairy, Poultry and Fishery

Bihar ranks fourth in term of meat production in India. However, there is no abattoir and no processing facilities within the State. No value addition is currently taking place. The buffalo meat production in India is growing at a CAGR of 5 per cent and the outstripping of demand *vis-a-vis* supply of lamb and mutton presents a huge opportunity for Bihar to tap into given its livestock resources. Poultry meat is faster growing animal protein but Bihar has negligible share in national poultry meat trade. Thus there is a need to gain by investing into and creating the right climate to spur the production of poultry and value added products.

Bihar produces about 2.9 million MT of milk out of which only 9 to 10 per cent of milk is processed by COMFED (Sudha Dairy in 11 places in Bihar). About 2 to 3 per cent milk is processed in the organised private sector. Milk processing presents a huge potential in Bihar even if it were to reach half of the country processing level or around 17 to 18 per cent.

Fish is one of the popularly consumed items in Bihar particularly in Mithila region and it is the fastest growing sub sector indicating a growth rate of over 10 per cent per annum (NABARD, 2006). Fish production in Bihar is showing increasing trend.

Honey

Bihar is one of leading honey producing states in India. The main regions in which bee keeping is done in Bihar are the district of Muzaffarpur, Vaishali, Sitamarhi, Champaran, Madhepur, Begusarai and Katihar. Bihar has the potential to produce about 40 thousand MT of honey with an estimated value of Rs. 200 crores annually and creation of more than 6 lakhs employment. Bihar is the only state producing litchi honey on commercial scale. In spite of great opportunities in the state there are few processing units in the organised sector and most of the processing units are in unorganised sector.

Confectionary, Bakery and Biscuits Processing Units

Globally bakery and confectionary industries are the first of the food processing industries. In India bakery is probably the largest among processed food industry. The two major bakery industries, i.e. breads and biscuits accounts of about 82 per cent of the total bakery products.

The Indian confectionary market includes sugar boiled confectionary, hard boiled candies, toffees and other sugar based candies. The total volume of sugar boiled confectionary market in the organised sector is around Rs. 2000 crores and unorganised sector has the market of Rs. 5000 crores. The Indian snacks market is around Rs. 1400 crores.

In Bihar though no production and consumption figures are available for this segment. The unorganised sector is burden with the use of outdated technologies and low quality and lower recovery.

Constraints

While the food processing sector offers several opportunities on the one hand, on the other hand it faces constraints as well as:

- Low income and the high share of basic food in the household consumption.
- Socio-cultural factors such as preference in India for freshly plucked/cooked food, variation in food habits across the country, easy availability of raw materials for cooking, preference for consumption of food at home, etc.
- Low productivity, high wastage.
- Inadequate infrastructure for sorting, grading, packing, etc. in addition to the high cost of raw material (at processor's level)

- APMC Act which restricts sourcing materials from farmers.
- Lack of common policy on contract farming.
- Lack of trained man power for various stages of processing, storage, marketing and branding.
- Lack of access to modern technology.
- Low share of sale of food products through organised retail, which are the usual drivers of quality, scale and integration.
- Access to credit for farmers as well as small and medium food processors is a key issue. Over 75 per cent rely on informal credit at very high interest rates leading to increase in cost of production affecting competitiveness.
- Inability to attract investment by large corporate houses who complain of unreliable sources of supply of raw material.
- Inability to induce investor confidence.
- Low inflow of Foreign Direct Investment, in spite of the permission for 100 per cent FDI in the food processing sector (except in food retailing, alcoholic beverages and plantations).
- Inability of Government Schemes to have the desired impact on productivity, technology and market arrivals.

VISION 2015: FOOD PROCESSING IN BIHAR

A developed food processing industry is sa prerequisite to not only reaping the benefits of commercialisation of agriculture, which has become a reality in the WTO mandated regime, but also in safe guarding the interest of the farmers. Bihar first has to catch up with the rest of the country in terms of agricultural development and also has to position itself to take advantage of the huge business opportunities in processed foods triggered by consumer needs of retail boom.

As the food processing is receiving intense and focused attention at the national level, the time is appropriate for Bihar to evolve strategies, which will ensure an accelerated growth of the food processing industry.

The Vision 2015 is a timely intervention by the government of Bihar to create a road map for food processing sector in the State. This is designed to 'tap the untapped potential' of Bihar's agriculture sector through accelerated of the food processing industry.

Strategy

The development of the food processing sector of Bihar calls for a product specific cluster-based approach under a public private partnership mode. The strategies suggested is aimed at attracting new investment and ensure technology infusion in the sector which can turn the food processing industry from the low capital, outdated technology industry to a vibrant industry emerging not only as a driver for the state economy but also a trend setter for the food processing sector in the eastern/central region of India.

The strategies require to achieve the goals are:

1. Identify existing and potential economic clusters and help them to move up the value chain.
2. Initialise the investment process by—(a) chanalisation of public funds, and (b) provide liberal financial support to private investment in the food processing sector.
3. Help to build a common brand for niche product unique to Bihar.

Action Plan

Short-Term Action Plan (1-3 Years)

1. Create a Directorate of Food Processing within the Department of Industry as a single window for catalysing the food processing industry.
2. Engage a professional project management agency to assist the Government of Bihar.
3. Develop a Food Processing Policy for Bihar and launch awareness campaign about the industry.
4. Identify the geographical and sectoral priority areas—including identification of existing and potential clusters.

5. Prepare Detailed Project Report (DPR) for the selected clusters-detailing supply chain and processing linkages aimed at creating models for replication.
6. Create a Market Development Fund for promotion of state products.
7. Design and Establish three Regional Capacity Building Centers for building capacities of unskilled labour force to tap the emerging employment potential from the food processing industry nationally and locally.
8. Create a panel of Sector Specific Experts.
9. Help to establish and operationalise Integrated Food Zones/'Mega Food Parks' in the selected clusters.
10. Establishment of modern Abattoirs and Fish Processing Units in the selected clusters.
11. Establish a state level institute for food processing in Bihar with Incubation centers.
12. Promoting Quality Awareness throughout the state including adoption of TQM, HACCP, ISO Standards, GMP, GHP, etc.
13. Establishment/Up-gradation of Quality Control Laboratory/Food Testing Laboratory.

Long-Term Action Plan (3-8 years)

1. Awareness Campaign based on success stories within and outside the state
2. Implement the various schemes taken up on pilot scale in the phase, state wide.
3. Based on the experience gained from the initial pilot projects, prepare an action plan for strengthening the backward linkages and implement the same. This may address the issue of processable varieties, appropriate models for community farming, etc.
4. Create at least one Safe Food Town.
5. Establish a Strategic Distribution Center for facilitating retail under PPP mode.

6. Strengthening the Board/Directorate to evolve polices for further development of the sector.

Directorate of Food Processing and Engagement of a Programme Management Agency

The state government may create a Directorate of Food Processing as a separate unit under department of industry headed by an officer in the rank of director and assisted by at least two technical experts. The directorate will be assisted by an independent professional Programme Management Agency (PMA) and roll out appropriate policies and guidelines and monitor their implementation. The primary role of PMA will be to assist the Bihar Government in effective implementation of food processing and action plan.

CONCLUSION

The above study reveals that agriculture development is crucial to India's overall progress in general and the progress of Bihar in particular. This can be achieved by intensifying the agricultural and allied activities as well as by diversifying and commercialising agriculture produce.

A strong and dynamic food processing sector could play a vital role in diversifying agricultural activities, improving value addition and creating surplus for export for agro products. The food processing industry will create a lot of job opportunities in the state. This would, however, require policies and plans for improvement of infrastructure including upgradation of technology and enforcement of quality standards and promoting investment in food processing.

In the era of economic liberalisation, a public private partnership mode will help in the development of food processing sector in Bihar. The state government should act as a catalyst for bringing in greater investment into this sector, guiding the industry in proper direction, encouraging exports and creating a conducive environment for healthy growth of the food processing industry.

Vision 2015 has been designed to tap the untapped potential of Bihar agriculture sector which will accelerate the processed food industry in this state.

References

Industrial Development Imperative for Bihar and Jharkhand—A Report, Bihar Industries Commission (2000-01)

Food Processing Industry in Bihar—The Road Ahead, Prepared by IL&FS Ltd. For the Govt. of Bihar.

Indian Journal of Commerce, Vol. 59, July-Sept. 2006.

Gitam Journal of Management, Vol. 4, July-Dec. 2006.

Kurukshetra, Vol. 52, May 2004.

Kurukshetra, Vol. 10, Aug. 2004.

Kurukshetra, Vol. 54, April 2006.

Kurukshetra, Vol. 9, July 2007.

Yojana, Vol. 48, April 2004.

Yojana, Vol. 4, July 2007.

Annual Report, 2006-07, Ministry of Rural Development, GOI.

9

New Strategy and Accelerators of Agriculture in Bihar

HARI NARAYAN PD. SINGH

"Earth has everything to fulfil everybody's need but not anybody's greed."

—Mahatma Gandhi

"Everything else can wait but not Agriculture."

—Jawaharlal Nehru

Agriculture is the backbone of India economy. Agriculture accounts for one fourth of India's National income and one third of India's workforce is directly engaged in agriculture for its livelihood. Nearly 95 percent of Bihar's population lives in rural areas and still majority of them are directly or indirectly dependent on agriculture and allied activities. 80 percent farmers are marginal and small. Since many decades, it occupies a place of pride in Bihar. People get their food from agriculture in various forms, i.e. cereals, fruits, vegetable, etc. many large and small industries depends on agriculture for raw material. Foreign trade also depends on agriculture as it supplies more for exports. Thus, the fact is that the development of the core agriculture is of Bihar economy.

Agriculture has all along been.the most curial sector of the Bihar economy. Large number of Industries depends on agricultural (Textiles, silk, sugar, rice, flour mills, milk products, etc.). Besides, the rural areas are the biggest markets for low priced and middle priced consumer goods including consumer durables and rural domestic sharing are important sources of resource mobilization. Any change in this sector, positive or negative, has a multiplier effect on entire economy. The agriculture sector, therefore, acts as a bulwark in maintaining food security and in the process, National security as well. The allied sectors like horticulture, animal husbandry, dairy and fisheries, have importance in improving the overall economic conditions of rural masses.

'Agriculture' the fiscal commission observes, "isn't merely an occupation or a business proposition of the people, it is a tradition, a way of life which for counties have shaped their thoughts, outlook and culture".

The Planning Commission of India is, therefore, "Convinced that without substantial increase in the production of food and raw materials needed for industry, it would be impossible to sustain a higher tempo of Industrial development". It is necessary however an economic as well as other grounds, first of all to strengthen the economy of the base and to create conditions of sufficiency and even plenty in respect of food and raw materials.

The term 'Strategy' refers to the dynamic process by which a programme is aligned with organisational structure to meet the demand of the environment. However, as far as Agriculture development is concerned, strategy means an approach that is adopted for the distribution of the real benefits of farmer. One of the crucial things is that strategy must be so designed as to ensure that desired results are created by the implementation of programme.

Agriculture development is a strategy designed to improve the economic and social life of a specific group of people—the farmer. It involves the extension of the benefits to development to the poorest among those who seek a livelihood in rural areas.

A strategy for agriculture development must recognize three points. First, the rates of transfer of people out of low productivity agriculture-related activities second, the rate of transfer people out of low productivity agriculture and related activities into more rewarding pursuits has been slow. Second the mass of the people in rural areas face varying degrees of poverty, their position is likely to get worse if population grows all unprecedented rate while limitations continue to be imposed by available resources, technology and institutions, third, rural areas have labour, land and at last same capital which, if mobilized may reduce poverty and improve the quality of life.

Almost the whole of rural population in Bihar is dependent on agriculture as owner cultivator, tenet cultivate, agriculture labourer, livestock various kinds of services to the farmers. A few families small traders, for example, which may have nothing to do with farming are among the first to be affected by failure of crops in their areas, the purchasing power of the people gets drastically reduced incase of crop failures. Thus agricultural development is imperative for rural development. It deserves the first priority. Only after agriculture gets moving fast that non-agricultural sectors of development will come into focus and will be become meaningful. Attention to non- agricultural sectors of rural development will then become absolutely necessary not only to diversify the economic activities but also to provide greater inputs to agriculture. From the onwards sectors of rural development will be mutually sustaining.

The first and foremost thing needed for agricultural development is the farm produce. Conditions have to be created so that producer gets remunerative price of the produce even when he sells immediately after harvest and in his own village of near by. For this, there have to be large number of urban regulated market up to the block levels.

Profit is the strongest motive for producing more. Increased profit also makes to possible to invest more in inputs to increase production. This history of agricultural development throughout Indian or the world is full of cases of production going down in absence of 'Market' for this product.

Agricultural production takes place not a very big factory its lacks of factories (farms) are scattered over the whole state and are owned managed by lacks of owners (farmers). Agricultural produce are pooled to the central place by the traders, government and the farmers similarly agriculture inputs are to be transformed to all the farms. The transport both ways is of bulky materials, which cannot be efficient or even satisfactory without modern transport system. For this a network of all whether *pucca* roads is a must. That network of *pucca* roads is an essential for agricultural and rural development. Agricultural economics says that a community (village) has to pay for the roads whether has it not. It pays more if it has not. The road is essential for agricultural development. However, I make suggestion taking into account the brood rural development scenario in Bihar that good network of roads can be gradually developed in Bihar with at providing heavy budget for the roads.

Land reforms are also essential for the agricultural development. Land reforms in Bihar, has been in the process from the beginning of independence but it continues to be incomplete even after half a century. Though significant, is to great extent a redundant idea. Every village requires for the general good of village some common land, which before zamindari abolition were to categories "Gair Mazrua Khas" and "Gair Mazrua Aam". The zamindars disposed of most of the Gair Mazrua Aam land and village community gradually swallowed all the Gair Mazrua Aam land by encroachment. Now common land have be again created. This is possible only during the process of land consolidation.

Another aspect of land reforms, which is very significant and reforms which is very significant and deserves urgent attention is fixing the lower limits of land holding. Higher limits of land holding under different situations have been fixed but not the lower limits unless this is done, very loon the land holding size will scientific production technology. Fixing lower limit might seem impossible but there seems to be no escape from that. It would not the wrong to say that nation on a whole has shifted from the ideology of socialism to be capitalism even though the use of word "Capitalism" may not be acceptable to us privatization, liberalisation and globalisation of economy, means capitalism. Thus, each of the farms and farmers have been exposed to global completion. The situation is going to be that of "Complete or perish". This situation us likely to prove very advantageous and suitable for some of the states like Maharashtra, Punjab and Haryana, which are producing for export.

Thus the only solution seems to be of organizing small co-operative societies at the village small co-operative societies to bigger societies at the Panchayat, block and district and state levels. Let there be as many federal set-ups of co-operatives as needed. Individual farmers may not the expertise and experience for global competition. But these co-operatives can face the challenges of global competitions.

As an accelerating force, agricultural extension system can show extraordinary result, once essentials mentions above are provided. What was been so far doing in Bihar and some other stats in that intensive network of agricultural extension services have been provided which are not giving as good result as possible in a absence of infrastructure for development. Bihar has excellent agricultural extension set-up but its workers are demoralised for want of supervision, guidance and encouragement. They are simply banged 7 condemned if targets are not achieved. Supervisions, as different from administration and an addition to administration is needed. However, it needs to be emphasised that even a well supervised and spirited agricultural extension agency cannot do much in absence of good technology and infrastructure. It may be like putting cart before horse.

There is a very wrong and discouraging belief in Bihar and more than outside the state that people of Bihar are backward. I can say with full sense of responsibility that this is not correct again the whole concept of people being considered backward and progressive has undergone change.

In the recent years, the Government has realized the need for restructuring of agricultural sector. The agricultural policy was governed by the planning framework. The quantum of plan outlay, its financing and the targets set far the agricultural sector were all decided through the planning process at the state and central levels. The first three five years plans concentrated on growth with the some institutional changes including abolition of intermediaries in agriculture, Zamindars and Jagirdars. In the mid-sixties, a new technology in the form of high yielding varieties (HYVs) was also introduced for cereals. Apart from the new technology, public investment in agriculture particularly in irrigation was stepped up significantly. The public sector played an important role in promoting agricultural research and education. Large investments were made for the development of research system under the aegis of Indian Council of Agricultural Research (ICAR) and State Agriculture Universities (SAUs). Simultaneously, a well-designed extension network was created for disseminating new technologies to the farmers and the system of administered price provided incentives to the farmers. Successive Five Year Plans aimed at improving the infrastructure through irrigation, stepping up the use of fertilizers, improved varieties of seed implements and machinery and supply of credit.

To conclude the pressure of population, which is generally a common feature in under-developed states, should not lead one to conclude that agriculture should be developed, because of such pressure, on labour-intensive methods. In fact agriculture like any other industry needs a 'push' of capital. *Maurice Dobb* has worked out the theory of such capital—"intensive production for an agricultural country with population pressure, since this will permit a more rapid increase in the rate of investment in the near future."

References

Sen, S.R., "The Strategy for Agricultural Development", Asia Publishing House, Bombay, 1962, p. 4.

Leibenstein, "Economic Backwardness and Economic Growth", Willy and Sons, New York, 1957, p. 94.

Prasad, D.C., "Agriculture in Bihar", 1987, p. 104.

Das, Arbind N., "Agrian unrest and socio-economic change in Bihar, p. 66.

First Five Year Plan, Planning Commission of India, 1952, p. 44.

Review of the First Five Year Plan, Planning Commission, Govt. of India, May 1957, p. 2.

Kurukshetra, 2007-08.

Yojana, 2007-08.

10

Innovations in Rural Marketing

Md. Imteyaz Hassan

INTRODUCTION

In rural areas Marketing has emerged as an important internal sub-division within marketing discipline particularly in the context of a large rural economy like India as well as in Bihar. The Indian rural market with its vast size and demand-base offers great opportunities to marketers. The marketers have identified the importance of rural markets and are concentrating their efforts to tap the same. Rural marketing has developed itself into a full-fledged stream, particularly Bihar. Marketing managers are looking out for developing new strategies, which would be applicable in the rural markets.

PRESENT POSITION

Our majority consumers live in rural areas and almost half of the national income is generated here. It is only natural that rural markets from an important part of the total market of Bihar. Our nation is classified in around 450 districts, and approximately 6,30,000 villages, which can be sorted in different parameters such as literacy levels, accessibility, income levels, penetration, distances from nearest towns. The Indian rural market with its vast size and demand base offers a huge opportunity that no company can efford to ignore. With 128 million households, the rural population is nearly there times the urban. Rural

India has a large consuming class with 41 per cent of India's middle-class and 58 per cent of the total disposable income.

The rise of the rural market in Bihar has been the most important marketing phenomenon of the nineties, providing volume growth to all leading companies using Agricultural produce as raw materials. The importance of the rural market for some durable marketers is underlined by the fact that the rural market accounts for close to 70 per cent of toilet-soap users and 38 per cent of all two-wheeler purchased. The rural market accounts of half the total market for TV sets, fans, pressure cooker, bicycle, washing soap, blades, tea, salt and toothpowder. What is more, the rural market products are growing much faster than the urban counterpart.

DEMANDING TASK IN RURAL MARKETING

A questions arises, "What, if any differences exist of between rural marketing and mainstream marketing?" The lack of clarity on this issue has led to proliferation of ideas, literature and managerial perspectives with loose and superficial interpretation and far removed from the ground reality. While the rural market certainly officers a big attraction to marketers, it would be naïve to think that any company can easily enter the market and walk away with sizable share. If has always been difficult to gauge the rural market. Many brands, which should have been successful, have failed miserably. Marketers need to understand to social dynamics and attitude variations within each village though nationally it follows a consistent pattern.

The rural market may be alluring but it is not without its problems which include low per capita disposable incomes that is half the urban disposable income; large number of daily wage earners, acute dependence on the vagaries of the monsoon; seasonal consumption linked to harvests and festivals and special occasions; poor roads; power problems; and inaccessibility to conventional advertising media. The rural consumer is unlike his urban counterpart in many ways. The major challenges, being faced by companies in rural markets include affordability, distribution; acceptability; awareness and communications.

CHALLENGES

The major challenges, facing marketers in rural markets is to ensure affordability of the product or service. With low disposable incomes, products need to be affordable to the rural consumer. It has to understand that most of the Indian rural consumers are on daily basis. Hence, marketers have to design products to suit the pockets of rural consumers.

Daily wage earners tend to have little stock of money, and therefore tent to make purchase only to meet their daily needs. The implication is that pack sizes and price points are critical to sales, and importantly, that rural consumers view the purchase-tradeoff dilemma across a much wider range of product categories. Hindustan Lever, among the first MNCs to realize the potential of India's rural market. Hindustan Lever, a subsidiary of Unilever coined the term nano-marketing in the early 90s when it introduced its product in small sachets. Recently, it started 'Operation Bharat' to tap the rural markets. Under this operation it passed out low-priced sample packets of its toothpaste, fairness cream, Clinic plus shampoo, and Ponds cream to twenty million households. It has launched a variant of its largest selling soap brand, Lifebuoy at Rs. 2 for 50 gm. It sells shaving gel, dishwashing liquid and toothpaste, to name just a few items in tiny pillow-like plastic packets that contain about 20 milliliters of product. Thus, sachets and miniature packs, as in the case of shampoo sachets priced at Re. 1 and Rs. 2 or toothpaste at Rs. 10, have become the order of the day in hinterland India and help improve market penetration.

The sachets answer the needs of rural consumers who cannot or are not used to, buying larger sizes and enables them to buy on a more frequent basis. Today, Hindustan Lever estimates its shampoo sachets are sold in around 400,000 of India's 600,000 villages. This strategy provides a viable entry-level price for many rural consumers who want to try new products, and follows companies to drive volume sales. The move is mainly targeted at the rural market. Coca-Cola has addressed the affordability issue by introducing the returnable 200 ml glass bottle priced at Rs. 6. The initiative has paid-off: eight per cent of new drinkers now come from the rural markets. Coca-Cola has also introduced Sunfill, a powered soft-drink concentrate. The instant and ready-to-mix Sunfill is available in a single-serve sachet of 25 gm priced at Rs. 2 and multiserve sachet of 200 gm priced at Rs. 15. Godrej recently introduced three brands of Cinthol, Fair Glow and Godrej in 50 gm packs, priced at Rs. 4-5 meant specifically for Bihar the so-called 'Bimaru' States. These price cuts have boosted volume sales. Companies can always provide low cost products to the rural consumers and achieve volume sales in the rural market. The volume sales can take care of the low profit margin of these companies.

MARKET STRUCTURE

The market structure consists of primary rural market and retail sales outlet. The structure involves stock points in feeder towns to service these retail outlets at the village levels. But it becomes difficult maintaining the required service level in the delivery of the product at retail level. Unlike developed markets where large retail distribution chains are commonplace, India is, by and large, a nation of small shopkeepers ("kirana"). This poses a tremendous challenge to consumer goods companies, which have traditionally used large retailers as their primary channel of distribution. Retail chains have not flourished in the rural areas of India because economics of scale do not exist. Rural consumers live in small homes with little storage space, lack refrigeration and do not own cars. As a result, daily purchases at the neighbourhood store are frequently preferred by consumers and may be the only avenue to buy goods in smaller rural towns.

ACCEPTABILITY

The acceptability for the product or service is another major challenge in the rural market. There is a need to offer products that suit the rural market. The rural consumer is suffering from various problems, which may not be encountered by his urban counterpart. Marketers have to design tailor made products so that they find acceptance with the rural consumers. As discussed earlier, most of the companies have started tinkering with pack sizes and creating new price points in order to reach out to rural consumers.

Driving consumption of goods in rural areas is not just about lowering prices and increasing volume sales. It is also about product innovation: developing indigenous products that cater to the needs of rural consumers who demand quality products at an affordable cost. This requires substantial R and D better understand consumer behavior our preferences. A case in points is the rural market for shampoo. Hair products were introduced to rural Bihar in an attempt to capitalize on a culture where hair grooming is taken extremely seriously by women. While rural women many wear faded saris and little jewelry, few step out without ensuring that their hair is in place. Consumer goods companies introduced a transplanted product from developed markets, the 2-in-1 shampoo/conditioner. Companies thought that women would be attracted to this product because it was cost-effective, however, initial sales were dismal. What companies failed to recognize is that most rural consumer had previously never used shampoo and did not value or understand the full benefits of conditioner.

AWARENESS AND COMMUNICATION

There is a difference in the kind of media mix that is used to convey the messages to the rural customers. There is a need to use different models and means to reach them as what appeals to the urban customer may not appeal to him due to varying lifestyles. Mass marketing through television and other forms of media is often seen as a more cost-efficient means to reach a large number of potential consumers in the rural markets. But, mass media reaches only 57 per cent of the rural population. Consumer goods companies cannot rely on conventional advertising techniques; particularly in India's rural areas where only one in every three households owns a television set and more than half of all villages are literate. Hence, building awareness is another challenge. Fortunately, the rural consumer has the same likes as the urban consumer—movies and music—and for the urban and rural consumer, the family is the key unit of identify. However, the rural consumer expressions differ from his urban counterpart. Outing for the former is confined to local fairs and festivals and TV viewing is confined to the state-owned Doordarshan. Consumption of branded products is treated as a special treat of indulgence.

Companies are turning to more innovative methods of advertising to reach their potential customer base. They are using methods of advertising like fairs of *haats* to reach their potential customer base. Some of the companies are employing customer video vans which carry infomercials to rural villages. A marketer invites people to the van to view the infomercial which incorporates the new product into an aspect of daily life. These potential customers are subsequently given a demonstration of the product, for example, toothpaste and toothbrush, and then provided free samples. This has provided to be extremely effective in advertising to the rural market.

Marketers need to understand the psyche of the rural consumers and then act accordingly. To effectively tap the rural market a brand must associate itself with the same things the rural folks do. This can be done by utilizing the various rural folk media to reach them in their own language and in large numbers so that he brand can be associated with the myriad rituals, celebrations, festivals, melas and other activities where they assemble.

CONCLUSION

The challenges and the opportunities which rural markets offer to the marketers, it can be said that the future is very promising for those who can understand the dynamics of rural markets and exploit them to their best advantage. Marketers of all hues are heading in just one direction—the rural markets. The rural markets, they echo, are the growth engines. And with the rural consumer becoming as discerning as his urban counterpart, the rural market is becoming that much harder to reach. To be successful, companies need to be innovative, dogged and culturally sensitive in developing rural marketing strategies. It is testament of both multinational and local consumer goods companies that they have been able to innovate and address the challenges offered by India's rural market to bring goods, to and improve the lives of so many people. These successful marketing techniques may even be introduced to large emerging markets in Bihar.

References

Berry, Leonard L., "Relation Marketing of Service-Growth Interest, Emerging Perspective", *Journal of Academy of Marketing Science*, 1995.

Kotler, Philip, Marketing Management, Planning Analysis, Implementation and Control, Prentice-Hall, 2000, New Delhi.

11

Strategy of Agrarian Crisis in Bihar: Special Reference to Land Reform

SYED ALAY MUJATABA AND PANKAJ PURSOTTAM

LAND REFORMS

> "There is only one fundamental method of improving village life namely, the introduction of a system of peasant proprietorship under which the tiller of the soil is himself the owner of its and pays revenues direct to the government without the intervention of any Zamindar or taluqdar."

By land reforms we mean direct state intervention in the agrarian structure to bring about fundamental changes. In Bihar, the need for land reforms, i.e. direct interventions of the state government of the state arose from the exploitative nature of the land revenue system that existed prior to Independence.

Bihar is one of those states in India where the agrarian structure has been very exploitative both in terms of land concentration and insecurity of tenure. Widespread oral tenancy is prevalent in the plains of Bihar, Legislative measures were undertaken to acquire surplus land and safeguard the interest of tenants with regards to the fixation of rent and ejection of tenants. However, the implementation of these various legislative pro-poor agrarian measures. Particularly the land ceiling and tenancy laws, has been rather dismal. The principal reason for non-implementation has been lack of political will and collusion of the bureaucracy with land owners. Studies have been shown that in many parts of the state, particularly in North Bihar, has been very inadequate implementation of the ceiling laws and that there is wide scope for acquiring much more surplus land (LBSNNA, 1991). In spite of the poor implementation, it is significant to observe that all such cases where cultivable lands were allotted, there has been some perceptible change in the socio-economic status of the allottees. They felt more confident and partly relieved from the clutches of the landlords. Provisions of land, however small, has given them a sense of identity and something on which they can fall back.

So far as the tenancy is concerned, many researchers have highlights the inter-linkage between landholdings, sharecropping and bondage which leads to the process of economic stagnation in the country side and immiserisation of the poor. In spite of large number of tenants in the plains of Bihar, who are mostly poor peasants and agricultural labourers, their pitiable conditions both with regards to security of tenure and fixation of rent hardly been the target of intervention of the government machinery.

The experience of neighboring West Bengal, the state which had broadly the same type of agrarian and social land and giving security of tenure—can be an important instrument for empowering the poor and channelsing their energies for agricultural and rural development by giving them facilites of irrigation and lending and integrating them with various schemes of rural development. Given the political and appropriate institutional machinery for implementation, there is no reason why what has been achieved in West Bengal cannot be achieved in Bihar.

OBJECTIVE OF LAND REFORMS

(1) To remove impediments in agricultural production arising from the exploitatative agrarian structure inherited from the past: and
(2) To eliminate all forms of exploitation and ensure social justice within agrarian system, to provide security of the tiller of soil and assure equality of status and opportunity to all sections of the rural population.

Measure of Land Reforms

Three types of measure were contemplated to achieve the above objectives:

(1) Abolition of Intermediaries
(2) Tenancy Reforms
(3) Reorganisation of Agriculture

LAND REFORMS IN BIHAR

The over all situation in Bihar as far as implementation of land ceiling is concerned, out of 3.69 Lakh acres of land acquired in the state, 1.47 Lakh acres are yet to be distributed. Some 91,000 acres are under legal disputes. 93 per cent of the land owned by the big landlords identified are located outside the village of actual residence. This demands a rigorous definition and implementation of the terms "Personal Cultivation". Most of the land ceiling cases were instituted between 1971 to 1975 which indicated the regors of administrative action during this period. Such regors were not followed-up further. Pending cases are rather few but they invariably belongs to large land owners. One of the striking features is that in districts like West Champaran 48 per cent of the allottees were not given physical possession of their land. Similar is the situation in other districts like Purnea. Surplus ceiling land should be overwhelmingly allotted to SC and ST but 'other castes' constituted 48 per cent in the number and 38 per cent in total area allotted. Though the extent of land allotted was not economically viable, yet the possession of land has given them a sense of identify and something on which they can fall back. The administrative slackness is quite severe as of the declared surplus 47 per cent area has yet to be allotted. In large number of cases the allotted lands are not under the physical possession of the allottees in view of the persistence of landlord powers. Land-lords by raising objections with regards to classification, unit and transactions of land can stretch the proceedings to an unending and agonising process, which involving from the lowest level of halka karamchari to the highest level of the appellate authority of the Revenue Board. The jurisdiction of the High Court further adds to the agony where the cases keep pending for years staying any further action in the matter. The multiplicity of the trial courts for land ceiling cases at the district level have made the matter worst in as much as the cases are frequently transferred from one court to another. Sometime without any perceptible reason, dislocating the proceedings for long durations. In addition to all this, the paper throws interesting light on the land-lord official nexus which operates in conspiratorial manner from the very beginning of the proceedings and gets reflected adequately in countless adjournments and accommodations given to the landlord. Section 45B of land ceiling act helps the evader of Jaw through reopening window of the case. Land ceiling act did not immediately follow the Zamindari abolition updating of land records was withdrawn at its very early stage on the strange ground that it would disturb the agrarian peace. Thus the bottlenecks to implementation of laws were provided within the provisions of the law and used actively for that purpose by the administration and big landlords. The concentration of land was widespread in many other districts. Besides East Champaran, like Purnea, Saharsa, Madhepura, Madhubani and others. Land reforms get implemented only when, bureaucracy, top political executive, and people's political pressure from below, is combined in one thrust.

The Tenancy Situation: The tenancy reforms remains an important question in the context of Bihar as the state has got significant area under tenancy. The area under tenancy in the state constituted 10 per cent of the total operated area as per

NSS figures of 1990-91. The incidence of tenancy is very large in some parts of North Bihar. Particularly in the districts of West Champaran North East Bihar and the tribal region of the-state show a very low level of tenancy, as was found by the study of LBSNAA. The prevalence of somewhat large area under tenancy in the district of Hazaribagh is evident where marginal farms and agricultural labourers, who improved large amounts or fallow and forest land with considerable amount of labour, were evicted or are being evicted from these lands as there is no provision of 'Bataidars' in the Chotanagpur-Santhal Paragna Tenancy Act. The LBSNAA study also reveals that the high incidence of tenancy is not only characteristic of areas with higher irrigation potentialities, but is equally characteristic of unirrigated areas. While overwhelmingly the tenants are landless agricultural labourers and the poor peasants with marginal holdings, it is found that under the demographic pressures and some other factors, better-off peasants have also started leasing-in land. The main factors responsible for somewhat large areas of cultivated land under tenancy are:

(i) Concentration of land holdings with a small number of landlords (thanks to the very poor implementation of ceiling laws in the state).
(ii) Social taboos forbidding a large section of the upper caste people to put physical labour into cultivation.
(iii) Widespread absentee landlordism including small landlordism and fragmentation of holdings.
(iv) System of usufruct mortgage leading into some kind of bondage, etc.

The inter-linkage of land ceilings, sharecropping, bondage and issue of agrarian transformation was highlighted by Tom Brass. Although much debate on land ceilings touches on the non-implementation of existing laws, yet empirical study in a district like Purnea, indicate that a land lord can retain legally substantial amounts of land. He can also lease in out to sharecroppers and resume it legally. Given that sharecropping leads to debt bondage, and that debt bondage places limits on the process of economic development, it was argued that this inter-linkage (big land-holdings, sharecropping, bondage) necessarily contributes to the process of economic and political stagnation. The system of tenancies is almost entirely concealed and informal and hence there is no security of tenure. Their plots are changed within a year or two thereby denying the privileges of the status of occupancy tenants. High-proportion of tenants have worked as tenants for more than 10 years with the same land-owners. The share-croppers are in a Very weak bargaining position *vis-a-vis* landowners. Even their awareness of the statutory provisions of ground of eviction, payment of fair rent, etc. is very low. There have been very limited attempts by the share-croppers to assert for the rights. The cases filled by the tenants are very few and far between as they neither the economic strength nor do they have the faith in the delivery system of judgment. The legal procedures are so clumsy, time consuming, expensive and biased towards landlords that tenants simply can not hope to benefit from it. Further, the tenants are required to furnish documentary evidence of their cultivating the tenanted lands, but the tenants are totally unable to provide such evidence as the tenancy is entirely oral and informal in the state.

The Case of Gair Mazarua Land: While narrating the situation of central Bihar, Mr. Priyadarshi observed that both the magnitude and cases involved in distribution of Government Gair Mazarua lands are high in Central Bihar compared to any other region of the state. The case of Bodh Gaya Math may be cited which had acquired about 10,000 acres of government land. Due to administrative inefficiency only 2,000 acres of such lands have been recovered from the Math and distributed among the poor peasants. The big landowners of the West Champaran district control the Gair Mazarua lands directly or indirectly through muscle power. Such lands forest department and railway department have also been under influential landlords who in connivance with the Government Officials acquire the lands with pro-people gesture, viz. for afforestation, cooperativisation of lands. The main results of the Survey conducted by the I.A.S. probationers from 14 villages spread to 11 districts of Bihar may be cited here. In this elaborate analysis of the data they covered the subjects like, magnitude of government Khas lands, its use pattern; encroachment of such lands by various castes, etc. The extent of government land located in the villages understudy generally ranged from 60 to 370 acres. The exceptions to this were the villages in Districts of Saharsa. Dumka and Aurangabad. In the village of District Saharsa only 10 acres of government land was located, in the village of Dumka it was only 39 acres where as in the village of District Aurangabad it was as much as 12433 acres. However, 83 per cent of this land HI the village Aurangabad District was covered with hillocks which was of no use. Excluding the land covered by hillocks, the average extent of Govt. lands identified in each village worked out to nearly 260 acres. It was rather astonishing to find that in the villages of Ranchi, Dhanbad, Samastipur, Madhubani and Dumka there was no government land which was under homestead. This looks rather strange for a state like, Bihar were houselessness of the underprivileged is quite rampant. This aspect needs to be probed further. The extent of land allotted for cultivation in the 14 villages was 602.43 acres which forms 16.58 per cent of the total government land in these villages (excluding hillock land) and 23.57 per cent of the extent of government land which were being used for cultivation. The SC allottees were 83.3 per cent, ST 4.2 per cent and other caste beneficiaries were 12.5 per cent of the total allottees. The average extent of land allotted to SC, ST and other caste beneficiaries was 0,73 acres, 1.08 acres and 0.94 acres respectively. In 71 per cent of the cases the allottees continued to have physical possession of the land allotted to them and in 83 per cent of the cases their names were also entered in the revenue records, only in the villages of Samastipur, Purnea and Madhubani the lands were not under the physical possession of the allottees. This was mainly due to the powerful land-owners in the village who prevented the allottees from occupying the land. Only in very few cases the allottees were integrated with the loaning and govt. Schemes. In quite a few cases the land allotted was of very poor quality which needed to be-reclaimed. Wherever the allottees were integrated with the developmental schemes, the land allotted was-economically viable. In all other cases the economic viability was very low. It, however, made a considerable difference in their social and psychological status and their dependence on the landlords was considerable reduced. Even those who were allotted homestead lands also felt considerable relief from the dependence and bondage of landlords. This shows that while the question of economic viability is one of the important determinants for allotment of land but in the Indian Situation and particularly in the semi-feudal set-up of Bihar, even the allotment of small plot of land relives the underprivileged from the dependence of landlords to a considerable extent. One of the most difficult aspect of the village life and specifically in Bihar is that considerable area of govt. land is under encroachment of people who are powerful, economically, socially and politically. The extent of the area encroached in the 14 villages under study was nearly 155 acres which constituted 4.26 per cent of the total government land. The encroached for cultivation purpose mainly by upper castes was quite substantial. The confirms the caste-class scenario of the powerful group in the villages of Bihar. The pattern of dominance was similar in all the districts.

REASONS FOR THE POOR PERFORMANCE OF LAND REFORMS PROGRAMME

In a forthright analysis, the Planning Commission Task Force headed by Mr. P.S. Appu mentions the following as the principal reasons for poor implementation of land reforms: lack of political will; absence of pressure from below because the poor peasants and agricultural workers are passive, unorganised and inarticulate; lukewarm and often apathetic attitude of the bureaucracy, absence of up-to-date land records, and legal hurdles in the way of implementation of land reforms. Tile Task Force categorically concludes: "In a society in which the entire weight of Civil and Criminal laws, judicial pronouncements and precedents, administrative tradition and practice is thrown on the side of the existing social order based on the inviolability of private properly, an isolated law aiming at the restructuring of property relation in the rural areas has little chance of success. And whatever little chance of success was there completely evaporated because of the loopholes in the laws and protracted litigation."

The basic problem in the implementation of a programme of land reform is to break the stranglehold of the vested interests in land and the legal support given by the judiciary the vested interests in me name of sanctity of private property. Obviously, the talk of strengthening administrative machinery without creating conditions for breaking the stranglehold of the holy trinity, i.e. landlord-moneylender-trader, is nothing but lip service to the poor peasantry. In case a frontal attack has to be made with a view to ensuring justice to the rural proletariat engaged in cultivation, the bold suggestions given by the Task Force on Agrarian relations must be implemented in letter and spirit:

1. Judiciary should not be involved at any stage in the implementation of land reforms. This suggestion has been given because civil legislation by its very nature is time-consuming and dilatory. Moreover, the decision of the Court depends upon the production of evidence and experience shows that the stronger party (viz., the landlord) has always been able to produce greater evidence by using all kinds of pressures both legal and illegal.
2. Organisation of Poor peasantry into a strong militant trade unions is a pre-conditioned of land reform and the state can provide representations to the poor peasantry, specifically in the administrative machinery at various levels, etc.

CONCLUSION

The exemption granted in favour of sugar mills should be withdrawn. Provisions of Section 12 to 14 of Bihar Land Ceiling Act relating to resumption should be applicable only to Land holders having less than 2.5 acres of irrigated/3.75 acres of Unirrigated/5 acres of inferior land. The provisions of Land Ceiling Act be made effective right from the date of promulgation of Bihar Zamindari Abolition Act in order to capture transactions manipulated before 22-10-1959 to evade land ceiling provisions. It was noted that Bihar Act 21 of 1987 provided for setting up of the, Bihar Land Reforms Tribunal. The said amendment has been struck down by the Patna High Court. An appeal has been preferred in the Supreme Court, Steps be taken to obtain decision from the Supreme Court at the earliest. There was need to-adopt a restrictive definition.of "Personal cultivation". This aspect has been dealt with in the paper on tenancy reforms. The list of bataidars/ Landless people should be prepared well in advance in every village to enable distribution of surplus land immediately after notification under Section 15. The process of distribution of surplus land shouldbe further strengthened by simultaneously mutating it in the name of settled/issuing rent receipt to create evidence in his favour.

12

Agricultural Crises in Bihar and Jharkhand

NAGENDRA KUMAR JHA, MANOJ KUMAR AND PARSHANT KUMAR SINGH

BACKGROUND

Agriculture today represent a third of Indian Gross Domestic Product (GDP), the highest proportion in the developed and developing world and countries to be the backbone of the economy for years to come. Nearly 70 per cent of Indian population depends on agriculture and in terms of total farm output it stands favorably but if in terms of production per unit area or per farm animal or per tree the position is extremely deplorable.

The performance of agricultural sector, the eastern region in general and in Bihar particular has changed over the years. Bihar, with its sound economy, was associated with West Bengal and Orissa was also a part of it. In cause of time, there was a demand of the day to bifurcate the province of Bengal. Reasons to get the proposal implemented were valid and sufficient, especially administration, control and smooth functioning were some of the basic reasons, which drew the attention of the government of those day. The Proposal was materialized through passing the Re-organization Bill under which Bihar along with Orissa was created in the year 1912 as an independent province named as Bihar Province. Further bifurcation of the State remained in the seen before the government, which was compiled to separate Bihar from Orissa through a Re-organization Bill. Thus, the province of Bihar come into existence in the year 1936 and similar status of province was also granted Orissa granted Orissa. History of creation of a province or state is the testimony which itself speaks that our state has been a rich state in terms of natural and physical resources besides above, the people of Bihar have their own universally accepted traditions, culture, agriculture and industrial base.

Indian agriculture witnessed a significant growth in the productivity of wheat and rice till 1980's which was the result of "Green Revolution". Therefore, a number of factors led to a slow-down in the growth-rate decline in the growth rate of foodgrain production in respect of productivity and input response or factor productivity has been observed recently, besides shrinking profit margins, degradation of natural resources base, declining water table and environmental quality in agriculture. This needs to look for immediate and long-term solution to meet the food demand of the growing population.

PRESENT POSITION

The 90 per cent of the total cropped area here are utilized for food crops against the national average of only 75 per cent. The State contributes 8 per cent of the total food grain production of the various crops of the State, rice is certainly the most important and accounts for about one-tenth of the total rice output in the country. Bihar's share is total maize output is about 9 per cent, in linseed 8 per cent and in turmeric 11 per cent.

So, here if we put a glance on the above collected data we come to see that in some way or the other Bihar contributes to the national economy to a great extent whether it is socio-economy, culture and polity. The contribution of the State can't be overlooked but at the same time for the maximization of the contribution, political will power has been in need. This need now arises more since the majority of contributing factors like mines and other resources with Jharkhand. And divided Bihar is left with agriculture, sorrow of rivers, sick or dead small industries, viz., sugar mills, paper mills and jute. Even in this position in India's economy the role of divided Bihar will be of immense importance.

The present status of Bihar economy after its bifurcation in the year 2000 has exposed four basic features. First, the dominance of agriculture in the State economy has become more apparent. Agriculture, thus holds the key to Bihar's development. It is a challenge well as an opportunity. Secondly, land and water are the dominant natural resource endowments, notwithstanding the fact that these are basic resources for agriculture. Thirdly, as a consequence, the rate of transformation of Bihar economy in terms of growing importance of non-farm and non-agricultural sector is much slow. Lack of opportunities in industries and poor rural-urban growth linkages retained agriculture's importance. This, of course, is a national trend but Bihar stands out as an extreme case. It is also notable that primary output dominates the agricultural economy of the State. There are very little agro-processing and even primary processing industries. Erstwhile Bihar which was, contributing 13 per cent of fruits

TABLE I

Basic Economic Features: Bihar *vs.* India

Item	*Bihar*	*India*
Agriculture as per cent of GDP (TE 1997-98)	43.8	26.5
Rural population as per cent of total population (2001)	89.5	72.2
Workforce participation in agriculture (%) 1993-94. NSS Survey	77.3	63.9
Human population density (per sq. km.) 2001	880	324
Livestock density (per ha) (1992 Livestock Census)	2.85	1.84

Source: Economic Performance – A Diagnostic view of Governance, p 17, J. Prasad.

and vegetables production in the country accounted for only 2.8 per cent of processing units. Also, the rural industries in the State have, by and large collapsed in recent years. Lastly, population pressure on natural resources is also exceedingly high. Human as well as livestock population numbers place high burden on agriculture resources.

All these basic features of the economy of Bihar after its bifurcation reveal the dominance of low-income agricultural sector and consequently, as also earlier observed, low per capita income and high poverty, particularly in rural areas. Thus, the basic strength of Bihar economy in its present status revolves around the primary sector-agriculture, livestock and fisheries.

CONTRIBUTION

Bihar's Gross State Domestic Product (GSDP) data indicates that growth performance has been quite weak, averaging barely 5 per cent during the 1980s, which was below the national trend rate of 5.6 per cent, and then turning flat in the first half of the 1990s when the national growth rate remained above 5 per cent (Table 6.14). Post-bifurcation, Bihar continues to lag seriously behind other States in India. Over the period 1994-95 to 2001-02, when data for the new State of Bihar is available, the growth rate averaged 3.8 per cent of less than two-thirds the national growth rate of 6.1 per cent per annum. This has widened the GSDP gap at an accelerating rate over the past decade.

Comparisons in per capita income growth reveal an even less favorable trend for Bihar. This is mainly due to the State's high population growth rate, which averaged 2.5 per cent between the 1991 and 2001 census, the highest in the country and well above the national average of 1.9 per cent. Moreover, unlike the other States whose population growth rates have been declining over the decades, Bihar's population growth rate in the 1990s was higher than the 2.1 per cent experienced in the 1980s. This has aggravated Bihar's population pressure and depressed income growth making fertility control an important development issue.

The sectoral composition of Bihar's economy reveals the

important role of agriculture in aggregate production. In undivided Bihar, the contribution of agriculture, fisheries and forestry in total output was 33 per cent during 1998-99 (Table 6.15). Bihar lost most of its industry and mining to Jharkhand after the bifurcation, and agriculture now represents 39 per cent of GSDP (as compared to 23% for the country). In contrast, Bihar's industrial sector is the smallest among India's major States, contributing only 12 per cent to GSDP (compared to 27% nationally) and employing fewer than 10 per cent of the workforce. The tertiary sector is Bihar's largest, generating 49 per cent of the State's GSDP, mainly in trade and transport services, finance, real estate, and Government (public administration).

The unsatisfactory performance of agriculture, Bihar's most important sector, is responsible for the State's low aggregate growth rate. Agriculture provides employment for three-quarters of the work-force, and is the main source of income for the majority of Bihar's rural poor. Hence improving agricultural incomes is the key to reducing income poverty. Agriculture showed negative growth in the early 1990s, and since the mid-1990s through 2001-02 it has grown by less than 1 per cent per annum, implying a negative growth rate of agricultural output per capita. In contrast, industrial growth averaged 10.5 per cent per annum from the mid-1990s, exceeding the national growth rate, though from a very low base. Small- and medium-scale enterprises predominate in Bihar's industrial sector. The performance of services has been higher than agriculture (6.4% p.a.), but is below the national average growth rate of 8 per cent per annum. Moreover, services appear to be relatively capital intensive and have not absorbed a share proportionate to their GSDP level in the workforce.

CONSTRAINTS

General Constraints: Specific Features of New Technological Package

HYV seeds, manures and fertilizers, and controlled water supply constitute the essential ingredients of a new technological package. HYV seed is the result of a selective process of breeding. It develops quickly into a short stemmed plant. It is highly responsive to the use of fertilizers and for fertilizers to be supplying nutrients, the water supply to the plants is essential.

The essential feature of the new technological package is that it resembles a chemical process. Like any chemical process the result (optimal output) can be achieved with the use of these inputs in a given proportion. For example, the use of a given amount of HYV seed is associated with the use of the particular types of fertilizers (depending upon the nutrients available in the soil) at some interval. Water supply is needed as and when fertilizer is used. To obtain the maximum yield, therefore, inputs are to be used in a fixed proportion and in a controlled manner.

HYV seed plants are further more vulnerable to pest attacks. The growth of weeds from the use of fertilizers may also necessitate the use of pesticides and effective weeding out practices. If the use of any inputs falls short of required dose, the output is adversely affected in varying ways.

Even if the proportionality in the use of these inputs exists, the inputs are said to be perfectly divisible and homogeneous. Hence, the inputs used are said to be scale neutral in purely technical sense. However, in so far as the new technological package raises the possibilities of multiple cropping, it is necessary to introduce rganization. The indivisible inputs—tractors, pumpsets, threshers and other agricultural appliances-are not scale neutral in a technical sense.

The farmers have to be dependent upon the market for the supply of HYV seeds, fertilizer and irrigation. The production, import and distribution of these inputs require institutional and rganization set-up to ensure that inputs are supplied timely to the farmers. Any lapse or the shortage of any of the inputs at required time may seriously damage the prospects of the crop.

Knowledge as to the timing and usage of the inputs and the scientific approach to the farming practices are extremely important if the use of these inputs are to provide maximum result (output). The new package requires that the farmer must be innovative, willing to bear the risk of investment in modern inputs as well as the risk of the substantial loss of output in the event of a crop failure say due to attack from pests.

The cost of production per unit of land is substantially higher with the new HYV seed-fertilizer-irrigation technology. The farmers, therefore, must have sufficient working capital to purchase these inputs from the market. Alternatively, credit institutions must provide adequate finance for purchasing these inputs from the market.

From the short-run point of view the availability and the timely use of the inputs in the production process may provide a higher yield. Even if the farmers, given the technical feasibility of the inputs, overcome the constraint, the new package has far reaching long-run consequences on the fertility of the soil and the environment. Moreover, it requires a dynamic search process to adapt to new conditions. If a farmer lacks dynamism to change to new conditions and the technology does not develop to changing requirements, the benefits of the new technology are bound to have diminished and its economic feasibility may be undermined.

Economic Constraints

96 per cent of the farmers operating 68 per cent of land operate at below subsistence or at subsistence level. They do not have enough working capital at the beginning of the production period. As a result, the extent to which the various inputs are applied in practice depends not on some technologically efficient dosage but on an economically optimum one, the latter being smaller than the former. The nature of the input use being complementary, the extent to which the application of a particular input can be profitably pushed, depends on the availability of, and the ability to purchase, other inputs. For most of the subsistence farmers in Bihar, therefore, the optimality in the use of these inputs cannot be achieved in the production of organization. As a result the yield of *rganizati* production is bound to be low. This also explains why the farmers in Bihar were not able to move away from *rganizati* to non-foodgrains production.

The economic imperative of the new technology drives the farmers to rganiza returns per unit of land and hence to the intensive use of the fixed factor by exploring the possibilities of multiple cropping. Besides, the HYV seeds are prone to damage from flooding, water scarcity and pests. This means that organization of farming is indispensable if the returns from land is to be organizate by raising cropping intensity. We have found evidence of rganization in agriculture in Bihar, albeit at a slow pace. However, the rganization could only be adopted by large and medium farmers. To the extent the large and medium farmers, were favoured/constrained to use fertilizer-water package in controlled manner, the effects of organization on the return from land varied considerably in different regions of Bihar.

External Linkage Activities to the Production Process

External linkage activities to the production process may relate to the (i) Procurement of necessary inputs such as seeds, fertilizers, pesticides, etc. from the market, (ii) Storage of products, (iii) Marketing of products, (iv) Use of organizational knowledge from agricultural experts, etc. Even if a farmer may remove economic constraints in purchasing these services, an organization and organizational farmer may not be able to procure these services from the market. Besides, each and every individual has to bear the cost on an individual sale of operations. The nature of many external linkage services are such that they are especially time consuming if carried out on a small scale. Also because of imperfect market of inputs, farmers sometimes may not get the required inputs in time. Clearly these problems can be solved more effectively by planning ahead with the framework of an organization.

Social Constraints

There are various social factors responsible for stagnation in agriculture. Social factors, such as, illiteracy, conventional beliefs and practices, the lack of scientific temper, etc. are no less important than economic factors in holding back the capital accumulation in agriculture.

These forces may resist change and reflect upon the attitudes of an individual. The new technological practices require the farmers to have knowledge as to the timing and use of resources, modern scientific attitude to farming practices, dynamism, innovativeness and risk-bearing ability. How far a subsistence farmer rooted in customary ideas and practices have the ability to break such social barriers.

Structural Constraints

In the specific context of Bihar the semi-feudal mode of agriculture is noted as one of the structural constraints tending to restrict the farmers to own cultivation. The restrictive assumption upon which the theoretical model is built has been pointed out by a number of economists. We shall not go into the specifics of the debate, suffice it to mention that there is no unique typology of agrarian structure that can explain the stagnation in agriculture. What is essential is the broader understanding of the village economic and social structure in its different dimensions. This is a broad area of research in agricultural economics and needs to be taken up to understand the structural constraints on agricultural production.

Specific Constraints Causes of Low Productivity in Bihar

The study of the most of the districts of the State clearly depicts certain reasons about the low productivity in agriculture. The list of causes is really very long and is of different types but here only important and common reasons which have been observed during physical survey are explained in the following paragraph.

FLOOD IN NORTH BIHAR AND DROUGHT IN SOUTH BIHAR

In Bihar approx 18 districts are flood prone and 20 districts are drought prone. Every year erratic behavior of monsoon resulted flood in some districts and drought like situation in other districts. About 41 per cent of geographical areas of the State is flood prone on the other hand 40 per cent of geographical area of South Bihar is drought prone.

Low Level of Input use

Growth of crop output is positively associated with the

use of modern inputs. Use of modern inputs has a great influence of the productivity of crops.

(a) Fertilizer

Fertilizer consumption was a mere 17 kg/hect. in 1980-81 but increase to a high of 110 kg/hect. In 2005-06, fertilizer consumption within a spectacular increase especially in the 1990s. Despite such an impressive jump in the use of chemical fertilizer the State is still far below the level of fertilizer consumption in State such as Punjab 173, Haryana 155 and Andhra Pradesh 143 kg/hect.

(b) Seed Replacement

Seed replacement rate for cereals is about 10-12 per cent, Gram it is 7.5 per cent and for rapeseed and mustard it is 30 per cent. It is desirable to have 30-35 per cent seed replacement rate for self-pollination crops and 50 per cent for cross pollinated crops. Maximum seed replacement for paddy 50 per cent Andhra Pradesh, for wheat 41 per cent in Maharastra, for gram 30 per cent in Orissa and for rapeseed and mustard it is 100 per cent in Gujarat.

(c) Consumption of Electricity

Per cent share of electricity towards agriculture sector is only about 13.5 per cent in Bihar whereas in Haryana and Andhra Pradesh it is about 45.12 and 43.45 per cent respectively.

(d) Low delivery of Agri-credit

The entire rural credit delivery system is not a good shape in Bihar. This hold true for all the three wings of rural credit delivery system. Rural branches of commercial banks, co-operative credit institutions and regional rural banks. Hence innovative approaches to rejuvenate the system are called for linking of self help group and non government with main stream financial institution is one such innovative mechanism. Upto 2005-06 only 14,50,779 Kisan credit cards has been distributed against the target of 30,47,536, which is only 47.6 per cent.

(e) Low Level of Mechanism

In Bihar number tractors per thousand hectares are about 2.5, which is much below in comparison 70 in Punjab and Haryana.

(f) Poor land reforms

Though Bihar was one of the first State to enact various law relating to land reforms, their implementation has been slow and far from satisfactory particularly the fragmented holding is posing a constraint on the optimal use of land and investment inland improvement measures.

(g) Marketing and MSP

There is a need to develop better roads, communication and market infrastructure and most importantly a commitment to procure all the food grain that comes to the market. Low level of procurement of food grain is hampering farmers for going large scale investment in production.

(h) Low Public Investment

A productivity seed agricultural growth requires large investment in creating and maintaining productive assets like irrigation and rural infrastructure as well as in promoting growth like agricultural research, education and extension. Unfortunately, the public investment in Bihar is one of the lowest in the Country, more frustrating is the decelerating trend of public investment in recent years.

(i) Low level of acceptance of crop insurance

During Kharif, 2004 only 2,93,442 farmers and during Rabi 2004-05, only 1,18,090 farmers are covered under crop insurance scheme.

(j) Problem areas

In Bihar, 1.00 lac hect of land is under Tal and 5.16 lac hectare is under Diara, 4.50 lac hectare under Chour and 4.14 lac hectare is under Saline and Alkaline Land which require urgent attention.

PROBLEMS

The poor performance of agricultural sector in Bihar is in sharp contrast to its endowment of natural resources. As far as agriculture-related endowment are concerned, the State even after separation enjoys congenial agro-climate conditions throughout the year having multiple crop seasons in the year. Geographically, Bihar now extends over an area of 94 lakh hectares having the total population of 82.9 million. More than two-third of its total land is cultivated. Both in rivers and the aquifers, there is abundance of water. According to 2001 census, 84.20 per cent of State worker's main source of income is from agriculture.

Since Bihar, after bifurcation, is predominantly agricultural State, the low rate of agriculture shall jeopardize the whole economy of the State. The particular question should, therefore, be why Bihar cannot be turned into another Haryana. Haryana ranked 10th in 1960-61, but moved up to second in 1988-89. Bihar's rank during fifties was fifth, but today it has reached the bottom. Needless to say, the importance of agricultural development has drawn the attention of policy-makers in the past but factors retarding growth could not be understood. Consequently, the efforts made so far could not bring about the desired results in achieving the targets of agricultural development in the State. It is not high time to understand what agricultural development in Bihar. Many explanations have been offered in terms of topographical, technological, institutional and resource constraints. It is generally conceived that changes in production may depend on technology but the technological changes are largely influenced by the institutional set-up and so, any analysis of agricultural growth in isolation from institutional constraints will be an exercise in futility.

The syndrome of non-development of agriculture in Bihar may be better understood in terms of agrarian structure. There are sufficient reasons for it. The available statistics on the use of important components of new technology in agriculture namely. HYV seeds, fertilizers and irrigation clearly indicate that with the same proportion of their use at all-India level, the crop productivity in Bihar is low. It may be noted that irrigation intensity (36.7%) in Bihar is higher than India (30.3%). Likewise, the area covered under HYV seeds has shown increasing trend in Bihar similar to the trend observed that though it is slightly less than all-India average but it is satisfactory. Thus, the comparative view of use of modern inputs presents the dilemma of technological impact on agricultural growth in Bihar. It seems that technological constraints are not so important to tardy growth of agriculture in Bihar as made out to be the past. Though the importance of technology in agricultural development cannot be negated, the main constraint to the high growth of agriculture lies somewhere else which may be seen in iniquitous agrarian structure, i.e. the institutional set-up of the agrarian economy.

The agrarian structure has remained highly iniquitous in Bihar since time immemorial. In fact, feudal characteristics of the agrarian structure were already in existence till the independence period. Since then some changes have occurred but it could turn into semi-feudal production relations in agriculture. This has been due to failure of land reforms which made the semi-feudal set-up inimical to rapid development of agricultural sector. Undoubtedly, the State government has failed to implement land reforms judiciously because of the vested interest of the bureaucracy and politicians. The dreams of land to the tillers as one of the most important agenda of land reforms have in fact miserably failed.

It concludes that, in the past five decades Bihar has suffered a lot due to non-implementation of land reforms as a basic instrument to transform agrarian structure. There has been persistence character of non-development of Bihar economy in terms of low agricultural growth, high incidence of poverty, rapidly increasing unemployment, strained relations between peasantry and rural oligarchy. The case for agrarian reforms, especially giving high priority to land reforms was never so strong as now. The emphasis on technological changes in isolation from institutional reforms for transforming agrarian economy will again prove to be meaningless in achieving the goals of agricultural growth with social justice. The need-based planning, for an integrated institutional reforms covering land distribution, marketing and credits is the most crucial area for bringing about agrarian transformation in Bihar.

SUGGESTIONS

In order to overcome the crises existing in the agrarian structure in Bihar and Jharkhand the following suggestions are considered to be useful:

Quality and Certified Seeds

The availability of quality and certified seeds is a major constraints faced by the farmers almost in all crops including vegetables during all the crop seasons. It has been found that resource use efficiency indicates negative seed elasticity which implies that farmers are losers even though they spent more on seeds. Quality seed production must find priority in any programme of agricultural development. Rajendra Agricultural University, Pusa may be entrusted to accept this challenge.

Farm Credit

A production-oriented agricultural system implies credit widening as also credit deepening. The former refers to bringing more and more farmers within the credit facilities whereas the later refers to increasing credit per hectare. In Bihar, the credit availability per hectare is Rs. 147 which is much low as compared to other States.

Agrarian Reforms

It has been usually accepted that there is lower utilization of HYV technology in Bihar than in India due to agrarian structural barrier. Therefore, agrarian reforms are required to make Bihar agriculture more conductive for technological improvement and full utilization of resources for development.

Further, given the declining per capita availability of land which has been severely affected after bifurcation of the State, and limited resource base of individual farmers there is an urgent need to remove the unproductive character to the agrarian structure. In order to make over 75 per cent marginal and small holdings economically viable, redical land reform measures are essential.

Integrated Farming System Approach

The declining trend in the average size of operational holdings poses a serious problem. The small and marginal farmers are, therefore, unable to meet both the ends with the income from cropping alone. The situation further deteriorates due to repeated failure of monsoon or due to floods. In this context, it is imperative to evolve suitable strategy for augmenting the income of farmers. Integration of various enterprises in a farm ensures recycling of residues, optimum resource use, higher employment, minimization of risk and uncertainties to increase farm and non-farm income. Various enterprises that could be included in farming system are crop (planning), dairy, poultry, goat rearing, fishery, sericulture, mushroom cultivation and silviculture. A judicious mix of enterprises, complementary to cropping and suited to the given agro-climatic situations and social-economic status of the farmers need to be introduced for promoting agricultural sector in the State. This will also facilitate the diversification of agriculture which increases the farm income. After all, the farmer's decision to adopt new techniques depends on their profitability as well as reliability.

Infrastructural Support

The pace and pattern of agricultural development in Bihar has been slow on account of poor infrastructure. The inputs supply system, service infrastructure, road and communication, marketing and processing, energy supply for agriculture and many other infrastructural development have been rather at low level as compared to the all-India figures. Due importance of infrastructural development in the State either with private investment or public investment needs to be given in the strategies for agricultural development in the State.

To conclude, the linkage between agriculture and industry commensurate with faster rate of agricultural growth need to be strengthened for the overall development of the economy of Bihar. The slogan of development in the State should be now put on as agricultural development led-industrialization. The day this slogan becomes a reality, Bihar can boast of eliminating poverty, inequality and unemployment. Like its past glory, it can once again be glorified. This would show the country a new path of social and economic development. Nobody would then say that Bihar is a sick State, a beleaguered and poor State.

References

Singh and Bright, Economics of Development.
Singh, Sukhpal, Contract Farming.
Sen, S.R., The Indian Economics Scene: Retrospect and Prospect.
Sen, Ranjit, Structural Adjustment in India.

13

Problems of Agriculture in Bihar and Its Remedial Measures

MD. MURSHID ALAM AND TALAT JABEEN

A serious crisis has broken out in the field of Bihar agriculture. The crisis is most glaringly manifested in the growing incidence of starvation deaths and farmers' suicides. While the largest number of starvation deaths are still routinely reported from the backward regions of the Bihar. the trend of suicides generally prompted by heavy indebtedness, crop failure, or inability to find a market for the produce, is noticed even among well-to-do farmers in Bihar.

The crisis has also led to a new phase of agrarian unrest. Peasants and farmers have strongly opposed the WTO, growing penetration of giant agribusiness firms and attempts to corporatise agriculture. Once again powerful farmers' movements are being witnessed in the green revolution areas. But the original exponent of farmers' movement in the country, Mr. Sharad Joshi, now stands on the wrong side of the fence. This erstwhile World Bank official-turned-farmer leader today advises the NDA government on matters of agricultural policy while the farmers are braving lathis and bullets on the streets.

While the WTO agreements and the thoroughly unequal competition with heavily subsidised big corporate farmers from the western countries have aggravated the present crisis situation, the root of it lies in the accumulated anomalies of the landlord path of capitalist development in Indian agriculture. For the overwhelming majority of poor and lower-middle peasants, the landlord path pursued in India under the slogan of green revolution has largely reinforced conditions of semi-bondage and extreme hardship. Of course, there were dramatic results initially in the late 1960s and all through the 1970s with foodgrains production recording major increases.

The green revolution thus helped in tiding over an alarming situation of extreme food scarcity and dependence on external aid, and part of the gains of this productivity also percolated to sections of the upper-middle peasantry. But its further spread to relatively backward areas was constrained from the beginning by serious infrastructural problems. With declining public investment in agriculture and rising prices of all key inputs, green revolution soon reached a point of saturation even in its initial strongholds. The farmers'movement in the 1980s with its loud demand for remunerative prices and cheaper inputs reflected this brewing crisis.

Against this backdrop, bourgeois ideologues within the farmers' movement started demanding liberalisation of agricultural trade and reversal of land reforms. Sections of big farmers started dreaming about exporting to the world market and securing super-remunerative prices. This was akin to the corporate clamour for freedom from 'licence-permit-quota raj'. But whether it be the would-be 'Indian' MNCs or the Indian big farmers eyeing their share in the world market, it did not take long for the dream to turn sour. And then just as the corporate sector started demanding a 'level-playing field' even while it was forging closer ties of collaboration with the MNCs, big farmers came up with the demand for insulation from the WTO even as they too were developing a nexus with agribusiness corporations. Just as the working class has to see through the corporate clamour for level-playing fields, so must agricultural labourers, poor peasants and their small farmer allies see through the rich farmers' 'crusade' against the WTO.

Barring small sections of big farmers the current agrarian crisis has adversely affected various sections of the agricultural population. The demand for remunerative prices has now been pushed back to the demand for minimum support price and guranteed procurement, or in other words, freedom from distress sale. Similarly, in the case of agricultural labour, the demand for assured employment has become one of the major demands even as wages often remain depressed way below the officially proclaimed minimum level. But with their relative economic power and much greater political clout, the rural rich, the kulaks and well-to-do farmers always try to transfer the burden of the entire crisis on to the rural poor. It is the latter who are being forced to make the greatest sacrifice and to surrender whatever gains they had achieved through years of struggle.

One look at the picture emerging from Bihar will indicate the extent of the growing burden of the accumulating agrarian crisis on the rural poor. We are singling out the case of Bihar. According to a recent status report released by the Land Reforms department of the Government of Bihar, over 13% pattadars (who had been allotted land under the land reforms act) have been dispossessed and among the recorded sharecroppers 3.02% have been evicted from their barga land.

Our agarian programme attaches a lot of importance to the issues and demands of the middle peasants and our class line calls for a close alliance with middle peasants. In practice, however, our reach within the middle peasantry remains quite limited. Given the intensity of caste-class divide in many parts of rural India, especialy in states like Bihar and UP, and the rise of kulak-based regional parties, it has been difficult for the party of the proletariat with its strong identification with the rural proletariat to make inroads among the middle peasantry. The present situation of agrarian crisis marks a major opportunity for us to boldly address the issues of the middle peasantry without in any way diluting our primary commitment to the rural proletariat.

It is against this backdrop that we have to review our ongoing agrarian struggles and decide our future course of action. Recent times have witnessed a surge in agrarian struggles not only in our traditional stronghold of Bihar, but also in pockets of UP, Andhra, Orissa, West Bengal, Jharkhand and Punjab. While land, tenancy, wages and employment remain the basic and most common issues of agrarian struggles, we also find many powerful initiatives on issues like privatisation of electricity, increased electricity rates, debt relief, procurement of food grains and various aspects of rural development and functioning of the panchayat system.

In Bihar, West Champaran district, which borders Nepal and Uttar Pradesh, has emerged as the latest stormcentre of land struggles. This district still has a very high incidence of well entrenched landlordism. Estates controlling thousands of acres of land are still quite common. Electoral politics in the district is directly dominated by these large estates and apart from having their own armed henchmen they also enjoy the loyalty of the local police. There is also the case of two MLAs who jointly own one estate (Vilaspur), one MLA elected on a Congress ticket serves as a minister in the Rabri Devi cabinet while the other MLA elected under the banner of the BJP sits in the 'opposition'! The agricultural labourers' association (khet mazdoor sabha) in the district has successfully redistributed 400 acres of land in Gaunaha block among 600 agricultural labourers. In Mainatand block, 300 acres of land belonging to one Markandeya Pandey of UP has been captured. The district administration is trying to suppress these struggles by unleashing barbaric police repression, but the masses are offering determined resistance.

In Bihar, the agricultural labourers' strike held on 22 July was implemented in nearly 2000 villages and demonstrations were held in 134 blocks. Some 70,000 agricultural labourers joined this class action all over the state to demand implementation of the minimum wages act, enactment of welfare legislation at central and state levels, CBI inquiry into the PDS (public distribution system) scam in Bihar and mandatory inclusion of all families with an annual income of less than Rs. 20,000 in the BPL (below poverty line) list. Earlier, a major campaign was conducted in the state on the issue of PDS scam demanding removal of the civil supplies minister and unconditional release of all arrested activists. Block level people's courts were organised in 116 blocks in 20 districts in which nearly 75,000 agricultural labourers and red card holders (those who are legally entitled to subsidised supply of essential provisions but who, in reality, are often denied this while the rich and influential corner all these facilities).

Now that we have launched a separate organisation for agricultural labourers, we are faced with the challenge of maintaining the separate identity of both agricultural labour and peasant organisations and yet combining the initiatives of the two organisations to raise the level of the overall movement. We should gradually move towards building an all-India organisation for agricultural labourers. With growing inter-state migration and the rise of common class demands including that of a comprehensive central legislation, elements of class-consciousness are growing among agricultural labourers and an all-India organisation with periodic national campaigns can accelerate and consolidate this process. In some areas where our work is concentrated primarily among either agricultural labourers or middle peasants, it is not necessary to rush immediately to form two separate organisations. In real life, agricultural labour and poor peasants are often indistinguishable and so a certain degree of overlapping between the agricultural labour organisation and the peasant association may be unavoidable. Any attempt to make a hard and fast distinction is liable to create a mechanical division and inhibit our overall initiative. Agricultural labour organisations may also be registered as trade unions and affiliated to our central trade union organisation. But this must be understood as a purely technical arrangement, agricultural labour organisations must not be confined to any narrow framework of trade union legalities or trade union mode of functioning.

INTRODUCTION

Agriculture occupies a very significant position in Indian economy. It plays a very vital role in the sphere of national income, employment, capital formation, food supply, industry, trade, transport, export, government budget and so on. But apart from this Indian agriculture is facing some difficulties and challenges, both internal and external. It is characterized by stagnating yield at a low level, a very large proportion of marginal, small and semi-medium holdings, burdened with high proportion of labour force, highly concentrated cropping pattern, very low income, lack for finance and credit. Over the period of time, the share of agriculture in GDP decreased to 26.2 per cent in 2001-02 from 59.1 per cent in 1950-51. So far as the labour force is concerned, 60 per cent of the total labour force is still employed in agriculture. So, 60 per cent of population contributes only 26 per cent in national income, it is not justifiable whereas in developed countries only two or three per cent of total work force is employed in agriculture and the contribution of agriculture in GDP is also two or three per cent.

In the case of Bihar's economy agriculture is a very significant. With carving of the new state, called Jharkhand, on 15th November 2000 the new Bihar is left with a geographical area of 94,163 sq. km. (2.86% of India) having population of 8,28,78,796 (8.07% of India) as per census 2001. With both large scale of industries and mines separated from the state of Bihar, agriculture and allied activities, are the only sector left on which the economy of the new Bihar has to thrive. 77 per cent of the population of Bihar depends for their livelihood on agriculture. In 2006-07, the contribution of agriculture and allied activities to the State Domestic Product was 29.26 per cent. Although this is a reduction from the level of 48 per cent in 1980 it retains among the highest in the country. With the separation of mineral rich and industrially developed area, Bihar is left with mainly agricultural lands and rivers. Bihar's agricultural growth is not satisfactory due some reasons such as uneconomic holdings, backward agriculture and industry, low rate of savings and investment, low per capita income, unemployment, under employment, poor infrastructure facilities, highest poverty ratio. Low literacy rate, less financial assistance, poor transport facilities, poor marketing and storing facilities, etc. The gangetic plains of Bihar, the bio-diversity of Bihar backed by good climatic conditions and firmly motivated and hard working farmers Bihar would become a world class producer of agriculture but Bihar not achieved well. In this paper we try to analyse the causes of hindrance the growth of agriculture and what majors to be taken for agriculture development in the state of Bihar.

PRESENT CONDITION OF BIHAR

Bihar has now a total geographical area of about 93.60 lakh hectare, out of which only 56.03 lakh hectare is the next cultivated area and gross cultivated area being 79.46 lakh hectare. Bihar has about 6,674.14 sq. ft. forest area which is 7.1 per cent of its geographical area. Bihar has flood affected area 68,800 sq. km. (73.06 per cent of total Bihar's land). Bihar has an irrigation potential of 93.38 lakh hectare out of this 53.53 lakh hectare is to irrigated through major and medium irrigation schemes and 44.85 lakh hectare through minor irrigation schemes. Upto March 2001, Bihar had 13,412.80 km. of *pucca* roads, including 2,461.73 km. of national highways and 10,951.07 km. of state highways and major district roads. In addition to this the length of rural roads in 15000 kms. Bihar's population division on the basis of urban and rural 10.5 per cent urban population and 89.5 per cent in rural populace. Bihar's 56 per cent population is below poverty line. The percentage of landless farmers, i.e. labourers working in the field is 48.18 per cent. According to 2001 census 16 lakh hectare land already engaged in non-agriculture activities. 68.80 lakh hectare land effected by floods and 19 lakh hectare land effect due to soil erosion. Irrigation facility available on 28.177 lakh hectare land only. Percentage of villages connected with *pucca* road in Bihar is only 19.0 whereas all India average is 36.8 percentage, per capita consumption of electricity was as low as 133.7 kwh. in 1994 as compared to 320.1 kwh in the country, the same figure for other industrially advanced states is much higher than Bihar. Financial facilities is lesser in the state. Bihar's Principal Food Crops are paddy, wheat, maize and pulses and main cash crops are sugarcane, potato, tobacco, oilseeds, onion, chilies, jute and mesta.

PROBLEMS OF AGRICULTURAL GROWTH IN BIHAR

There are so many causes for the low growth of agriculture in Bihar.

1. Increase Presence of Population on Agriculture

Absence of allied occupation and fast increasing population are responsible for the increasing pressure on agriculture. There are aggravating the problem of employment in the rural areas. Bihar's 77 per cent population depends on agriculture. Bihar's rural population is 89.5 per cent of the total population. Due to increase presence of population affect the growth of agriculture in the state and per capita cultivated land decrease day-by-day.

2. Land Tenure System

The most important reason of low agricultural productivity has been the Zamindari system. This system drained out the very capacity, willingness and enthusiasm of the cultivations to increase production and productivity. The abolition in the post-independence period has been able to break the stronghold of the zamindars on the rural economy. The only changed the grab and became large landowners. A major part of the cultivable land is owned by big landlords. Bihar's 8 per cent agriculture land occupied by only 0.85 per cent landlord which have more than 10 hectare land each. 47 per cent of the gross cultivated land of Bihar is below 2 hectares holding. The large landowners themselves do not till their land but give it to tenants on crop share system or tenary revenue. The tenants are mostly indifferent to the improvement of land because they know a big chunk of the increased production will go to the land. Under the Zamindari system the cultivator was only a tenant who could be turned out the land. Even though the Zamindari system has now been abolished and tenancy legislation have been enacted to protect the tenants, the position of tenants is far from satisfactory. Under these difficult conditions, it is impossible to expect the tiller to increase agricultural productivity.

3. Uneconomic Holdings

The average size of holding in India and even Bihar is very low, less than 2 hectares or 5 acres. Bihar's 47 per cent Gross cultivated land holdings below 2 hectares. Mostly holdings is the hands of the cultivators is too small to allow use of any new methods and use of tractors, etc. Mechanised farming is not possible in such small holdings. Many times the field are left even untilled. Small sized holdings lead to great waste of time, labour and cattle power, difficulty in proper utilization or irrigation facilities, quarrels and consequent litigation among farmers, wastage of crops in the absence of fencing, etc.

4. Joint Family System and Fragmentation and Subdivision

Joint family system prevails in the villages which discourages the tendency of hardwork. It gives rise to disguised unemployment and reduces per capital productivity. The father's land is divided among the sons and the holdings go on being subdivided and fragmented after successive division. In small holding there are no irrigation facilities nor crops can be well looked after, the result is low productivity.

5. Poor Techniques of Production

In spite of some progress after independence even now old and primitive implements and methods of cultivation are used. Wooden ploughs and bullock are an integral part of India and Bihar's cultivation. Although the use of tractor is on the increase yet it is so costly that it is practically impossible to make use of it by poor farmers with their small holdings. Bihar's mostly farmers are agricultural labour. Who don't have any resource for their land development. One of the reasons of low productivity of Bihar farming is that the farmer still uses old seeds and traditional modes of production. Only in recent years and to a limited extent the farmers have started adopting improved implements like steel ploughs, sugarcane crushers, small pumping sets, water lifts, barrows, hoes, seed drills, fodder cutters, etc. Increase in production is possible only if proper and adequate manures are used. To revitalize fertility and to utilize fallow lands, the use of various kinds of manures is urgently called for. The use of chemical fertilizers has been steadily increasing but because of high cost they are not yet used by poor farmers.

6. Inadequate Irrigation Facilities

One of the basic causes for the weakness of Bihar agriculture has been that most of the farmers throughout the state of Bihar depend upon rain fall and very a few of them can avail of the facilities of artificial irrigation. Bihar has an irrigation potential of 93.38 lakh hectare out of this 53.53 lakh hectare is to irrigation through major and medium irrigation schemes. Due to poverty most of the farmers of Bihar not in a position to avail of the facilities of artificial irrigation they depends on rainfall.

7. Flood

Flood is a chronic problem for Bihar state specially in North Bihar, certain parts of the region experience flood problems almost every year. This region has a dense network of river streams. Many of these, rise in the hills in Nepal and are subject to violent floods as their beds have been raised by silt deposits and streams flow on elevated channels. The heavy rain in monsoon both in Nepal hills and in the command area pose the problem of discharge. The shallow streams do not cope with the volume of water rushing down and that causes several flood. Construction of a number of public and private bounds for protection of villages also caused greater danger to the villages situated relatively in lower reaches and water stagnation for months if flood water enters into low land. In Bihar nearly 68.38 lakh hectare land is under flood prone ecosystem which is 16.5 per cent of the total flood affected area of the country and 37 per cent of the geographical area of the state. North Bihar alone occupies 44.47 lakh hectare of land under flood-prone ecosystem accounting 90.5 per cent of total flood affected area of the state, 76 per cent of the total geographical area of North Bihar and 25.6 per cent of the total geographical areas of the state. The state rice is cultivated in 4.8 million hectares of land in kharif season. Out of total area, nearly 50 per cent area is under flood prone ecosystem which is not all suitable for rice. In spite of that, rice is grown in this area where production and productivity of rice is very low. In rabi season nearly 85 per cent of rice area is converted by wheat crop which due to silt deposition in the soil is harvested comparatively better yield but not at par with the yield which is obtained under favourable ecosystem. The low productivity under large area reduces the average productivity of rice and wheat in Bihar. It is really a matter of concern to the agricultural scientists and policy-makers to study the situation and to search out the ways to improve the productivity of crops under flood prone ecosystem.

8. Lack of Marketing Facilities

The farmer cannot sell his products on reasonable prices. He is being exploited by a long chain of middleman. For fear of his exploitation he likes to sell his produce locally to the village moneylenders at through away prices. No wonder he thinks of farming as a method of subsistence only. He does not introduce reforms in cultivation.

9. Lack of Credit and Financing Facilities

Bihar farmer is already poor and then due to low productivity he fails to raise the income. Therefore both savings and investment are low. The indebtedness to the village mahajan keeps his caught in vicious circles of poverty. Although after the nationalization of commercial banks, there has been some improvement in the availability of credit, yet the benefit has mostly been reaped by big landlords. Banking system play a significant role in the supply of funds for agricultural development. It is true that during recent years considerable expansion has been recorded in terms of the number of bank branches established in Bihar and the amount of deposits mobilized by different banks and has also been substantial. But the flow of credit from these sources to meet the financial requirement of the agriculture or business sector has not been satisfactory. This means that large amount of funds collected in this part of the country has been shifted to other states or used elsewhere. The resultant situation is such that banks often fail to confine the interest in the agriculture and business prosperity of Bihar. There has been no change in the financial position of poor small farmers.

10. Problem of Infrastructure

Economic development to a great extent depends both on physical and social infrastructure, physical infrastructure, in case of roads, railways, sports, electricity, etc. have hardly made any contribution to the agricultural and industrial development of Bihar. Length surface of roads for every 1,00,059 km. of area in Bihar comes 167 km. whereas the all India average is 326 km. (1991-92) many other states in India have much larger length surface road. In Tamil Nadu it comes to 1015 km. percentage of villages connected with pucca road in Bihar is only 19.0 whereas all India average is 36.8 per cent, per capital consumption of electricity was as low as 133.7 kwh in 1994 as compared to 320.1 kwh in the country the same figure for other industrially advanced states is much higher than Bihar. Thus Bihar is far behind the rest of the country in respect of infrastructure hold back the state from taking benefits of whatever natural advantages it has.

11. Lack of Suitable Varieties of Seeds and Hybrids

Suitable variety and hybrids seeds of crops is a key factor in improving the productivity and lowering of production cost. Unfortunately, while the state government lacks initiatives towards developing or providing suitable varieties, besides having remained unconcerned about unsuitable of its varieties. Most of the released varieties deteriorated within 34 years. Other states enjoyed significant support in developing new suitable varieties of crops which help the rapid agricultural growth.

12. Lack of Agri-based Industries

There has been inadequate growth of medium scale, small-scale and household or cottage industries. Food and other industries based on agricultural, live stock and forest resource has also not grown on a very substantial scale, and two of the major industries in this group namely sugar and jute have been declining over the years due to very largely raw material problems. Food processing and agro-based industries helping the agricultural growth but unfortunately these industries not developed in adequate manner.

In short lack of infrastructure, under-developed marketing facilities and inadequate technological inputs, including dismal financial support are some of key factors, determental the growth of agriculture sector. Cumbersome land holding system of Bihar and obsolete processing units with inadequate of financial assistance, are the major roadblocks to the growth of cultivation/agro-based industries in the state. Again the absence of cold chain technology and lack of entrepreneurship, including inadequate technological inputs related to packaging methods and preservation of fruits and vegetable are the major handicaps to the food processing industry.

MEASURES TO IMPROVE AGRICULTURAL GROWTH IN BIHAR:

To boost agricultural productivity the whole of India and Bihar Agricultural will have to be reconstructed and reorganized. Institutional factors have to be reformed and new techniques of production have to be used in mechanization and modernization have to be adopted in right-earnest.

(i) Improvement in Volume of Cultivable Land

There is need to increase the cultivable land. For this purpose barren and uncultivable land can be brought under plough with the use of modern scientific methods of cultivation. Bihar geographical area about 93.60 lakh hectare, out of which only 56.03 lakh hectare is the net cultivated area. The rest has forest, deserts and uncultivated.

(ii) Development of Irrigation Facilities

To improve agricultural productivity the dependence

on monsoons has to be cut-off and permanent means of irrigation have to be developed.

(iii) Improvement in Land Tenure System

Productivity cannot be increased unless the farmers are made the masters of land, i.e. ownership right should be granted to tillers.

(iv) Implementation of Land Reforms

To improve and raise productivity it is essential that the reforms in land tenure system uneconomic holdings should be stopped. At the same time the other programme of land reforms should be speedily, and effectively put through.

(v) Increase in Credit Facilities

It is also essential that the farmers should be provided with cheap credit facilities so that they may be able to invest in land reforms and improvement.

(vi) Fixation of Economic Holding

To check further sub-division and fragmentation of land ceiling suitable for the living of the farmer's family should be fixed. Consolidation of holdings has also proved helpful in this direction.

(vii) Encouragement to Cooperative Farming

Due to small and uneconomic holdings mostly it became uneconomic to introduce land reforms or cultivate the total cultivable land. Therefore, the government should encourage cooperative farming so that the total area of cultivable land may be put to an ideal use.

(viii) Determination of Proper Price Policy

To encourage sufficient investment in land by farmers it is essential that he should get a profitable price for his produce. Thus it becomes imperative for the government to fix minimum price for food grains and other crops to break the instability in prices and uncertainty of the farmer's income.

(ix) Co-ordination Between Various Agricultural Activities

A proper coordination between different activities of agriculture from the purchase of inputs to the marketing or produce should be established so that the farmer may perform all these activities easily and efficiently.

(x) Crop Diversification Strategies

Crop diversification is an important strategy to be adopted for agriculture productivity. Fruits and vegetables occupy 10 per cent of the gross cropped area in Bihar, the account for 50 per cent of the income from farming. The area under litchi, mango, banana, guava and makhana will be increased after identification of the area suited for the crop. Vegetable cultivation will be promoted to areas with assured sources of irrigation. Area under sugarcane cultivation will be substantially stepped up.

(xi) Training and Necessary Information and Services given to Farmers

For increase productivity of agriculture balanced and integrated fertilizer use will be promoted, soil testing infrastructure will be extended to the block level and agro-climes will be encouraged to bring soil testing services to the farmers. Chemical pesticides will be replaced by vigorous promotion of integrated pest management approach. Organic farming will be encouraged and vermiculture technology will reach every farmer. Agricultural mechanization will be promoted for timely sowing, harvesting and post harvest activities. Training should be given to farmers far modern technological use and new varieties of seeds, use of fertilizer, etc.

(xii) Flood Control

In Bihar nearly 68.38 lakh hectare land is under flood prone ecosystem which is badly affect the productivity of agriculture government should adopt measures to control the flood.

(xiii) Improved Varieties of Seed to be Provide to Farmers

The above measures can introduce a total revolution in

agricultural line. If these measures taken honestly for the development of the agriculture, the agriculture will be sure developed and agragarian crisis to be solved amicably.

REFERENCE

"Bihar at a glance" published by Directorate of Statistics and Evaluation, Govt. of Bihar, 2004.

Ghatate, Subrata and Ingersent, Ker., Agriculture and Economic Development (New Delhi: Select Book Service Syndicate, 1984).

Roy, A.K.: Industrialising Bihar: The Option, *The Economic and Political Weekly*, July 29, 1995.

Prasad, K.N. (2000): "What Ails the Bihar Economy: A Non-Economic Diagnosis", *The Bihar Economic Journal*, Vol. 1, No. 1.

Desai, Vasant (1983): "A Study of Rural Economic", Himalaya Publication House, Bombay.

Rakesh Moha, "Industrial Policy and Controls", in Bimal Jalan (Ed.), *The Indian Economy: Problems and Prospects* (New Delhi, 1992).

14

Impact of Agricultural Price Policy in Jharkhand's Eco-Development

N.C. JHA

Basically India is a fast growing developing economy, currently the world's fourth largest in terms of real GDP, after the USA, China and Japan, the second fastest growing major economy averaging at an annual growth rate of 7.7 per cent; in character an agrarian economy having 17.5 per cent of the share in GDP in 2006-07, giving 70 per cent of total population the minimum subsistence directly or indirectly. Over the years the share of agriculture has a declining trend because in 2000-01, it was 23.4 per cent in GDP which goes down to 18.8 per cent and 17.5 per cent in 2007 and 2008 respectively where as the share of the Industrial sector as well as Service Sector has gone up from 26.2 per cent and 50.5 per cent in 2001-02 to 27.5 per cent and 53.7 per cent in 2004-05 and 27.9 per cent and 54.6 per cent in 2006-07. In the 11th Plan the share of agriculture would be 15.3 per cent where as the share of Industrial and Service sector would be 28 per cent and 56.6 per cent respectively which is a good shine of the accelerated growth of the Indian economy in the world perspective. The Land Use Pattern of Indian Economy in 2005-06 is as follows:

TABLE I

Area Used	*Percentage (%)*
Net Sown Area	46.8
Forest Area	22.6
Not available for	–
Cultivation	13.6
Fallow land	3.3
Waste land	4.6
Trees and groves	1.2
Pastures	3.6

Source: Chronicle, India, 2007

From the above table it is evident that the net sown area has the highest percentage and the Indian economy is, undoubtedly growing at the rapid rate as in the 11th Plan the growth rate of agriculture is projected at 4 per cent with its effect the people living below poverty line would be reduced to less than 15 per cent of the total population.Thus agriculture plays a substantial role by providing adequate food supply, thus maintaining a stable price. In the development of agriculture agricultural price policy plays a crucial role but it has generally been used negatively-to keep "Bread and Raw materials cheap for the growing Industrial sector and maximize and transfer to the city for investment the profits of trade in agricultural commodities. For stability in the economic zones, the agricultural price policy plays a crucial role by making a halt in inordinately increase in the price of food and non-food variables and also not allowing them to go down below the critical minimum level. It also checks the corrupt and unfair profit making traders to use artificial tools to have an impact on the agricultural prices. In India generally on the recommendation of the Agricultural Price Commission, the minimum prices as well as procurement prices are announced. Minimum prices are in nature of long term guarantee to the farmers so that in the event of a glut, prices are not allowed to fall below these announced minimum prices. Procurement prices are fixed at a higher level as compared to the minimum support prices and are meant essentially for the purchase of quantities needed by the government for maintaining the Public Distribution System and for building Buffer Stocks. Issue prices indicate the prices at which the government supplies foodgrains through fair price shops and Ration Depots.

The chief goal of the Agricultural Price Policy is to provide a security to the farmers at its highest level so that they should have certainty and confidence in agricultural activities. But this Agricultural Price Policy might have positive as well as negative effects. In India year after year the A.P.C has issued the Minimum Support Prices but it is proved a negative policy because the agricultural output has not increased significantly and planners have felt compelled willy-nilly to turn to a positive policy

TABLE 2

Minimum Support Price for Important Crops in India

(Rs./Per Quintal)

Name of Crops	*1990-91*	*2002-03*	*2004-05*
Paddy-Common	205	530	560
Grade-A	225	560	590
Wheat	225	620	640
Coarse Cereals	180	485	515
Maize	180	485	525
Barley	200	500	540
Gram	450	1220	1425
Arhar (Tur)	480	1320	1390
Moong	480	1330	1410
Sugar Cane	23	69.5	74.5
Cotton H-4 (peril)	620	1875	1960
Jute	320	1355	1500

Source: CHRONICLE INDIA. 2007.

From the above table it is evident that MSP for different crops over the years has undoubtedly an increasing trend and its effect, according to the Indian Economists, is not efficient enough to cover even the cost of the farmers, henceforth, if we go through its effect on the Area, Production and Yield of the different crops, if not positive even in Indian context.

Jharkhand which is the 28th state of Indian union reflects all the characteristics of backwardness and multi-dimensional economic social and political problems especially the peasent's associated alround problems. The low per capita income, high incidence of poverty, low agricultural growth rate,high illiteracy,over dependent on agricultural,social backwardness. Political wilderness mass malnutrition among the weaker section, etc. are some of important indicators of the new state's backwardness. The state mainly known as a mineraly rich state, having 2.7 million population of which 27.67 per cent is tribal population, predominantly rural one because 94 per cent of tribal population resides in villages or hilly forest areas, has the largest poverty status population, i.e. 43 per cent in rural areas and 32.9 per centin urban areas. The total geographical area of this state is 79714 sq. km. of which the rural sector and urban sector have 77876 sq. km. and 1838 km. respectively. out of total population in Jharkhand, 86.26 per centpopulation is directly or indirectly dependent upon agriculture for their livelihood. if we go through the land use pattern of the state, about 18.4 hectares land gross cropped area, 20 lakh hectares is barren and current fallow land and 2 lakh hectares is non-agricultural land such as grazing, gardening, etc. and 23 lakh hectares is forestry which is 29.2 per cent of total geographical area of the state. The land use pattern of India and Jharkhand can be explained as follows:

TABLE 3

Land-use Pattern of India and Jharkhand

(In%)

Items	*India*	*Jharkhand*
Net sown area	46.80	22.54
Forest area	22.60	29.20
Fallow land	3.31	3.86
Waste land	4.60	1.09
Trees groves	1.2	1.30
Pastures	3.6	1.63
Non-cultivable land	13.6	14.72

Source: Chronicle India, 2007 and Jharkhand Hand Book, 2006.

From the above table, it is evident that only 22.54 per cent of total geographical area of Jharkhand is available for agricultural purpose which is quite less than the national net sown area. If we go through the crop wise area in Jharkhand. it is evident that the major area is devoted to rice, wheat and maize which we may explain with the of following table:

TABLE 4

Area Under Different Major Crops in Jharkhand

Name of crops	*Area in '000 hect.*
Rice	1701.0
Wheat	90.0
Maize	877.0
Barley	28.9
Rage	103.7
Gram	27.0
Tur	29.0

Source: Jharkhand Hand Book, 2006.

From the above table it is evident that the largest area is devoted to rice, wheat and maize which is due to lack assured irrigation because 1.63 per cent of total net sown area is under assured irrigated area in Harahan and in the recently published economic surrey of Harahan under F.R.B.M. act it is also revealed that the low rate of agricultural growth is due to larger dependent on monsoon, low development of irrigation projects, low infra-struture, low social development and higher influence of 'ultra-forces' or anti-government forces in the rural orhilly Jharkhand.

In the development of agricultural sector agricultural price policy has generally been used negatively to keep bread and raw materials cheap for growing industrial sector and to maximize and transfer to the urban sector for investment. For stability in the economic zones, the agricultural price policy plays a crucial role making a halt inordinate increase in the price food and non-food variables and also not allowing them to go down bellow the critical minimum level. It also controls the corrupt and unfair profit making traders to use artificial tools to have an impact on the agricultural price. The chief goal of the agricultural price policy is to provide a security to the farmers of its highest level so that they should have certainly and confidence in agricultural activities but some opine that this agricultural price policy might have positive as well as negative effects. The positive aspect the farmers might have the general programming issue of the rate of growth of agricultural output or the corrected issue of the proportion of development expenditure to be devoted to agricultural. The negative aspect may create uncertainty among the farmers and without taking any risk, the economy can not achieve the desired rate of growth. The role agricultural price is crucial in the around development of agricultural sector but under the present political scenario, administrative set-up and the classification of peasants, its influence is somewhat doubtful because majority of peasants in Harahan is either marginal or small who cultivates their land for subsistence objective. Out of total peasants 80 per cent is marginal and small farmers who produce the agricultural products mainly for let subsistence consumption not for marketable surplus since the state itself is deficient on its own cereal supply.

RESPONSIVENESS TO ACREAGE OF THE CEREALS

The agricultural price policy does play a great role to accelerate growth of agricultural output whole by influencing the responsiveness output as a whole by influencing the responsiveness of acreages of individual crops to relative price movements than on market supply or aggregate output function. The price elasticity's of acreage in case of Harahan for single crop proves in effective because the area under different crops remain more or less unchanged where as the minimum support price of rice and wheat over the years has a rising trend which was Rs. 205 per quintal for rice in 1990-91 has got to Rest. 530, Rs. 550 and Rest. 560 per quintal and Rest 225 per quintal for wheat in 1990-91 to Rs. 629, Rs. 630 and Rest 640 in 2001-02, 2003-04 and 2004-05 respectively. The fixity of rice of rice wheat in Harahan according to many economic thinker is due to lack of proper irrigation lack development of small and medium sources of irrigation, facilities, subsistence thinking of marginal and small farmers, unchanged cropping pattern, skewed and uncertain monsoon, no effect of agricultural price policy etc because the assured irrigated areas is only 8 per cent of total cropped area. The pattern of acreage responses which emerges from the Table 2 is more or less nil or response group. In view of factors constraining peasant behavior is dual or mostly single crop agriculture, this pattern is rationally accountably in case of Jharkhand. Moreover, the subsistence grain crops wheat, maize, barley, ragi, gram, tur, repond little to relative price variations.

RESPONSIVENESS OF AGGREGATE OUTPUT AND YIELD

In case of Jharkhand the formulation of a price policy for agricultural development for the all agricultural products can also be assessed its responsiveness of aggregate output to its fixed minimum support price. In general the popular concept sometime a go was about the existence of backer sloping supply curves in peasant economics have not be confirmed by recent empirical work in respect of the acreages (output) of individual crops in many parts of peasant world as remarked by Gerald Memoir (in leading issues in eco-development (p. 427). The responsiveness of agricultural price policy to some important cereals such as such as rice, wheat and maize in Harahan shows that it is more or less inflective or it's very low in comparison to the minimum support price. This we may explain with the help of Table 5.

From the above table it is evident that the responsiveness of individual crops to relative price move mints may be prohibitive and still the responsiveness of aggregate output may be zero or negative in case of Jharkhand because the per pita coral availability in Jharkhand is 130 kg against the national.

On national production and yield level in case of rice, wheat and maize Jharkhand's production and yield level are far behind which shows that the state certainly needs a suitable and inductive agricultural policy which in turn affects the production and yield of the major crops produced

TABLE 5

Showing Production, Yield of Rice, Wheat, Maize of India and Jharkhand

Name of Crops	*India*		*Jharkhand*	
	Production in '000 tonnes	*Yield in kg per hact.*	*Production in '000 tonnes*	*Yield in kHz percent*
Rice	91100	2051	1424	836
Wheat	73700	2707	115	1250
Miaze	14700	1983	580	814

Source: Chronicle India, 2007, Year Book.

by the farmers' policy-markers will therefore do well to remain content with a price policy which has the modest objective of guranteeing farmers a minimum objective of guaranteeing farmers a minimum costs-based price for a few selected crops to close the serious excess demand gap and to line with some of the unintended consequences of doing so; In Jharkhand the size of olding is not as large as in Punjab Hariyana because more than 84 per cent of holding belongs to marginal and small farmers who infect are not aware of the minimum support price because their total need is even not dull filed. The government also is providing input subsidization but the subsidization is not being felt by these farmers. The agricultural price policy in Jharkhand proves fruitful if the production and yield starts to and becomes nearer to the national average. For marking the agricultural price policy more advantageous these important steps should be reinforced for the government of Jharkhand.

1. The farmers of Jharkhand should be given an element of certaintly and confidence regarding protection from the cereals protection from the abrupt fluctuation of price of the cereals as well as non-cereals production.
2. The farmers should be make more alert as well as literate about minimum support prices and procurement prices which is out of knowledge in Jharkhand.

3. The farmers should be protected from the inflationary pressures of inputs or the they be provided sufficient inputs subsidy as practicable as possible.
4. In Jharkhand, like Punjab and Haryana, as many centers as maximum to absorb the maximum area for purchasing or procurement centers or should be protected from the exploitations of local Mahajanas or purchasers.
5. The minimum support price or procurement price in Jharkhand should be flashed at every important rural marketing are a like the advertisement of the government of Jharkhand so that it should be channelised of Jharkhand.
6. The distortion in cropping pattern should be made uneflected to the Jharkhand peasant's because it favors rice and wheat peasants to other cereal peasants.
7. The minimum support price should be decided on realistic criteria than the faulty one by the Jharkhand government.
8. It's the general perception of the marginal and small farmers that minimum support price is always changed in favors of large farmers because the procurement center of the state and the marginal and small farmers fail to take the advantage of the M.S.P.
9. The P.D.S. should be made more favourable to the marginal and small farmers of Jharkhand so that the agricultural price policy in terms of subsidies should be reached to them.
10. With increase in M.S.P. and procurement price, landless labourers, marginal and small farmers who constitutes about 73 per cent of total working population in Jharkhand creates many hardships and fails to accrue the benefits of high prices because they are subsistence on producers and are dependent on the market meeting marketing their day to day cereal consumption So the agricultural

price policy for Jharkhand should be supportive to these groups.

11. According to J. Mohan Rao and Serves storm when agricultural prices rise as a consequence of price incentives, public investment relevant to potential output in agriculture actually declines because of a consequent fiscal squeeze.

In conclusion we may say that the agricultural price policy in case of Jharkhand can be proved effective if above suggestions are to be put in practical way and thus be suitable mostly marginal and small farmers than the big farmers. Raj Krishna in his finding concluded that national policy markers and international development bankers will therefore do well to devote at least as much attention and effort to the development of technology, infrastructure and human capital as to the price environment hence in the context of Jharkhand the agricultural price policy be such that keeps technological innovations, subsidies to marginal and small farmers and helpful in the level of income and employment to the agricultural farmers, workers by improving the irrigational facilities as well as informative awareness method to the concerned class.

References

Bihar Economic Journal, Conf. Volume, 2004, 2005.

Chronicle Year Book, 2007.

I.E.A Annual Conference, Parts 1 and 2, 2006.

Indian Economy, Rudradutt and KPM Sunderam.

Jharkhand, 2003, S.K. Singh, Readers Corner, Patna.

Jharkhand—Ghanshyam.

Kurukshetra—Different Issues

Leading Issues in Economic Development, Gerald M. Meier-Second Edition.

Prabhat Khaber—Special Hul, Alex Ekka, 30 June, 2005.

Yojana—Different Issues.

15

Agrarian Crisis in the Womb of Industrialization—A Case Study of Bokaro Steel Plant

N.N. MAHTO

A number of studies that attempt to testify the unit root behavior of velocity of agrarian crisis conclude that its velocity possesses a unit root that would satisfy the very aim of rural land management. Gould and Nelson in the year 1974 promoted this line of research conclude that the velocity of agrarian crisis in any economy is well characterized by its peripheral development walk. A recent study of Prof. Thornton in year 1995 also supported the unit root behavior of velocity in the process of rural land management conclude that using four different measurements of the crisis aggregates simple sum of production, marketing, financial and social obligatory existence of a existence of a single unit root.

The problem of this study arises due to take over of land to install Bokaro Steel Plant from the rural so the present so the agrarian crisis emerges for us fault of the peasants, who have been displaced and their fate became foreland.

CSR (cooperate social responsibility) of SAIL manifests a long term sustain and multi-level initiatives would be taken off as a caring and sharing of its brands towards caring a better future for the people living beyond its boundary. Almost 320 villages have been selected by all units of SAIL to provide peripheral development facilities within 20 km. radius of its units.

The public sector in India is conceived of with certain goals in adoption to production. So is the goal of BSP. In fact, it is the instrument of charge for the economic emancipation of the teeming million of the country, SAIL, particularly BSP as a corporate entity has adopted social goals as some of its auxiliary objective recalling the belief of Mr. K.C. Khanna, M.D, 1974-76 that "Bokaro is a large family, here if any one is unhappy, all of us are". This sum of the managements deep concern for human welfare, specially for displaced persons living in and around its periphery.

The first step was taken by BSL, 15 resolve the crisis was to ask and obtain from the DPLR a comprehensive list of displaced persons, village wise and family-wise. The list was received by the labour and Employment Department of the Government of Bihar in October 1971. It was prepared by the DPLR, Dhanbad, on basis of survey conducted in 1962-63 as, revised in the middle of 1971. The department also produced information regarding employment and other development benefits already given to such persons either in BSL or HSCL. The lists were verified by the Employment Directorate with the consent of various Trade Unions and details information were laboriously compiled. Initially 83 revenue villages had been notified for acquisition for Bokaro Steel Project and thus periphery of BSP is defined. A total of 56 villages have so far been acquired, 37 of which included both lands and homes and 19 were such of which only were acquired. Further 33 addition villages will be required up to the 10 MT stage beyond the plants present requirement. All such villages come under the administrative jurisdiction of 8 Prakhands of Bokaro districts—they are Chas, Chandankiyari, Jaridih, Gomia, Peterwar, Bermo, Kasmar and Nawadih.

Thus, the present study has been designed on the basis of the peripheral definition framed by the joint collaboration of Bureau of Public Enterprises (BPE) and Trade Unions in the year 1971 covering 20 kms radius of BSP center of which is Adm. Buildings, B.S. City to resolve the crisis of the 320 agrarians tic villages.

In the literature on regional planning and peripheral development defining a region a distinct spatial entity has always been and intricate problem and has engaged wide attention the concept of region varies with the criteria adopted. Traditionally three types of regions may be distinguished (a) Homogenous region (b) nodal of financial region, (c) Programme of Planning regions.

The first deal with the homogenous characteristics usually a combination of spatial and economic aspects of a region, the second analysis the polarization around some market or urban place within a region and the third method of classifying region is a division into planning region which is some times called programming region to cover the area specifically meant for. The geographical periphery of the research moves around the boundary line of BSP, a unit of Steel Authority of India Ltd. (SAIL). The BSP has been set-up on Jan. 1964 with the objective of socio-economic development of the Nation predominantly peripheral development of its surroundings, though this study is believed to be a fresh in this regards, but a preliminary acknowledgement has been found in the study of Dr. N.R. Srinivasan, Research fellow and published by BSP in the year 1988. This study emphasis that, the steel city are islands of affluence amidst on ocean of poverty. BSL has been alive to the humanitarian concern to help in the betterment of brethren in the neighborhood. About 3 dozen village have been helped which fall on the periphery of this steel city. During the last eight years the peripheral development work has taken the form of construction and renovation of 23 school building in 19 villages provision of 45 hand pumps in 35 villages and 6 open well in 3 villages and desisting of Topcachi lake. Roads and bridge have been constructed and the most recent instance being the opening of four course ways on the Garga, on October 2, 1987, thus providing vital communication to 25 villages benefiting a populations of about 36,000 persons. A mobile dispensary unit renders free medical aid. Training and motivation, adult education, a forestation, opening of four poultry farms and training in sewing for women are some of the activities under peripheral development. The total expenditure on this account from 1979 to 1986 has been Rs. 24.4 lakhs. The actual expenditure in 1987-88 has been Rs. 10.5 lakhs, while that for 1987-88 stands of Rs. 14.3 lakhs. Despite the positive attitude and effort of BSL, the response from the villagers has not been reported to be receptive. It is felt and attitudinal change is called for in the villagers to help themselves with external assistance offered by BSL at their doorsteps.

Nevertheless, Dr. C. Ashokavardhan, in his wok Human Resources Development in BSP in the year 1989 revealed that basis development works done by BSP in its periphery covers the basic amenities such as maintained public health education medical, Road and communication, Water Supply, employment and welfare facilities have been provided to the people of its periphery in an adequate, it not abundant measure. In maintenance of infrastructure in its periphery the latest cost accordingly to the 1987-87 amount of Rs. 2.50 crore, for the maintenance of Roads, Rs. 1.62 crores, for the water and electricity Rs. 1.96 crores and other operasational expenditure to the tune of 0.30 crores.

The objectives of the peripheral development are to provide financial assistance to the families of the displaced employed. Thus as at the present maintenance cost for peripheral Development around Rs. 4.4 crores per annum and its bound to increase, as the area grows further.

In the studies of the Research and Development, BSP, first and second issues published by R & D wing, Bokaro Steel Plant in the year 1986-87 and year 1992-93 it has been further witnessed that Bokaro being situated in Bihar and having the largest share in employment by the inhabitants of the State has organizations whose immediate concern is the welfare of the "Local People". It may not be out of place to remark that, in certain quarters of society and State intended to can note people of the immediately surrounding region and district. Persons genuinely coming from other parts of this State are foreigners. However, Chhatanagpur has been conceded as a district region, with a predominantly Adiavasi population. Against this background it would be seen that some organization are motivated by considerations of regional tribal welfare. The Chhatanagpur plateau Praja Parisad owes its origin to the propagation of the cause of Jharkhand was formed in 1952. Its limb at Bokaro has long active in expounding the cause of tribal, in the matter of agrarian crisis. It lease with the State and Central Government authorities continuously. For educating children and adults, its runs a school and night classes. It is proud of its past heritage and organizes fairs and festivals to educate the youth in the "Dhamkuria" and "Gittore" traditional Brisa Jayanti is celebrated annually and statue of Brisa Munds is to be erected. The Chhatanagpur Sahayog Samitti started in 1980 is socially oriented and work in close association with the Praja Parisad, formerly the Bhojpuri Samaj, was started in 1967, with the sole aim of getting the maximum employment to the prople of region in BSL. Its efforts were success. In October 1985, it participated in them international youth year. Adivasi through which the Samaj expresses its objective are folklore. Dances and cultural functions. A year later, the Sama Samaj comes on the scene, to cater to the cultural life of the Adivasi. It organizes the seasonal festivals of Bihar.

Thus, the methodology of study covers the area of the present study covering 56 villages acquired so far, 37 of which includes both lands and homes and 19 were such if which only lands were acquired. This study will also cover 33 additional villages, which are yet to be acquired, as and when required. The present study area limits the survey to be under taken 6019 displaced families, out of which 554 are SCs, 1103 are STs and 4362 are others, living in 8 Block areas of Bokaro district—Chas, Chandankiyari, Jaridih, Perterwar, Gomia, Nawadih, Bermo, Kasmar.

Thus Mr. S.K. Roongta, the than Director Personal SAIL said that we cannot live as a island of prosperity. Our periphery has to develop in tandem. The basic approach of peripheral Development Scheme of BSP has revolved around three basic components—Economic Social and Environment this belief of BSP reveals that it is duty of BSP as a responsible cooperate.

SAIL through its various peripheral development

activities has been supporting educational, Charitable and welfare institute within and outside the steel township. The activities include schemes relating to health and Medical welfare, education sports and culture ancillary development roads and other infrastructure, water and sanitations self-help groups, etc. The infrastructure created by SAIL includes 39 primary health centers 18 reproductive and child health centers and four supper specially hospitals and have provided relief to about 22 millions people cumulatively over by the year. SAIL has opened about 150 schools in the steel townships that employ more than 6000 teachers providing modern educations to around 122000 students. Apart from managing its own schools SAIL also supports other public schools managed independently.

It is obvious that land tenures in India before independence were of there kinds: (a) Raiyatvari System, (b) Mahatvari System, (c) Zamindari System. These System were abolished after independence and new tenure were set-up as—(1) Teneney reform, (2) Fixation of ceiling on land holdings, and (3) Abolition of zaminadars those set-up have to be kept in mind to preserve the interest of the Peripheral land while installing on industry.

During study it was found that peripheral development authorizes of BSP have not heathered to the security of tendency right as regulation of displacement right or ownership for tenants retained unsettled.

As a result of this, the condition of the small and marginal farmers as who, did not got neither employment in BSP nor uplifted otherwise and whose condition fall under the periphery of BSP, has been precarious they became land less farmers. Since inception of BSP, the Agrarian crisis of Peripheral people retained unsolved a result of which intradance and inequitable distribution of income and wealth have emerged giving birth to terrorist activities like noxlite movement in Jharkhand.

Reference

Bhatia, Satindra, Bokaro Steel Plants, *Some Economic Aspects*, 1991, Popular Prakashan, Bombay.

Srinivashan, N.R., *The History of Bokaro Steel Plant 1988*, Thomson Press (India) Ltd., Faridabad.

The Indian Economic Journal, Vol. 45, July-September, 1997-98, No. 1.

Sail News, Vol. 33, No. 3, April-July 2006.

Bokaro Durpan, Jan. 2007.

16

Economic Reforms and Agriculture

PASHUPATI RAY, VINAY KUMAR SINGH AND
INDU RANI KESHARWANI

INTRODUCTION

After Independence of India in 1947, a planned attempt was made to bring about the agrarian transformation in the country with a view to improving the lot of the peasantry. The role of agriculture in the economy was then very vital as it contributed more than 55 percent to the GDP of the country and employed about 70 percent of the total workforce. As in most underdeveloped and developing countries, the agriculture sector of the Indian economy was then most backward. Collin Clark[1] attributes the casuse of this backwardness of agriculture to the high density of agricultural population with low productivity. But it must be realized that immense improvements are possible in agricultural productivity in most parts of the world. What is needed is eduction and technological knowledge and of course, capital. But this Paper would not be directly confined to these requirements but to the agricultural growth and diversification of the agrarian economy of Eastern India since Independence and more particularly since 1991 when economic reforms were launched in India.

AGRICULTURAL GROWTH

Agrarian Reforms after Independece

After Independence the most important refomrs introduced in Indian agriculture dealt with (i) the abolition of zamindary (intermediaries) system, (ii) the indroduction of tenancy reforms, (iii) the imposition of ceiling on landholdings, and (iv) the distribution of the surplus lands among the landless and small landholders.

As a result of the abolition of intermediaries and the introduction of tenancy reforms, the area under tenancy declined farily considerably in the four States of Eastern India during the 40 years from 1953 to 1993 as Table 1.

TABLE I

Area under Tenancy as Per cent of the Total Area in India

States	*1953-54*	*1992-93*
Bihar	12.40	3.91
Orissa	12.60	9.48
West Bengal	25.40	10.40
Assam	16.70*	8.87
All India	20.55	5.28

Note: *Assam figure relates to 1971-72 (NSS 26th Round).
Source: National Sample Survey on Landholdings, NSS (8th Round 1953 and 48th Round 1992).

The percentage of area leased out varied from 11 to 26 percent in different parts of India, though the all-India average was 20 percent in 1953-54 which fell down to 8 percent by 1992-93.[2] Thus as the above table shows the areas leased out in each State of Eastern India in 1992-93 was still abvoe the all-India average.

The imposition of ceiling on existing landholdings appears to have failed in India due to mala fide and benami transfers, and the proportion of small and marginal farmers obviously increased instead of decreasing. This is apparent from the trends of the average size of operational holdings shown Table 2 so far as the States in Eastern India are concerned.

TABLE 2

Average Size of Operational Holdings in Eastern States

States	*1970-71 (ha.)*	*1990-91 (ha.)*
Bihar	1.50	0.93
Orissa	1.89	1.34
West Bengal	1.20	0.90
Assam	1.47	1.31
All India	2.28	1.57

Source: Ministry of Agriculture, Agricultural Situation in India (1981) and Agricultural Statistics at a Glance (1995).

Although the extent of the area operated by the farmers with larger size of holdings is not readily available, it can be inferred from the above table that a bulk of the peasantry subsists on marginal holdings and unless these peasants are either provided with alternative non-agricultural employment or are employed in medium and large farms by increasing their productivity, the chances of eradicating the rural poverty in Eastern India will ramian bleak. Nevertheless, the position in West Bengal is different where security of tenure of the tenants and determination of fair rent have been successfully implemented.[3] On the whole, the preponderance of small and marginal farmers with low production base continues to pose a great institutional challenge to the Eastern Region of India.

TECHNICAL PROGRESS AND AGRICULTURAL GROWTH

Besides the agrarian forms, the upgradation of production technology is another very important factor for agricultural development in India, which took place after Independence. This includes development of irrigation facilities, rural electrification, construction of roads and communication, establishment of agricultural universities, development of research infrastructure, seed-fertilizer technology, etc. It was these technological inputs that had led to the green Revolution in 1970-71. But the revolution was limited to wheat, maize and bajra only and took place in Punjab, Haryana, Western U.P. and in certain districts of Andhra, Maharashtra and Tamil Nadu.

The technological inputs were further upgraded. Hence in the second phase of the green revolution in the period from 1972-73 to 1982-83, the new technology had gradully extended to some parts of Eastern India and to the coastal areas of Andhra and Tamil Nadu in Southern India. The third phase from 1982-83 to 1990-93 marks a turning point in the agricultural development of India. During this phase, agricultural growth had accelerated not only in the few irrigated regions but it also extended to most regions including the rainfed regions. The agricultural growth rate increased to an unprecedented level in the Eastern States particularly West Bengal when achieved the growth rate of 5.4 percent per annum.[4] The Table 3 shows the agricultural output region-wise from 1962 to 1999.

TABLE 3

Region-wise Growth of Agricultural Output (1962-62 to 1990-93)

(in percent)

Regions	*1970-73 over 1990-93*	*1980-83 over 1962-65*	*1990-93 over 1970-73*	*1996-99 over 1980-83*
North-West Region	3.60	3.21	3.55	1.91
Eastern Region	1.57	1.09	3.63	1.25
Central Region	0.73	3.13	3.33	4.50
Southern Region	2.40	1.38	3.43	2.19
All India	2.08	2.38	3.44	2.83

Source: G.O.I., Ministry of Agriculture, Area and Production Crops in India (Various issues of the Report).

The above Table shows that Eastern Region had creditably performed among all regions during 1990-93 due to unprecedented growth in West Bengal.

The unprecedented growth in the output and yields of wheat and rice resulted to the self-sufficiency in foodgrains production in India during the 1980s. But the table further shows the deceleration of agricultural growth rate during the 1990s which hit the Eastern Region the most.

GLOBALIZATION AND DECELERATION OF GROWTH DURING THE 1990s

The introduction of economic refroms failed initially to bring much bouyancy to agricultural secroth which was someshat neglected. Therefore during the 1990s the trend of growth rate in agriculture has shown a significant deceleration as compared with the growth rate during the 1990s. The growth rate of the Gross Domestic Product from agriculture decelerated from 3.91 percent per annum during 1980-91 to only 1.94 percent per annum during 1991-99. The joining of WTO and the signing of GATT in December 1994 was expected that it would lead to increasing international rade in agriculture. The expected abolition or reduction of export subsidies by the developed countries was thought that it would bring about an increase in agricultural exports of developing countries. But that did not materialize and instead the agricultural sector in India is faving some serious problems. After high growth during early 1990s, deceleration had visibly appeared in the export at the end of 1996. This should have clearly affected the Eastern States whose agricultural growth had already slumped to the lowest level as shown in Table 3.

Productivity Improvement

A major challenge before India is to reduce costs and raise productivity and quality of agricultural produce to global standards. In the long-run, productivity increase has to be seriously considered, as the possibilities of expansion of farm area are minimal except the region stretching from north Bihar to Assam. The potentiality of expansion of farm area still exists in this region.[5] What is important is the enhancement of capital formation in agricultural productivity. It was very disheartening to observe that the Indian agriculture was starved of capital at the initial period of the economic reforms. That was the main reason for the subsequent deceleration of growth in agriculture. While the public sector investment declined, the private sector investment kept on fluctuating as can be seen from the Table 4.

TABLE 4

Public and Private Investment in Agriculture (1980-81 prices)

Year	*Public Sector (Rs. in crores)*	*Private Sector (Rs. in crores)*	*Total GCF in Agriculture*	*Share of Agri. GCF in total GCF*
1980-81	1892	2972	4864	18.9
1984-85	1822	3066	4888	14.8
1985-86	1631	3010	4641	12.1
1992-93	1179	4694	5873	11.2
1993-94	1269	4295	5564	10.8
1994-95	1426	5397	6823	9.6
1995-96	1394	6193	7587	9.9

Source: Ministry of Agriculture, Agricultural Statistics at a Glance (Various Issues of the Report).

From the above table, it is clear that the percentage share of Gross Capital Formation (GCF) in agriculture keeps on decreasing until 1995-96 when it started increasing by a small margin. It must, however, be mentioned that public sector investment from 1980-81 till 1984-85 was always above Rs. 1,800 crore each year. Thereafter, it declined while private sector investment kept on rising from 1987-8 onwards. The deceleration of agricultural growth has some serious repercussions. The region-wise data of capital formation are not readily available. But it could be surmised from the foregoing analysis that deceleration must be more serious in Eastern States with the exception of West Bengal. The main consequence of deceleration in agricultural growth is the falling income of the cultivators. Secondly, the expected gains from increased trade have not actually materalized because the growth rate of exports has deceleated. Further, there has been adverse impact on employment and trend reduction in poverty in rural areas.

AGRICULTURAL DIVERSIFICATION

The main rationale of economic liberalization and globalization was the expected increase in agricultural exports of developing countries of the markets of developed countries because of increased market access. Since agriculture is labour-intensive, increased export were expected to provide more productive employment to agricultural workers of developing countries not only in agriculture but also in the agro-processing industries. This is turn was likely to lead to gradual diversification of labour force from agricultural to non-agricultural occupations. But all this does not happen. The exports of major agricultural commodities from India did register an increase in the early 1990s, but his increase was short-lived. For instance, rice exports which had reached the level of 5 (five) million tonnes in 1995-96 declined to 1.8 million tonnes by 1999-00. The slow-down in the exports of agricultural commodities from the country must have affected the exports from the Eastern region more since the deceleration in its agricultural growth had been the lowest among all regions as can be seen from Table 3.

Crop Diversification

The deceleration in agricultural growth duringf the 1990s had not only resulted in the slow down in the exports of agricultural commodities but it had also painfully led to the slow process of workforce diversification away from low productivity ariculture in the country as a whole. The slow rate of agriculturaal diversification of rural workforce equally applies to crop diversification. The strategy in India initially was to raise foodgrains confining to two crops only, namely, wheat and rice, leaving aside other cereals and crops, the production of which remains stagnant for many years. India, the Eastern Region in particular, would do well to change its strategy in crop diversification. The entire region of Eastern India along the foothills from north Bihar to Assam and the Hills States in the North-East, is the potentially attractive area for crop diversification through horticulture development. The region could be converted into a National granary of horticultural produce with the potential to export these produce to other States in the country and abroad. The rest of Eastern India also has the potential of productivity increase if some more efforts and use of nutrients are adopted. With the brightening scenario of the plains in foodcrop production, the hilly regions in the north and north-east can go all out for horticultural development.

CONCLUSION

It must be the aim of agricultural development to diversity the rural economy of Eastern Region which is lagging behind the rest of India. The development of activities allied to agriculture would tremendously contribute to the diversification of agriculture in the region. There is also the nened to develop rural industries based on aricultural outputs. The diversification would not only lead to higher incomes and employment of the rural population but would also result into even self-sufficiency and exportable surplus of agricultural produce from this region.

Rural Infrastructure

The entire rural infrastructure has to be refurnished to make rural activities viable. The Union Government has an ambitious plan to achieve Universal Rural Connectivity before 2007 through the National Rural Road Project. It is hoped the Eastern States are fully geared to fully implement the project. Beside rural transport facilities, minor irrigation works are to be built through public sector investment. Both these components of infrastructure will help the exploitation of extensive waste or fallow lands in Eastern India. The recent law passed on Rural Employment Guarantee Schemes and the Food-for-work Programme, if sincerely implemented and intensified, would nfot only lead to gradual diversification of labour force also help in better food distribution and creation of durable rural assets.

NABARD and RIDF

The Union government had created a corpus fund known as the Rural Infrastructure Development Fund (RIDF) in NABARD with an initial amount of Rs. 2000 crores to extend loans to State governments to enable them to complete the implementation of the existing rural infrastructual projects relating to irrigation, rural roads, rural bridges, watershed development, flood development, inland waterways, etc. The RIDF has since grown to a massive Rs. 23,000 crores. It all depends on the capability of the Eastern States to fully draw or utilize funds from RIDF in order to gain maximum benefits from the Fund.

Both agricultural diversification and building of rural infrastructure would create demands in rural areas for more specialized agro-processing, more sophisticated trading and repair services and more professional education, health and personal services. They would also mitigate the excessive rural-urban migration that has been witnessed by the slums and shantytowns in various cities. A prosperous ariculture is therefore the only determining factor for jobs for the rural poor. While the Economic Reforms Policy of the country has been directed towards liberalization, the public sector policy has still to play a leading role in accelerating the pace of development in Eastern Region of India. And, for this to happen, a responsive government in each State of the Eastern Region has to keep in mind the welfare of the masses.

Notes and References

1. Collin Clark's Paper in A.N. Agarwal and S.P. Singh (ed.), *The Economics of Underdevelopment.*
2. R. Datt and K.P.M. Sundaram (2004), *Indian Economy,* (S. Chand and Company Ltd.), p. 552.
3. G.O.I., Ministry of Agriculture, *Area and Production Crops in India* (Various Issues of the Report).
4. P.M. Passah, "Agricultureal Growth and Diversification in N.E. India: A Keynote Address" in the *Proceedings Volume of the 4th Conference of the Northern Economic Association* held on Septemeber 8, 2001, p. xix.
5. R. Datt and K.P.M. Sundaram, *op. cit.,* p. 598.

17

Agrarian Crisis in India: Causes and Remedies

R.K. Shah

The last ten years have witnessed a fatigue in the green revolution with the growth rate in food grain production falling below population growth. Thus, human numbers are increasing faster than our capacity to make the goal of ***'food for all'*** *a reality. At the same time, consumption is not going up due to inadequate purchasing power at the household level. A famine of jobs/livelihoods as a result of poor growth of opportunities for employment in the rural non-farm and off-farm sectors is leading to a famine of food at the household level. According to the National Planning Commission, we are off-track in achieving the UN Millennium Development Goal of reducing the number of hungry persons by half by 2015. Our Prime Minister has rightly emphasized the need to double annual food grain from the present 210 million tonnes to 420 million tonnes within the next 10 years, i.e. by 2015. Since land is shrinking resource for agriculture, the pathway for achieving these goals has to be higher productivity per units of arable land and irrigation water.*

I. INTRODUCTION

Agriculture is termed as spine of Indian economy. There are a couple of reasons that make agriculture as the most important component of the economy. Firstly, more than 65 percent of the country's population is involved in agricultural activities and secondly; it still contributes a major share (26 percent) to the national income, hence, making it the largest industry in the country. Nevertheless, the share of agriculture is sizeable; it is considerably declining in recent years giving way to manufacturing and services. However, the significance of agriculture for development is not something to argue about. As agriculture provides the basic necessities for human survival and the major inputs for manufacturing and services, it is of crucial importance for economic development in any circumstance. Concurrently, It is equally important to see what is the reason to produce crisis in the field of agricultural sector in India.

India's economic growth is largely dependent on agriculture as it contributes about 27.4 percent of the country's Gross Domestic Product (GDP) and supplies the bulk of wage goods required by non-agricultural sector and raw material for a large section of the industry. Similarly, India's economic development substantially rests on agriculture that employs about 67 percent of the country's work force and microscopic development in the agricultural sector is bound to be reflected as a change in the quality of life of this major chunk of India's population. Thus, agriculture plays a pivotal role in the economic betterment of India. Agricultural productivity in India has been very low and far below the mark to result in any substantial export (we only started to boast of being self-sufficient in food production after 1960's Green Revolution).

II. OBJECTIVES AND METHODOLOGY

The main objectives of the study are as follows:

- To define the concept of inclusive growth,
- To know the causes of agrarian crisis in India,

- To find out which factors are responsible behind these causes,
- To discuss about the agricultural economy of India, and
- To suggest some remedial measures to reduce the agrarian crisis in India.

The present study is covered regarding the Indian Agricultural Crisis that based on completely secondary data, which collects from journals, periodicals, Internet, books, etc.

III. INCLUSIVE GROWTH DURING ELEVENTH FIVE YEAR PLAN

The Indian economy is experiencing a high rate of growth of above 8 percent per annum, and it is anticipated to grow at a higher rate in the near future. It is already being considered as a "transforming" economy, as one of the best performing economies in the world, and not a developing economy any more. The impressive economic growth and the economic reform policies being vigorously followed also lead many to fear that the high growth might be exclusionary in nature and be characterized by jobless growth, ruthless growth, voiceless growth, rootless growth, and the futureless growth, that the United Nations Development Program (UNDP, 1996) warned against. That the growth of the Indian economy has been exclusive and that there is a need to make it inclusive is, in fact, long felt [e.g. K.N. Raj Mody, 2006; Kannan, 2006]. Clearly now India is recognized as an economy with a "stunning" but "jobless growth" [UNDP-ILO, 2007], and a "booming economy with growing gaps" where the spectacular successes make have not been shared by all equally [World Bank, 2006]. The Planning Commission has also realized that economic growth has failed to be sufficiently inclusive, particularly after the mid-1990s. It has noted in the approach to the Eleventh Five Year Plan, "While the performance reflects the strength of the economy in many areas, it is also true that large parts of our population are still to experience a decisive improvement in their standard of lining. Far too many people still lack access to basic services such as health, education, clean drinking water and sanitation facilities without which they cannot be empowered to claim their share in the benefits of growth. These problems are more severe in some states than in others, and in general they are especially severe in rural areas" [Planning Commission 2006:1]. Further, given the experience of most other countries which saw a high rate of growth in a decade followed by a big fall in the subsequent decade, it is feared that the growth in India may not be sustainable, unless it is made inclusive. Thus, inclusive growth has become the new mantra of development. After pursuing a policy of vigorous growth ever since the introduction of economic reform policies in the country, as it was believed that "there cannot be inclusive growth without growth itself" [Ministry of Finance, 2007:15], India has adopted, as recommended by the World Bank (2006), a development strategy of inclusive growth and set "faster and more inclusive growth" as the focus of the Eleventh Five Year Plan (2007-12).

As the World Bank (2006) described it, inclusive growth is "the only sure means for correcting the deeply ingrained regional imbalances, inequities and for consolidating economic gains", as inclusive growth is the growth "with emphasis not only on the distribution of economic gains but also on the security, vulnerability, empowerment, and sense of full participation that people may enjoy in social life". Inclusive growth is, however, not new, though it seems to be a new concept. The *Oxford Dictionary* defines inclusive growth as growth that "does not exclude any section of society". It is akin to the development strategies such as "growth with justice", "growth with equity", "growth with distribution", "growth with a human face", "pro-poor growth", etc. suggested by many starting with Dadabhai Naoroji in the beginning of the 20th century, and attempted at one point of time or the other by many countries during the last 50 years. The new mantra is now at the hearth of mainstream development economics [Ali, 2007]. Inclusive growth is expected, like the above mentioned earlier development strategies to focus on the poor, the marginalized, the neglected, the disadvantaged and deprived sections of the society, and the backward regions of the country. An added dimension of the new development strategy also includes linking growth to the quality of basic services like education and healthcare.

Inclusive growth presupposes inclusive education-good quality education that is accessible to all. The role of education in ensuring inclusive growth is very critical. As noted in the *Economic Survey, 2006-07,* "the inclusive nature of the growth itself will be conditioned by the progress that is made in the areas of education" [Ministry of Finance, 2007:16]. Hence education need as special attention as an instrument of achieving as well as a constituent of inclusive growth. The Planning Commission recognizes this and notes, "a strategy of inclusiveness and broad-based participation in the development process calls for *new emphasis on education,* health and other basic public facilities."

IV. SITUATION OF AGRICULTURAL ECONOMY OF INDIA

Agriculture is the core section of the economy of India. This section provides new material to industries, employment to a large number of people revenue to government and ground to earn foreign exchange. More then 70 per cent of people in India depend upon agriculture and allied sectors for their livelihood. Thus, agriculture plays a very crucial role in the economic development of the country.

The average farm size is going down and nearly 80% of the farm families belong to the marginal and small farmer categories. Fortunately, the ownership of livestock is more egalitarian. Enhancing small farm productivity, and increasing small farm income through crop-livestock integrated production systems and multiple livelihood opportunities through agro-processing and bio-mass utilization, are essential both to meet food production targets and for reducing hunger, poverty and rural unemployment. Programs designed to achieve these goals must be engendered, since there is increasing feminization of agriculture, poverty and under-nutrition. The umbrella of NREGP has spread to all the districts. The program should be made free from excessive bureaucratic webs.

After the independence in India, agriculture and rural

development became the concern of the government. Thus, the government took the initiative in this matter. The government launched a number of programs and projects for agricultural and rural development in India.

India's GDP share from agriculture sector is on continuous decline. It was slightly more than 50 percent in the early 1950's, which decreased currently to 20 percent as indicated in Table 1.

TABLE I

Share of Agricultural Output in India's GDP

Year	*1950*	*1965*	*1976*	*1985*	*1999*	*2004*	*2005*
Percentage Share	52.2	43.6	37.4	32.8	24.4	22.0	20.0

Source: Agricultural Situation in India, 2006.

V. CAUSES OF THE AGRARIAN CRISIS

1. Lack of Modern Technology and Fertilizer

Fertilizer is one of the major inputs, which influences the crop production. Indian 70 percent of the population depends upon the agriculture and the large number of farmers in interior areas does not have the knowledge on the use of chemical fertilizers, High Yielding Varieties (HYV) seeds, pesticides, adoption of new farm technology, etc. It is hoped that assured irrigation facility, agricultural support services and effective extension programs and motivate the farmers in adoption of improved farming techniques with increase in the use of chemical fertilizer. The low level of fertilizer consumption among the farmers is the outcome of present subsistence nature of agriculture in India. In such situation there is not scope to improve the existing position to achieve higher production, higher yield per unit of area. The under developed status of agriculture is not due to want of programs and policies of the government, but is a case that modern technology like HYV seed, application of fertilizer are not adopted due to certain constraint. Fertilizer plays a crucial role in boosting up of agricultural production.

2. Uncertainty of Monsoon

Agriculture in India has been widely held to be heavily dependent on two major domestic factors, i.e. monsoon and irrigation. Due to uncertainty of monsoon losses the seasonal crop production by farmers. Fertilizer use in India is very low mainly due to combination of a number of physical interacting factors like high monsoon rainfall, recurrence of floods, impeded drainage, lack of irrigation facilities, acidic soil, non-availability of fertilizer in time, lack of awareness about the benefit of fertilizer in time, lack of awareness bout the benefit of fertilizer user, etc.

3. Less Effect of WTO Agreement on Agriculture

Another important reason for agrarian crisis in India is less effect of World Trade Organization (WTO) agreement on agriculture. The liberalization, globalization and economic reforms is putting a lot of stress on the improvement of agriculture produce particularly food related health and safety concerns and standard of living. It is well known fact that the Uruguay Round, Agreement on Agriculture (UR AoA) could not immediately achieve any major breakthrough in streamlining large distortions in production and trading of agriculture, expect bringing agriculture into the fold of global trading rules. However, the agreement entails the review of its progress before the end of 1999, which had been a major concession to developing countries.

4. Unsatisfactory Environment

The most important cause of decline in growth rate of agricultural production in India is the inadequacy of favorable environment for agricultural growth. Most of the rural areas in the country suffer from infra-structural facilities which include rural electrification and timely supply of power roads, markets storage, extension services, etc.

Credit facilities are also not easily available to the farmers. Co-operators in the country are also inadequate and weak.

5. Lack of Moisture in Soil

In India, soils lack moisture. Sandy soils require

frequent water than the alluvial or black soils. Residual moisture is not available in the soil in dry season, which may support multiple cropping. Thus, crop production in India is insufficient due to this factor also.

6. High Cost of Modern Inputs

The cost of modern inputs required for agricultural production, such as high yielding varieties (HYV) seeds chemical fertilizers, pesticides, agricultural machinery of these inputs by the state governments, yet these are beyond the reach of the poor, small and marginal farmers. The new technology of agriculture is not only expensive but it involves risks also. The small and marginal farmers who are in majority in the country cannot use modern inputs on their hands. Thus, our agriculture growth rate has been declining rapidly.

7. Problems of Agricultural Finance

- India is a vast country based on agriculture. Hence more than two-third people depend upon agriculture for their earnings. But the financial needs of rural farmers cannot be matched with the finance provided by the Financial Institutions.
- The repayment of loans of farmers is very poor. It is severely affected the financial performance of such institutions.
- Political intervention in the lending programs creates serious problems to identity the right beneficiaries.
- The farmers in India generally are not utilizing the financial assistance provided them in commensurate manners.
- At last, the lack of awareness among the rural people leads to so many problems in rural credit.

8. Other Causes

Other causes are also hampering our agriculture growth such as:

- Lack of proper management of available water supply to cultivated lands,
- Traditional thinking of Farmers,
- Small and scattered pieces of lands,
- Lack of organization among farmers,
- Delay in implementation of development plans and projects,
- Lethargic attitude of agricultural machinery,
- Non co-operation attitude of farmers and farm laborers, and
- Lack of proper agricultural extension services, etc.

VI. REMEDIAL MEASURES TO REDUCE AGRARIAN CRISIS IN INDIA

It is discouraging to note that despite the implementation of various plans, projects and schemes to improve the agricultural growth in the country, the practical side of their implementation and their results in terms of desired impact are very dismal. After analysis and close observations of the facts, at various levels, the following remedial measures should be taken to improve growth rate and productively of agricultural lands in India:

1. More Irrigation Facilities and Suitable Water Management

It is bare fact that irrigation has great influence structure and productivity. Thus, efforts should be made to increase irrigation facilities especially in those areas where irrigation facilities are deficient.

It is also essential that water supplies be put to utmost efficient use. In agricultural technology, water requirement is an essential step now. Water management requires suitable system of soil surveys, crop patterns, crop rotation, use of High Yielding Variety (HVY) seeds, quantity of fertilizers and pesticides, used and adoption of improved agricultural facilities, etc. Further, leveling and grading of land preparation and designing proper lay out for irrigated farming are important. Effective demonstrations should be given to convince the farmers of the proper use of irrigation water for different crops and areas.

The government tube-well, which is static, should be repaired at all costs. This view should not postpone by the state government. The state government should also increase the efficiency of minor irrigation by installing new tube-wells in their state at the village levels. In the owners of private tube-wells should also be encouraged to install new tube-wells and to repair the defective ones. The state government should corporate with them in this matter.

2. Adequate Supply of Electricity

The adequate supply of electricity is a very serious problem for the farmers. In the absence of power supply taken wells and electrical pump sets cannot operate. The state government should ensure regular supply of electricity in the rural areas for agricultural purposes. Besides, the electricity supply rate for irrigation purpose should be none moderate.

3. Supply of High Yielding Variety (HYV) Seeds

The high yielding variety (HYV) seeds are neither supplied to the farmers by the government in time nor in required quantity. This position compels the farmers to go to the private dealers for their supply, who do not supply good quality seeds resulting in poor yield to the farmers. It is, therefore, required that the timely and adequate distribution of pure variety seeds should be regularized by the government. Moreover, the government should ensure that the germination capacity of the seeds supplied of superior level and there are no administers in handling and storing such seeds.

The state government should appoint inspecting agencies whose task should be to prescribe and enforce standards of purity, quality and genetic entity of the seeds. This agency should be made responsible to conduct careful field survey and laboratory investigations of all seeds produced and offered for sale. Thus, proper arrangement of distribution and ensuring quality seeds to the farmers should be made by the state governments.

4. Proper Utilization and Management of Chemical Fertilizers

The chemical fertilizers are note given to the farmers at

the appropriate time and in adequate quantity. Thus, farmers are forced to approach the private dealers for their supply who charge high prices and show no liberal attitude. Thus, the state government should ensure the adequate and timely supply of fertilizers to the farmer. The government should also give incentives to small and marginal farmers in supply of fertilizers. The use of chemical fertilizers should however, depend upon the results of soil survey of particular areas or regions. Further, all precautions should be taken before using chemical fertilizers as their over doses may be harmful.

5. Cheap Availability of Pesticides and Insecticides

As pesticides and insecticides are very highly priced there use is made by the farmers as a very limited scale. The government should, therefore, take steps to reduce their prices so that these may use in greater quantity by the farmers to combat plant diseases effectively. The state government should give attract 7 percent subsidy on pesticides and insecticides to be supplied to small and marginal farmers. The government should also ensure timely availability of pesticides and insecticides to the farmers

6. Program of Plant Protection Scheme

As a plant protection measures, the farmers should be provided facilities free of charges for trading seeds against seed bone diseases. Moreover, in each District Development Block in the one extension officer with special training in plant protection should be appointed whose task should be to provide all assistance in this respect. If the possibilities for given warning against the out break of epidemics and plant diseases are explained by the government, the production and productivity of land can further increase in the country.

7. Using New Agricultural Machines and Implements

The holdings of the small and marginal farmers are small. Thus, they cannot use modern machines and implements on their farms. Under these circumstances, only selective mechanization is possible. The government should encourage the small and marginal farmers to use the new machines and implements, which can be used conveniently on their lands. Owing to high cost of modern agricultural machines and tools the small and marginal farmers who have almost no savings cannot purchase them. It is, therefore, suggest that the state governments should provide this facility against very nominal charges (rent) with the condition that these machines should be returned by them after use. This will encourage these farmers to use new machines and implements on selective basis.

8. Arrangement of Financial Institutional Support

The credit should be made available to the farmers on easy terms. The long productive in granting credit adopted by the financial institutions should be discarded. The co-operated credit societies, commercial banks and other financial institutions should adopt such measures, which may benefit the farmers in this respect. In this matter credit needs of the small and marginal farmers should be given priority and no room should be left for non-institutional credit and the exploitation of the farmers. The commercial lands should show liberal attitude in grouting loans to small and marginal farmers and should bring their credit plans to the notice of all, the farmers by launching effective campaign in rural areas. The Regional Rural Banks are functioning in almost all the states of the country. These banks can do a lot in granting loans to prove farmers and farm laborers. The agriculture credit to the farmers should be provided at the lowest rate of interest, which should range from 5 to 6 percent.

The government should provide financial security to the small, marginal and sub-marginal farmers and labors that are financially unsecured.

9. Provision of Technical Staffs

The District Agriculture Department in every state should make effective efforts to transfer new agricultural technology to all categories of farmers. The technical staff for this purpose served is appointed by the state governments.

10. Proper Management of Demonstrations and Training Programs

To attain higher lands of productivity and production,

the government should grant incentives to small and marginal farmers such as subsidy on inputs and should organize demonstrations on their farms and provide effective training to motivate them.

It is also required that the farmers are given adequate training in farm management techniques by the experts from agricultural uncertain in the country. The prevent day agriculturė is technology sensitive and therefore is requires proper management.

11. Provision of Co-operative Joint Farming

The co-operative joint farming should be encouraged in the country. It will improve the efficiency of forearming.

12. Quick Implementation of Plans and Projects

All plans and projects prepared for agricultural development should be implemented without delay.

13. Provision of Cheap Agricultural Machinery

The attitude of the agricultural machinery at the state and district levels should be co-operative and helpful to the farming community.

14. Extension of Agricultural Services

Agriculture extension services should be properly organized at the district levels and they should provide their effective services to solve the problems of the farmers.

15. Using Advanced Agricultural Technology

Technology is the need of the hour, as it is the prime mover of change. The aim should be to enhance income per hectare on an environmentally sustainable basis. Lab to land demonstrator should include post harvest technology. For land less agricultural labor, the aim should be to convert them into skilled workers, thereby, adding economic value to their time and labor. There should a pro-nature, pro-poor and pro-women orientation to technology development and dissemination.

The government should take all steps, as directed, to increase agricultural production and productivity and only

then the present agrarian crisis in the country will be our. It is really very sad that even after 60 years of our independence, we have not been able produce enough food grain for our population.

VII. CONCLUSION

Apart from all these developments and crisis, Indian agriculture is not achieving so much yet. For this the Government of India should initiate bold measures to ensure that the WTO regime dies bit deviate from the trade-related approach and considerations like environmental and labor standards should not be brought into trade issues. India's GDP share from agriculture sector is on continuous decline. It was slightly more than 50 percent in the early 1950s, which decreased currently to 20 percent. Agricultural production extremely affect the over all growth of GDP.

In a globalized economy, we should develop appropriate institutional instruments and policies to safeguard the livelihood security of nearly 70% of our population who depend on crop and animal husbandry, inland and marine fisheries, forestry and agro-forestry; agro-processing for their work and income security. Farmers need appropriate institutional support to enhance their agricultural competitiveness. Institutional support to confer on small farm families is vital to enhance the productivity and profitability of small farms.

REFERENCES

Das, Sarada Prasanna (2005); *Globalization and Agriculture*, Third Concept, Vol. 19, No. 236.

—— (2005); *Reason for Low Level of Consumption of Fertilizer in the North-Eastern Region*, Agro Economic Research Center for North-East India, Agricultural University, Jorhat—Assam.

M. Selvekumar and N. Manicka Mahesh (2006); Agriculture Credit in India, Third Concept, Vol. 20, No. 233.

Nair, Dr. Reji D. (2006); African Agriculture in the New Millennium: Lesson from the Twentieth Century, Third Concept, Vol. 20, No. 230.

Pradhan, Manoj (2002); *Indian Agriculture and Challenges for Foreign Policy*, Third Concept, Vol. 15. No. 180.

Prasanna, N. and R. Asokan (2006); *India and World Agriculture Trade Liberalization,* Third Concept, Vol. 20, No. 229.

Raheem, Dr. A. Abdul (2006); *Globalization of Indian Agricultural Trade: An Alternative Approach,* Third Concept, Vol. 20, No. 232.

Rao, B. Dayakar and M. Pavan Kumar (2005); *Indian Agriculture in Changed Scenario of Globalization,* Agricultural Situation in India, Vol. LXII, No. 5.

Ratnam, Dr. N. Vijaya (2002); *A Review of the Corporation of Agriculture in Andhra Pradesh,* Third Concept, Vol. 16, No. 182.

Singh, R.P; Singh, Alka and *et. al.* (2005); *Indian Agriculture in the Global Contest: Calls for Competitiveness,* Agricultural Situation in India, Vol. LXII, No. 5.

William and Paul Paddock, (1967); *Who will Survive;* Boston, Little Brown.

18

Role of Commercial Bank in Agricultural Development of Bihar

SHYAM CHANDRA GUPTA

The state of Bihar constituting 2.85 percentage of the geographical area of India and about 8 percent of its population (8.29 cross as per 2001 census), is the third most populous State of the country and it frequently characterized as the ("most back ward state of India"). After the division of the state, it is left with cultivated land in the Indo-Gangetic Plains and plenty of surface and sub-surface water. It is practically devoid of forests, mining and industries. In this study attempt has been made to analyse the strengths and areas of concern so far as the opportunities for Commercial bank credit and limitations are defined by the demographic, agro-climatic and social-economic infrastructure of the state. A brief presentation of the state profile is given. The opportunities and limitations of the agricultural sector are discussed below.

After bifurcation of the state natural resources in Bihar are now dominated by cultivated land and water. The three emerging core areas with substantial potential are agriculture, allied activities and agro-based industries. Bihar lost most of its industry and mining to Jharkhand after the division and now 39 percent or two-fifths to the total GDP as compared to 26 percent for the country is accounted for by agriculture sector. Agriculture now employs three-quarters of the work force and is the main income source for the majority of the Bihar's rural poor.

Behind Bihar's low aggregate growth performance is the weak agriculture sector which showed negative in the early 1990s and since mid-1990s through 2001-02 the sector has grown by less than 1 per cent p.a. in divided Bihar revealing negative growth rate for agricultural output per capita.

POSITION OF AGRICULTURE SECTOR IN BIHAR

Among the major States of India, Bihar State has the lowest per worker gross value added from agriculture—Rs. 5941 in 1998-99 as compared to Rs. 12,201 for India as a whole—the former being a little less than half the level of the latter. Despite the fact that due to the natural fertility of the soil per hectare yield of some of the crops mainly food grains are better than those in many other states. Per capita food grains production is partly due to the heavy demographic pressure in the state. The average per capita holding in the state is 0.75 hectare (19991-92) as against 1.3 hectares for India as a whole. Other than 80 percent of the landholding are marginal in which average landholding was only 0.31 hectares- or can be classified as nearly landless category.

Irrigation Facilities Covered in Bihar

Average ground water exploitation in the state is 39 percent, leaving a very large potential gap. The ultimate irrigation potential of the state has been assessed at 106 lakh hectares which far exceeds the gross sown area of 80 lakh and net sown area of 56 lakh hectares. Thus even if the cropping intensity of the state cross such the 200 percent level, its irrigation potential will be sufficient to cover such situation. The need is to increase investment both public and private in this sector. The state's investment on this sectors has taken more than 25 percent of its total plan expenditure.

Consequently gross irrigated area in the state has increased from 18 lakh hectares in 1951 to 50 lakh hectares in 2001, i.e. at the rate of 1.90 percent per annum. A large part of the public investment on irrigation tube wells and lift irrigation structures lie unused due to lack of electricity supply. In case of major and medium irrigation sector maintenance of the distribution system is reported to be a serious concern.

Coverage of Irrigation in Bihar

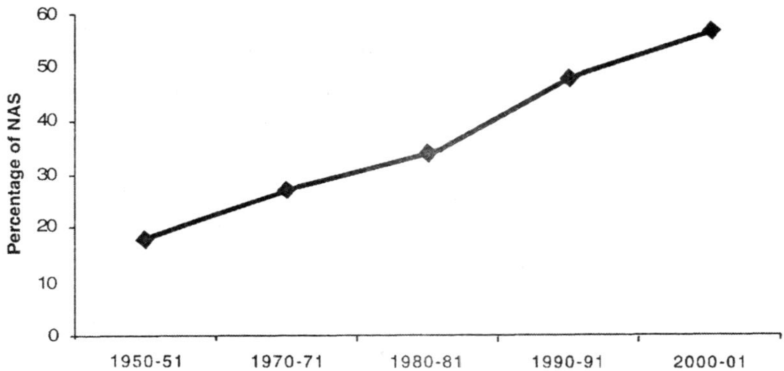

Fertilizer use in Bihar Agriculture

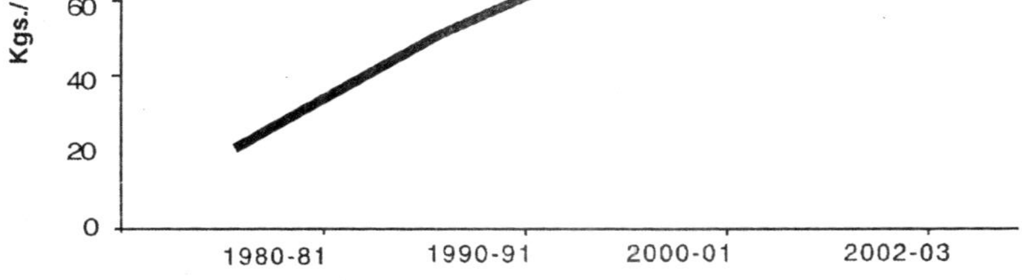

Low Capital Formation in Public and Private Sector—Shyness of Credit

Bihar's weak and declining level of investment is a major contributing factor to low growth performance. Public investment per hectare of net sown area at constant prices in seventh plan (1985-90) was Rs. 139 and Rs. 187 in Bihar and India respectively. In the Eight Plan (1992-97) public investment per hectare in Bihar fell drastically to Rs. 79 per hectare of net sown area. The private investment per hectare also does not show any encouraging trend. It rose from Rs. 76 to only Rs. 82 per acre between Seventh and Eighth Plan.

Steps taken by Commercial Bank and Other Banks

Flow of credit to Agriculture Announcements made by the Unoin Finance Minister on June 18, 2004:

- Doubling the flow of Agricultural Credit in three years- 30 per cent increase in 2004-05 by all all lending institutions over the previous year to Rs. 105,000 crore by—
  - o Enhancing coverage of institutional credit, including through KCCs, in line with the higher goal of agriculture credit in 2004-05 for.
  - o Energising the 33,039 rural and semi-urban branches of scheduled commercial bank and 14,051 branches of RRBs to enhance the flow of agriculture credit.
  - o Bringing under the fold of Commercial Banks, on an average, at least 100 new farmers at each rural and semi-urban branch during the current year so as to fulfil the goal of enlarging the number of farmers borrowing from banks by about 50 lakh.
  - o Each rural and semi urban branch of commercial bank to take up on an average at least 2-3 new investment projects in agriculture and allied areas.
  - o All commercial bank put together to finance on an average 10 agri-clinics in every district during 2004-05. the programme for agri-clinics

will be finalized by NABARD after discussions in the State Level Bankers' Committee (SLBC).

- o Public sector bank to lend more to small and margin farmers and progress in this regard to be monitored.
- o Lending institutions to view agriculture as a sector with immense commercial opportunities to lend and earn dynamic profits.
- o Scales of finance to be reviewed by the District Level Technical Committees (DLTCs) to meet the realistic needs of farmers, especially capital-intensive agricultural operations. These will only be indicative in nature.
- o NABARD to implement a special package to promote technology upgradation in agriculture, agro processing and agri-biotech, including concessional finance and support for dissemination of technology.

Debt Restructuring

- o Restructuring of Debt by Commercial Bank, RRBs and Cooperatives for farmers in distress, farmers in arrears and OTS for small and marginal farmers.
- o Farmers in distress, i.e. those who have suffered production and income loss on account of successive droughts. Floods and other calamities in districts declared as calamity-affected by the State. Government concerned, to be given debt relief and their debts rescheduled/restructure. Interest outstanding to be clubbed with principal outstanding as on 31 March 2004, and the amount thus arrived to be repayed over a period of 5 years at current interest rates, including a moratorium of 2 years.

Farmer in arrears, i.e. those who have become ineligible for fresh credit as their earlier debts have been categorized as sub-standard or doubtful, to be given debt relief in the form of rescheduling of loans in default so that such farmer will become eligible for fresh finance.

OTS for small and marginal farmers- A one time settlement scheme for defaulting small and marginal farmers who have become ineligible for fresh credit from lending institutions to enable them to settle their accounts in a transparent manner and thereafter access fresh credit.

Farmers indebted to non institutional lenders, such as moneylenders, to be provided relief in the form of loans advanced to them against appropriate collateral or group security.

FLOW OF GROUND LEVEL CREDIT IN BIHAR

The total ground level credit flow in Bihar during 2004-05 at Rs. 5040.73 crore registered a growth of 32.31 per cent over previous year. The priority sector credit has shown an impressive share of 68 per cent as compared to 32 per cent share of non-priority sector credit. The total ground level credit flow in Bihar during the past three years is furnished in Table 1.

TABLE I

(Rs. crore)

Year	*PS*	*NPS*	*Total*	*PS % to total*	*NPS % to total*
2002-03	1710.97	1342.25	3052.22	56.04	43.96
2003-04	2212.53	1597.06	3809.56	58.07	41.93
2004-05	3421.27	1619.46	5040.73	67.87	32.13

Source: SLBC.

Agency-wise Analysis

The state of Bihar has a banking network of 30 commercial bank with 2075 branches. 14 RRBs with 1486 branches, 22 DCCBs, Bihar State Cooperative Banks and Bihar State Land Development Banl with 118 brnches. Three RRBs viz. Begusarai, Bhagalpur-Bank and Munger have been merged into one RRb named Bihar KGB with effect from 12 September 2005.

The agency-wise targets and achievement under priority sector during 2004-05 are shown in Table 2.

TABLE 2

(Rs. crore)

Agency	*Target*	*Achievement*	*% Achievement*	*% Growth over previous year*
CBs	4492.72	4025.86	89.61	132.36
SCB/CCBs	341.09	273.75	80.26	93.57
SCARDS	108.18	20	18.49	98.60
RRBs	1077.3	741.12	68.80	126.26
Other	17.61	0	NIL	NIL
Total	6021.69	5060.73	84.04	128.73

Source: State focus paper 2007-08, NABARD, Regional Office, Patna.

Table 2 shows that Commercial Banks have shown as extra-ordinary performance by registering a growth of 132.36 per cent during 2004-05 against a growth of 29.99 per cent during 2003-04. the SCB has also recorded a remarkable growth of 93.57 per cent during 2004-05 against 39.19 per cent growth during the year 2003-04. the performance of RRBs during 2004-05 has also been overwhelming with a growth of 126.26 per cent as compared to 18.58 per cent reported during 2003-04. However, the performance of SACRDB during the year 2004-05 was not up to the satisfactory level with only 18.49 per cent achievement although SCARDB, in absolute terms has shown 98.60 per cent growth, the relative achievement was not satisfactory.

Commercial Bank

The achievement of Commercial Bank *vis-à-vis* the target fixed for them in the Annual Credit plan for 2004-05 is given in Table 3.

As can be seen from the above table, Commercial Banks have shown 95.58 per cent achievement against the

TABLE 3

(Rs. crore)

Sector	ACP-Target	Achivement	% Achivement	% Growth over Previous year
Crop Loan	1386.29	542.74	95.58	67.21
Agrl. Term loan		782.32		
Total Agrl. Credit	1386.29	1325.06	95.58	67.21
Non-Farm Sector	443.63	193.51	43.62	34.73
Other Priority Sector	926.17	1023.35	110.49	28.49
Grand Total	2756.09	2541.92	92.22	46.71

Source: State Focus Paper, Regional office, NABARD, Patna.

target of Rs. 1386.29 crore under agriculture sector. With credit disbursement of Rs. 193.51 crore, the industries sector has shown 34.74 per cent growth during 2004-05 against 25.78 per cent growth recorded during the previous year. The credit disbursement under other priority sector has also registered a significant growth of 46.72 per cent during 2004-05 whereas achievement was 110.48 per cent. Overall, against the target of Rs. 2756.09 crore for the year 2004-05 under priority sector, Commercial Banks have achieved 92.22 per cent of target thereby showing the remarkable performance.

AGENCY-WISE REFINANCE DISBURSEMENT

The agency-wise refinance disbursement for the last three years is given in Table 4.

Bihar Regional Office disbursed refinance assistance of Rs. 176.454 crore during 2004-05 against the target of Rs. 95.20 crore. During the previous year 2003-04, an amount of Rs. 96.70 crore of refinance was disbursed in the state. There has been a growth of 82.47 per cent over the previous year. Future, the sanctions of Rs. 34.99 crore to CBs were not disbursed during the year and if included in saction then the total sancton would amount to Rs. 211.44 crore.

TABLE 4

(Rs. in crore)

Agency	2002-03		2003-04		2004-05		2005-06@	
	Amt.	*Share*	*Amt.*	*Share*	*Amt.*	*Share*	*Amt.*	*Share*
CBs	7.27	8.9%	0.17	0.18%	88.76	50.30%	13.05	57.13
RRBs	74.83	91.1%	90.00	93.07%	77.69	44.01%	9.79	42.87
BSCLDB	NIL	NIL	6.53	6.75%	10.00	5.66%	NIL	NIL
BSCB	NIL	NIL	NIL	NIL	NIL	NIL	NIL	NIL
Total	82.10	100%	96.7	100%	176.45	100%	22.84	100%

@ As on 31.12.2005.

Commercial Banks

We can analyze from the above table that the refinance off-take which was increased signification from 0.17 crore to Rs. 88.76 crore. The refinance availed of by the Commercial Banks during the year 2005–06 (upto 31.12.2005) is Rs. 13.05 which is expected to be picked up in the next three months.

Following are the major factors affecting the overall refinance flow under investment credit:

- Almost negligible industrialization,
- Fragmented land holdings,
- Lack of Infrastructural facilities such as roads, transport, communication and power,
- Poor CD ratio,
- Lack of Infrastructural facilities such as roads. Transport, communication and power,
- Inclination of banks for investment rather than providing credit due to availability of excess liquid and zero-risk approach, and
- Inadequate land reforms.

Eradication of Agrarian Crises by Commercial Bank and Others

The credit flow to agriculture in Bihar through financial institutions, which deteriorated in real terms in the post reforms period, showed signs of improvement since 1999-

2000. The total flow of institutional credit to agriculture in Bihar in 1989-90 was Rs. 138 crores, which marginally increased to Rs. 142 crores in 1992-93 and further to Rs. 380 crores in 1999-2000. In the wake of inflation and rise in fertilizer prices, it certainly denotes a declining availability of credit in real terms. However since 1999-2000 the growth in ground level credit flow for agriculture suddenly took an upward inflection and rapidly rose to Rs. 548 crores in 2001-01 and further to Rs. 1148 Crores in 2003-04. The sudden increase in credit flow for agriculture was a result of three developments—firstly, grounding of the Kisan Credit Cards (KCC) gave an effective instruments to the Commercial Banks and the RRBs to enter the crop loans segment and show continuous exponential growth subsequently. Secondly the launching of the MSTP gave a convenient platform to the Commercial Banks and the RRBs for increasing their involvement in the investment credit segment in the State. Thirdly the growing agriculture sector in the late 1990s gave a boost to the financing of the Farm machnization especially tractors by the Commercial Banks and the RRBs. But for the sickness of the cooperative sector the growth in the ground level credit flow for agriculture would have been much more spectacular. The BSCB gained a major advantage through the historic one-time settlement of outstanding old dues and rationalization of scales of finance by the BSCB in 1990-2000 resulting in making earlier defaulters eligible for the crop loans and also increasing the maximum credit limit of the borrowers. These steps led to spurt in the flow of crop loans in 1999-2000 and 2000-01. However this advantage was soon lost as the overdues again mounted restricting the flow of crop loans. Although some new developments in the BSCB's recovery drive are heartening yet sustainability of such recovery climate would require much more that periodic recovery campaigns.

The GLC in Bihar has been recording consistent growth since 1999-2000. Commercial Banks are the major financial institutions showing persistent growth since the year 2001-02. The overall growth rate has increased from 15.72 per cent in 2001-02 to 128.82 per cent in 2004.05.

TABLE 5

Agency-wise Flow of Credit to Agriculture

(Rs. Crore)

Year	*CBs*	*Coops*	*RRBs*	*Total*	*Growth*	*Share*
2000-01	325.45	145.60	76.90	547.95	–	1.15
2001-02	461.96	82.78	75.18	619.92	15.72	1.14
	(75%)	(13%)	(12%)	(100%)		
2002-03	604.73	101.60	153.84	903.85	45.80	1.04
2003-04	792.44	141.43	204.87	1138.74	26.00	–
2004-05	1325.06	293.75	431.30	2050.11	128.82	

Policy Initiatives by Govt. of India to Eradicate Agriculture Crises in Bihar

Backward Regions Grants Fund—A Backward Religion Grants Fund has been establishes with an allocation of Rs. 5.000 crore for 2005-06 and an equal amount to be allocated every year in the next four years. Consequent upon the establishment of the fund, suitable transition arrangement will be made in respect of existing Rashtriya Sam Vikas Yojona (RSVY).

- *Rural Infrastructure*—Government to focus on providing basic infrastructure to the poor. Especially those in rural India and in urban slums. The Rural Infrastructure Development Fund (RIDF) with NABARD provided a corpus of Rs. 8,000 crorre in 2005-06 also.
- *Bharat Nirman*—In his address to parliament, the president outlined an overarching vision to build India, and called it 'Bharat Nirman'. Bharat Nirman has been conceived as a business plan, to be implemented over a period of four years, for building infrastructure, especially in rural India. It has six components, namely, irrigation, roads, water supply, housing, rural electrification and rural telecom connectivity. The GoI's target is:

- o To bring an additional one crore hectares under irrigation.
- o To connect all village that have a population of 1000 (or 500 in hilly/tribal areas) with a road.
- o To construct 60 lakh additional houses for the poor.
- o To provide drinking water to the remaining 74,000 habitations that are uncovered.
- o To reach electricity to the remaining 1,25,000 village and offer electricity connection to 2.3 crore households.
- o To give telephone connectivity to the remaining 66,822 villages.
- o An outlay of Rs. 30,000 crore (till 2009) is being considered of which Rs. 4000 crore per year (till 2009) is being rougted through NABARD.

- *Roadmap for Agriculture Diversification*—The Ministry of Agriculture to prepare a roadmap for agricultural diversification. To focus on fruits, vegetable, flowers, dairy, poultry, fisheries, pulses and oilseeds.
- *National Horticulture Mission*—The National Horticulture Mission launched on April 1, 2005. An amount of Rs. 630 crore allocated in 2005-06 for the Mission. The Mission to ensure an end-to-end approach having backward and forward linkages covering research, production, post-harvest management. Processing and marketing, under one umbrella, in an integrated manner. As the Mission gathers pace, more funds to be provided.
- *Agriculture Marketing Infrastructure*—A new scheme called "Development/Strengthening of Agriculture Marketing infrastructure, Grading and Standardization" introduced by Government to induce large investment from the private and cooperative sectors for setting up agricultural

markets, marketing infrastructure and support services such as grading, standardization and quality certification. Assistance available in the form of credit-linked, back-ended subsidy. The scheme to be implemented through NABARD and NCDC in those Stated which amend their Agricultural Produce Marketing Committee (APMC) Acts. Rs. 72 crore allocated for the new scheme.

- *Water Resources, Flood Management and Erosion Control*—The National project for the repair, renovation and restoration of water bodies launched in the month of March 2005. the pilot project planned for 16 district in 9 States and to cover nearly 700 water bodies, and 20,000 hectares of additional land to come under irrigation. The allocation for the pilot project increased to Rs. 100 crore in 2005-06.
- *Micro Irrigation*—Water-use efficiency in India agricultural being one of the lowest in the world, Government to promote micro-irrigation technology, comprising drip and sprinkler irrigation, on a large scale. Coverage under micro-irrigation to be increased to 3 million hectares by the end of the tenth plan and 14 million hectares by the end of the Eleventh plan. Rs. 400 crore allocated for promoting micro-irrigation in 2005-06.
- *Rural Credit and Indebtedness*—Reserve Bank of India (RBI) to examine the issue of allowing banks to adopt the agency mode, by using the infrastructure of civil society organizations, rural kiosks and village knowledge centers, to provide credit support to rural and farm sectors.
- *Credit Flow to Agriculture*—Commercial banks. RRBs and cooperative bank to increase the flow of credit by another 30 percent in 2005-06. further, the public sector banks to cover 50 lakh new

borrowers during 2005-06 also cooperative banking system accepted by Govt. of India, in principle. The process of implementing the recommendations in the States that show willingness to accept the recommendations to be initiated.

- *Farm Insurance*—The National Agriculture Insurance Scheme (NAIS) to continue in its present from for kharif and rabi 2005-06.
- *Micro Insurance*—Government to see that insurance benefits percolate to rural India and to the vulnerable sections of the population. The Insurance Regulatory Development Authority (IRDA) has published draft Religions for micro-insurance. NGOs, SHGs, cooperatives and MFIs to be invited to become micro insurance agents.
- *A Knowledge Centre in Every Village*—The National Commission on Farmer has recommended the establishment of Rural Knowledge Centers all over the country using modern information and communication technology (ICT). Mission 2007 is a national initiatively launched by an alliance comprising nearly 80 organizations including civil society organization. Their goal is to set-up a knowledge centre in every village by the 60th anniversary of Independence Day. Government to join the alliance and route its support through NABARD. NABARD to provide Rs. 100 crore out of RIDF.
- *Agricultural Research*—A Task force headed by Dr. M.S. Swaminathan has recommended the creation of a National fund for Strategic Agricultural Research. Initial provisions of Rs. 50 crore made for operationalizing this fund.
- *Rural Electrification*—A massive programme for rural electrification to being in 2005-06 with the objective of covering 1.25 lakh village in five years with focus on deficient states.

In this why commercial Bank played a better role to providing Agricultural finance in Bihar. It performance is satisfactory in the field of Agricultural Development of Bihar.

References

Kurukshetra, 2007.

NABARD, State focus paper 2007-08.

Yojna, 2007.

19

Land Reforms: A Dismal Picture in Bihar

Sofia Fatima and Priyanka Sinha

> *"Article 39 of the Indian Constitution stipulates that states direct policies to ensure that all citizens have the right to adequate means of livelihood, and that all community resources be distributed so as to serve the common good. Land reform is carried out under this directive."*

Land reform is basically all about reform programmes in context of ownership, utilization, management and development of significant factors of production. It is a free gift of nature with limited supply. The law of diminishing returns is operative in case of production in land. Land reform is an essential pre-condition for the conversion of feudal and semi-feudal society to modern society, i.e. the capitalist society. It refers to all sorts of policy-induced changes associated with the pattern of ownership, tenancy, and management of land. Directly or indirectly it has certainly covered the entire agrarian structure of the country. The idea behind land reform was agricultural grown with attainment of social justice. It aims in at re- distributing ownership holding with justification. It also aims at reorganization of operational holding for optimum utilization of land. Land reform was designed in such a way which focussed on the accomplishment of agricultural growth with elimination of inequitable agrarian structure.

It is an admitted fact that productivity is based on technological as well as institutional factors. Institutional factors viz: feudal system, sub-division and fragmentation, high rents, etc. adversely affect the growth of agricultural production is does not motivate the farmers to save and inject their money in agriculture, besides enjoying the fruits of their labour. It was strongly felt that land reforms and technological change were inevitably required for the all-round development of agriculture. The purpose of land reform is to rationally use the land (the resource which is scarce in nature) and also to redistribute the agricultural land to the less privileged classes.

The objective of land reform can be introduced by stating that it is to confer ownership of land rights to the landless and to give security of land holding to marginal and small farmers, the major objectives of land reform in India are:

- to restructure the agrarian relation,
- to eliminate exploitation in land relation.
- to actualize the target of "land to the tiller",
- to improve the socio-economic condition of the rural poor,
- to enhance the level of productivity and production,
- to facilitate the development of land base, and
- attainment of higher equality in local institution.

There are three very important types of land reform which have been enacted after independence in India are:

- the abolition of intermediaries,
- regulation of the size of holdings through imposition of ceilings of land holdings and redistribution, or through land consolidation, and
- settlement and regulation of tenancy.

The land redistribution is marked with several positive impacts such as:

- it put a check on burning of forest for cultivation,
- helps in substantiating the people's livelihood and also prevent migration,
- it has the prospect for economic growth and alleviation of poverty, and
- provides a platform for political participation at the grass root level.

Before independence a substantial part of agricultural land was held by intermediaries under the Zamindari, Mahalwari and Ryotwari systems. The tillers of land (i.e. tenant farmers) were charged high rents and they were also exploited by other means. The abolition of intermediaries began in 1950s. The purpose of the related legislation was to leave no scope for intermediary level in between the state and the cultivators. It was also emphasized that the compensation is paid to the owner. As a consequence of such laws, 20 million cultivators became owners of the land where they had been tilling. 57.7 lakh hectares of land were redistributed. Zamindars received compensation, but the abolition of intermediaries brought no changes in alleviating the problems of inequalities in landholding, it rather aggravated the problem by restraining the land, landholding ceilings and surplus land distribution.

Whereas the legislation for ceiling on landholder had an appreciable impact in some states but it was not that effective

The tenancy reforms were of three types viz: regulation of rent, security of tenure and ownership rights to tenants. This reform has been counter-productive.

The laws regarding ceiling of land were enforced in many states in 1950s and 1960s. Such laws were subjects to some modification as per directives of the Central Government in 1972. The enactment of the very legislation declared that there was 73.95 lakhs acres of land (up to 30th of September, 1995) which was surplus, out of which 65.58 lakhs acres of land was taken over by the Government and

51.68 lakh acres of land was distributed among 50.33 lakh landless labourers (including 36% SC and 14% ST beneficiaries). Under the legislation of ceiling, no land was declared as surplus in the states of Bihar, Karnataka, Orissa and Rajasthan. This clearly reflects that enough deficiencies and loopholes were present in the very low. Statistical data reveals that 1875.37 lakhs acres of land was taken up for the process of consolidation of land (up to November, 1995). The process had been successful in some states like Maharashtra, Uttar Pradesh, Punjab and Haryana. The law relating to ceiling also has a provision of paying Rs. 2500 per hectare as financial assistance for cultivating on the land which is not of good quality and which is also covered under the legislation for ceilings.

In the process of land reform new classes are born and take place of old classes. There is also a change of hands for economic, political and social power. These new classes result in evolution of new agricultural production, changed techniques, etc. Due to there new social and cultural changes, the entire social fabric changes.

COMPUTERIZATION OF THE LAND RECORDS

There are two schemes under the sponsorship of Central Government viz: (a) Computerization of the land records (CLR), (b) Strengthening of revenue administration and up landing of land records. The administration of these two schemes lies in the hand of Land Reforms Division in the Department of Land Resources.

The CLR schemes was channelised in 1988-89 in eight districts of Assam, A.P., Jharkhand, Gujarat, M.P., Rajasthan, Maharashtra and Orissa with the motive of eradicating the difficulties and shortcomings related to manual maintenance and updating of land records. Computerization data of land records for better developing and transparency. It was emphasised also to make it available to the group of users and public. It also helps the State Government to utilize funds in relation to the same for effective results. Since the inception of the CLR scheme, Government has released Rs. 346.13 crores till 31st March, 2005, Rs. 226.34 crores has been utilized by the state or UTs to which is around nearly 65 per cent of the total funds released for the purpose.

Bihar

The glory of ancient India is synonymous with the glory of Bihar (the then Magadh). The message of peace and coexistence by Emperor Ashoka in unparalleled in world history. Biharies are identified as good people and it has been testified by great personalities, and eminent leaders like Mahatma Gandhi and Dr. Rajendra Prasad. But Bihar is now identified as a State with extreme poverty. Backwardness in agriculture is one of the major factors of rural poverty in Bihar.

The area of the state is 94 lakh hectare. The net irrigated area is 33.5 lakh hectares. It's population is 8.3 crore, it's literacy rate is only 48 per cent against national rate of 65.4 per cent. 33 per cent of the population is living below poverty line. Bihar is now considered as a textbook care of stagnation, backwardness and poverty, which is an outcome of political and bureaucratic mismanagement.

Land Reforms in Bihar

Bihar is the pioneer among states is India for introducing land reforms after independence land reform was actually a commitment by the Indian National Congress during the liberation movement. These were some predetermined targets of land reform, the very first of which was the abolition of Zamindaris System. It was not at all an easy task. This system was completely engrossed with the exploitation of the less privileged. They were termed as parasites. Zamindars were the affluent ones, they were quite powerful also. At the independence of India in 1947, Bihar got a radical man, Dr. Sri Krishana Sinha as it's Chief Minister. He took initiative in this matter and the Zamindari Abolition Bill 1950 (Bihar Act 30 of 1950) was passed. And it is also true that Jawahar Lal Nehru, the then Prime Minister was highly impressed by this very move in Bihar.

The second decision step towards land reform, i.e. fixation of ceiling area and acquisition of surplus land to under privileged/landless (Harijans or Adivasis) was the enactment of Bihar land reforms (Fixation of ceiling area and acquisition of surplus land) Act, 1961 Bihar Act XII of 1962. Binnodanand Jha was then the Chief Minister of Bihar.

The key feature of land reform in Bihar are quoted below:

The Bihar Lands Reforms Fixation of Ceiling Area and Acquisition of Surplus Land Act, 1961, stipulates a ceiling of 6 hectares per holding for irrigated land.

The Act only provides for a ceiling, and does not extend to tenancy reforms. Ceiling is applicable to both owned and tenanted land. There is no legal provision in the state to record informal tenancies. Thus, a tenant is neither protected nor secured.

Bihar has the legislation for land consolidation but it lag behind as far as implementation is concerned. Planning Commission report of 1964 shows that either one or one and a half lakh acres of land could have been acquired if the law had efficiently be operated. The ceiling process accumulated 3,85,013 acres of spare land, of which 2,77,490 acres land was distributed among 3,52,703 families as of January, 2001. In 2000-01 449.73 acres land was distributed among 844 families. However, the extent of land distributed to each family worked out to about 0.53 acres, which is quite small plot to be cultivated profitably. The landless rural people of Bihar had an idea of negligible improvement in their livelihood, so they thought of migrating to cities where they compose a major chunk of the working population. This process of migration is a kind of set back for the ethnic agrarian structure, this also cause paucity of labourer on agricultural fields.

For a better understanding of land reforms it is important to know the composition of rural class right before the land reforms. 1950s, just before the abolition of Zamindari system there were 2,05,927 regularly revenue paying, permanently settled holdings. They accounted for ninety percent of land area. Legally the Zamindari were considered to the owners the land. But the reality they were mere middlemen appointed by the Government to collect revenue from the title-holder. Revenue which was paid to the Government was in the form of cash and which was about 90

Land Ceiling in Various States

[Acres per family (consisting husband, wife, minor children, unmarried daughter)]

	Double cropped *irrigation land*	Single cropped *irrigation land*	Unirrigated land *(Dry Farming)*
A. Proposed in National guidelines of 1972	4.05 to 7.28	10.93	21.85
B. Real maximum land ceiling			
1. Andhra Pradesh	4.5 to 7.28	6.07 to 10.93	14.16 to 21.85
2. Assam	6.74	6.74	6.74
3. Bihar	6.7 to 7.28	10.12	12.14 to 18.20
4. Gujarat	4.05 to 7.28	6.08 to 10.93	8.09 to 21.85
5. Haryana	7.25	10.9	21.80
6. H.P.	4.05	6.07	12.14 to 28.33
7. J & K	3.6 to 5.06	3.6 to 5.06	5.95 to 9.20
8. Karnataka	4.05 to 8.10	10.12 to 12.14	21.85
9. Kerala	4.86 to 6.07	4.86 to 6.07	4.86 to 6.07
10. M.P.	7.28	10.93	21.85
11. Mahrashtra	7.28	10.93 to 14.57	21.85
12. Manipur	5.00	5.00	6.00
13. Orissa	4.05	6.07	12.14 to 18.21
14. Punjab	7.00	11.00	20.50
15. Rajasthan	7.28	10.93	21.85 to 70.82
16. Tamil Nadu	4.86	12.14	24.28
17. Sikkim	5.06	–	20.23
18. Tripura	4.00	4.00	12.00
19. Uttar Pradesh	7.30	10.95	18.25
20. W. Bengal	5.00	5.00	7.00

per cent of total revenue paid by the title-holder of the Zamindars. In the structure of operation of revenue collection, Zamindars used to collect the revenue from the title-holders (the amount of revenue depend upon the desire of Zamindars). Then at the second level there were title-holders to have obtained the right from the owners of the land or from other title-holders who collect revenue. At the third level there were the occupancy ryots who had to make the payment of revenue for the land they had occupied and cultivated. They could transfer their rights to someone else. At another downward stage of this hierarchy, were the non-occupancy ryots. These non-occupancy ryots had to pay revenue for occupying the land on a temporary basis. They used to let land to sub-tenants who used to pay revenue for getting land on a temporary basis. The labourers were the lowest level of this arrangement. They had to work really hard but had no right on the land. They were the victims of several exploitative agrarian relations.

This composition is an index of existence of various level of revenue collectors in between the Government and the tillers of the land. These levels are identified as intermediaries. The actual producer would get only negligible portion of the produce after 90 per cent of the next went into the hands of the intermediaries. In such dilapilated condition they was presence of no ray of hope for any type of development or capital formation.

In 1930s and 1940s, a flood of peasant movement was pushing forth in Bihar. The occupancy and non-occupancy ryots played a major role in the movements for Zamindari abolition during the British Raj. The tenants-at-will and labourers also participated for the cause and the occupancy and non-occupancy ryots received the biggest benefit of Zamindari abolition.

Despite innumerable ups and downs, the first substantial step towards attainment of land reform was successful enough. Land reform emphasised much on equity than on productivity. According to experts the rural development programmes should be assimilated with land reform measures. It is found that the concrete conditions of Bihar small holdings are tailor-made as far as optimum productivity is concerned, but it may not keep pace with the economies of scale on a scientific basis.

Bhoodan: A Flight of Fantasy

Right after independence of India, a movement popularly known as *"Bhoodan Movement"* was led by Vinoba Bhave. Bhoodan literally means land gift. Vinoba Bhave with his follower observed a *"Padayatra"* where they used to go to the villages in order to convince the larger land owners to donate at least one-sixth of their land. The land so donated was to be distributed to the landless people. 1951 th movement penetrated in Bihar also but within a few years it lost its sheen. The target of Bhoodan Movement was to receive 50 million acres of land, i.e. around 1/6th of the total cultivable land in India, as donatation for distribution to landless. But merely 8,72,000 acres of land had been distributed by 1961. Thus the goal of peaceful revolution could not be achieved. The zealous work for the peaceful revolution could not bring wonders.

Bhoodan in Bihar

Vinoba Bhave remained in Bihar resolve the land related problems in the state. The legislation which facilatated the land gift movement in Bihar were:

The Bihar Bhoodan Yagna Act, 1954 and the rules and regulation made under it including the Bihar Bhoodan Yagna Rules, 1955 and Bihar Bhoodan Yagna Regulation, 1960. The cause of these legislations could not gain momentum.

"Dhan Aur Dharti Baat Ke Rahenge, Apna Apna Chhod Ke" (the wealth and land would be definitely distributed, but barring one's own wealth and land), was a slogan in Bihar, pointed out by a functionary of the state unit of Kisan Sabha.

The shortcomings or lack of will in respective departments were the hindrances in the way of successful implementation of the land gift movement. For instance, no separate register for Bhoodan Land was mainted by the Anchal Adhikaries where a district register was required to be maintained by the order in 1960 of the revenue department (land reform) in Bihar, to disclosed the details of Bhoodan land. Another example to substantiate the ineffectiveness in channelising the movement, was the district administration's failure regards to furnished the verification reports of work done by Bhoodan Yagna Committee to the Governemnt and this was against the instructions given by the revenue department in the year 1989 to all the Collectors and the Deputy Commissioners. All these things indicate that the legislative measures were deregulated and this resulted to a comment by the working group on land reforms of the

National Commission on agriculture in 1973. The very comment is quoted below:

> "By their abysmal failure to implement the laws, the authorities in Bihar have reduced the whole package of land reforms measures to a sour joke. This has emboldened the land owing classs to treat the entire issue of agrarian reform with the utter contempt."

The working group had already identified that the land owners were orgnized and aggressive also had the unique suppport of the administration. This strength was enough for the big land owners to defy the spirit of Bhoodan Movement. They denied to give up even an inch of their rights, privileges and economic dominance.

The Present Context

The Bhoodan Movement could not be accelerated in the correct direction and it is now identified to be a White Elephant because of it failure in performing its assigned role. A few years ago, Bhoodan Board was proposed to be disbanded by the minister of Land Reforms in Bihar, along with the adjustment of its workers in some other department.

The Bihar Bhoodan Yagna Committee reported that 10 lakh acres of land received under the movement was not fit enough for distribution. Land received by the committee could not be distributed to landless persons due to non-availability of technical approval require under the state Bhoodan Act.

Therefore, it may be safely concluded that one should stop bewailing and consider Bhoodan as a dream which has not yet come true.

CONCLUSION

Even after more than 60 years of independence, the pre-determined and announced goal of land reforms have not yet been achieved. The reform is too far from over. In past years no direct link could be weaved between the Government and the peasant class. The rural parts of the state are still dominated by the landlords. These landlord classes are the obstacle in the path of instilling enterprising spirit of broad peasantry.

The defects in legislation gave birth to transfer of land to fictitious holders. The regulation of size of holdings through the imposition of ceilings and the distribution of land thus declared surplus alongwith generous ceiling limits and poor execution of the law resulted in some 'Benami' transactions. The quantum of such Benami transaction was so appaling that all calculations made by concerned officials about the quantum of surplus land that would be obtained for distribution among the landless proved deceptive and unreal.

The process of land reforms is in complete, biased and still ineffective. But some advocates that some new classes have emerged in rural societies. Apart from families of Zamindars, middle peasantry group, free labourers, etc. have stepped forward. This change has transformed the method of cultivation also. Besides tenant cultivation, cultivation is getting done by free labourers also. The advocacy for the motion has stressed on increased usage of pumpsets for irrigation, fertilizers and high-yielding seeds. Infusion of more capital in agriculture through Banks and Goverenment agencies and blocks is also seen as the positive side of the story. But the other side of the story is fulminated by the fact that the designing and execution by the respective legislation has been turned in the interest of landlord class and it is deviated and is far from benefitting the real tillers, i.e. it's true beneficianries.

Land reforms have been mispositioned and had been caught in the trap of rules, regulations, laws and litigation. It is a matter of bewilderment that the land reforms which were expected to serve good to the less privileged had actually provided legality to the landlords' rights over the land. The reform in Bihar is not been contended and has the potential to accelerate the matter. The knavery of the concerned people and authorities has resulted in a flop show of land reform programmes.

The constitution has already been amended 13 times to erase the legal obstacles in the way of land reforms. Even then, a lot has to be done to make the inception of land reform a grand success.

New Agency for Land Reforms

Separate agency for land reforms and upgradation of waste land has been setup by the Government. New agency named Jai Prakash Mission for Land Reforms and Wasteland Development will actual worked under the ministry of rural development. This body will be authorised for formulating policies and implementing them for land reforms and wasteland upgradation.

In Bihar, the present Government has set-up a commission on land reforms. It is a three members panel headed by Mr. D. Bandyopadhyay. This Commission is bestowed with the task of land reform exercise in the state.

Land to a landless person is not to be seen as a supplement to the productive asset with him but it becomes his sole means of livelihood on which he can rely. Accessiing the sources of livelihood is a fundamental right of every single person in the society.

Various legislations for land reforms were made and initiated, but it never proceeded to any meaningful and effective implementation of the measures. The reasons behind non-effective execution such measures were the lack of political will and resistance from the landed sections.

SUGGESTION

The spirit both in formulation and implementation is inevitable for successful lunch and conduct of any programme. Therefore, genuine and honest participation from all concerned streams shall have a glorious future of the state agrarian structure.

There should be impartial, unfetttered and positive participation and contribution of all. All should join hands for the successful implementation and enforcement of the programmes. Then only we can boast of having perfect, equitable and sustainable growth as well as overall development of the people of Bihar.

Thus, the entire theme of land reforms programmes shold not "end in fiasco."

REFERNECES

Indian Economy: Dutt and Sundaram and I.C. Dhingra.
Pratiyogita Darpan: Special Issue.
India Together: Bhoodan Betrayal in Bihar, January, 2004.
The Hindu: Online Edition.
Mainstream: December 22, 2007.
File://E:landreformsinbihar.htm

20

Commodity Derivatives Markets and Prospects for Cotton Futures in India

S.P. SAHA AND K.K. AGRAWAL

INTRODUCTION

While the concept of derivates is certainly not new it is only in last decade of twentieth century it is only in last decade of twentieth century that the use of these risk management tools have proliferated. The basic purpose of derivatives is to hedge unwanted risks to remove them from those who do not want them and pass them to those who are willing to bear them. These instruments therefore provide financial players with the flexibility to unbundle and manage risks, which previously was not possible. In the context of investments and investment management, hedging instruments offered by derivative markets makes investors more willing to hold and trade cash positions. These instruments provide a low-cost means of entering and existing from financial markets and contribute to the downward pressure ontrading costs. So, Derivatives provide three important economic functions (i) risk management, (ii) price discovery, (iii) transactional efficiency. Riskmanagement protects existing profits and does not create new profits, price discovery represents the ability to achieve and disseminate price information and transactional efficiency is the products of liquidity. When derivatives are used for speculative purposes—as they often are—they are not being applied towards risk management. Such uses have given rise to the impression that derivatives create risk which is uninformed judgment and generally untrue. Derivatives are then used to manage financial risk in market place having four basic types of financial risk; equity risk, foreign exchange risk, interest rate risk and commodity price risk.

Derivatives have been freely used in most of the developed markets of the world to share risks among individuals has also seen exponential growth in several developing countries. For example, derivatives markets in Brazil are some of the largest markets in the world. The first derivatives in the world started with commodities like wheat, sugar, cows and pigs as the underlying. In India, there has always been derivatives markets on commodities. These derivatives mostly stopped trading with the ban of 1969. Trading is now established in only six relatively minor commodities—hessian, potatoes, castorseed, turmeric, pepper and Jaggery. Recently, there has been an increase in derivatives trading and commodity futures have come back into limelight, with the Kabra Cabra Committee recommending another 14 commodities to start futures trading on, one of these recommended commodities is cotton.

The East India Cotton Association, which is based in Mumbai, has been granted permission to start a cotton futures exchange in terms of determination of India cotton prices. The Indian cotton faces competition internationally with firms in Brazil, Turkey and China and if our raw materials costs are too high, them our exports are rendered uncompetitive. Therefore, Indian cotton market will definitely look way to lock in cotton prices using world futures. The commodity derivative markets in India have now occupied a key position in Forward Market Commission worldwide. The Government of India (GOI) has been taking steps to improve the business potential for commodity derivatives exchanges, by—(i) liberalising policies in the underlying commodity market, and (ii) by permitting derivaties on more commodities.

In this article, we examine the rationale for starting cotton futures trading—beginning with understanding the importance to cotton in the Indian economy the economic need futures on cotton and implementation issues in setting up the futures market.

OBJECTIVES

(i) To review the commodity Derivative Market with special reference to the Indian Commodity derivative Markets.

(ii) To conduct a comparative appraisal of need for cotton futures trading.

(iii) To identify the users of cotton futures and the role for the regulator.

(iv) To suggest some measures and recommendation to improve the cotton derivative market internationally by making a strong like between foreign exchange volatility and cotton prices.

RESEARCH METHODOLOGY

Data used in this paper are secondary in nature. They have been collected from the published documents of the Indian Cotton Mills Federation and other Government reports concerned with commodity market. Report on various aspects of Cotton futures trading in India, 2002 and 2003 and from websites of data on same aspects for the time period of 1996-97 to 2003-04. For analysing the prospects of futures in India various statistical tools have been used.

BACKGROUND OF COMMODITY DERIVATIVE MARKET

The first derivatives in the world started with commodities like wheat, sugar, cows and pigs. In India, trading is established in only six relatively minor commodities—hessian, potatoes, castorseed, turmeric, perpper and Jaggery. Recently, there has been an increase in derivatives trading and commodity futures have come back into limelight, with the Kabra Committee recommendations another 14 commodities to start futures trading on one of these recommended commodities is cotton.

A commodity futures trading has been in existence in India for a very long time; it was only in the recent past that futures trading was banned. Pepper was a politically non-controversial commodity in comparison with commodities like cotton, sugar or rice, and therefore one of the six commodities permitted to run futures contracts· on by the Government India. The external impetus for the international pepper futures markets came from the UNCTAD in 1994. The study proclaimed a need for global pepper futures contracts that would serve the need of pepper-producing countries such as Brazil, Indonesia, Malaysia, Vietnam, Thailand, Sri Lanka and India. The India Pepper and Spice Trade Association (IPSTA) submitted a proposal, which was received favourable by the UNCTAD. This along with the approval of the international futures market.

After the pepper market, the next commodities derivatives market that the government has sanctioned to become an international market is the castor future market, currently housed at Bombay Oil and Oilseeds Exchange (BOOE). But castor futures market has a lot of hurdles such as the delivery of the commodities and fear born in the minds of the domestic traders of their ability to trade in the minds of the domestic traders of their ability to trade in the same field as international participants who are much capitalized than they are much more progress have been witnessed of the IPSTA by creation of the clearing corporation by IPSTA-ICE (International Commodities Exchange) combination haring much interest to see how they resolve and work with these issues.

All users of IPSTA-ICE have to be registered either as non-members or members of exchange and with the Forward Market Commission (FMC). Secondly, all the members with foreign customers, both international and domestic, have to be registered with RBI, to take care of currency flows. Thirdly the members have to have not own funds to be developed in India, as kind of fallback amount capital invested in the country. Lastly, clearing members have to subscribe to some amount of equity in first commodities clearing corporation of India (FICCI), which is crucial in carrying the trade guarantee up to the trading member.

This makes four categories of members: (a) a composite clearing member who can trade and clear their own as well as for customer, (b) composite trading members, who can trade their own well as for customers, but can not clear any contracts, (c) clearing members, who can trade and clear on their own contracts, and (d) trading members, who can trade their own contracts. In addition, there are three banks that have been admitted as institutional clearing members (ICM) who clear customer contracts, but do not trade on their own account.

Two other issues that impact questions of payment are taxation and the foreign exchange rate. IPSTA has to resolve the double taxation issue. The tax treatment of mark-to-market profit or losses is not yet very clear. In addition, the export tax is different for different countries which means that for delivery in different countries would imply different futures prices at the time of maturity. Lastly, there is the problem of resolving foreign currency rates affecting the prices the solution is to choose a common currency to denominate the futures prices in. There have been string suggestions to have a dollar-denominated contract.

FORWARD MARKET COMMISSION AND GROWTH OF COMMODITIES DERIVATIVES MARKET

The commodity derivative market in India are currently a far way off from welt functioning financial marketplaces for commodities, in comparison with their status prior to the 1690s. Today, the fraction of the commodities markets covered by commodity futures is very small all the current six commodities accounts for just around 1.2 percent of the GDP of this, around 0.5 percent is concentrated in potatoes, which is not a very successful markets in terms of volume.

With such percentages, there is very little real volume for the exchanges to build strong business foundations on. This is reflected in the movement of people and smalls out of the industry into alternative careers, skills that have been developed over the last forty years. The government of India has been taking steps to improve the business potential for commodity derivatives exchange, by (a) liberalizing policies in the underlying commodity markets, and (b) permitting derivatives on more commodities. The exchanges can take steps to—

(i) Increase their financial strength,
(ii) Improve their systems—trading, clearing, settlement with strong managing systems for risk management, surveillance systems of prices and members for fraud management, etc.
(iii) Improve their administrative structure.

With the Kabra committee report, at least four new commodities have been approved for futures trading by GOI-pepper, castor oil, cotton and jute sacking. But without investing in the above listed improvement the exchanges will be far but to do a good job as providers of financial services. There have been suggestions, 60th from Coimbatore Stock Exchange (CSX) and from the National Stock Exchange (NSE) to utilize the existing infrastructure of the CSX and the NSE to trade commodities. This would be a practical solution, given the following conditions are met:

The sizes of commodities being traded have to be substantially larger than what exists today (i.e. 0.7 percent of GDP) to justify a national exchange.

A lot of investment has to be made in understanding the systems, if not in building the systems from scratch.

There has to be an adoption of the infrastructure from the people who know and understand the commodities. There are a lot of features in trading that are particular to certain commodities and to have the need of correct human capital if the traded prices are conformant with prices on the underlying commodity.

COTTON FUTURES: TRADING AND DERIVATIVES MARKETS

India is the third largest producer and second largest consumer of cotton in the world (See Table 1). Cotton has a large share in the Indian agriculture output itself, accounting for about 2.5 percent of the agricultural crop output and more than Rs. 10,000 crore in absolute value. Cotton provides 7 million jobs in farms, at least a million jobs in mills and many more jobs in trade, ginning, power-looms, garment and other sectors.

Apart from being an important agricultural output, cotton plays an important role in industry and export itself as well cotton provides 68 percent of the raw material of the India textile industry (see Table 2).

Cotton's dominance in the Indian textile industry is much higher (with a share of 44.7 percent) compared to the share it has in the world fibre market. In absolute value, cotton consumption is still growing in India (See Table 3) and the trend is expected to continue because of growth of cotton textiles export. The working groups on textiles industry has estimated a growth of 4 percent in the consumption of cotton in Tenth Five Year Plan.

The textile industry is the largest exporter of goods in India and the export are growing at a rapid pace. Cotton based textiles account for 73 percent of all textile exports (See Table 4) cotton textile play an important share in exports from India. accounting for nearly 22 percent of the total (See Table 5). in the Tenth Five Year Plan, accelerated growth is projected for textiles exports more than doubling the present level of exports (See Table 6). It is expected that cotton based textiles will account for major share of this growth.

As mentioned earlier, Indian cotton plays an important role in the world cotton scene as well. Apart from being in the top three by world-wide production and consumption, India also have started integrating its cotton economy with that of the rest of the world. Cotton has been imported into India under Open General License (OGL) with zero import duty from 1994 on wards. Exports of cotton from India with a quantitative quota is now permitted while the exports of

TABLE 1

Estimated World Production and Consumption of Cotton (2001-02)

(In Million Kg.)

Country	*Production*	*Consumption*
China	4203	4600
U.S.A.	4124	2422
India	3000	2797
Pakistan	1615	1530
Others	6623	7845
Total	19565	19194

Source: Proceedings of the 56th Plenary Meeting of International Cotton Advisory Committee, 1997.

TABLE 2

Consumption of Raw Materials in the Indian Textile Industry

(In Million Kg.)

Raw Materials	*1999-2000*	*2000-01*	*2001-02*
Cotton	1960	2484	2438
Others	890	1020	1170
Total	2850	3204	3608
Cotton/Total (%)	69	68	68

Source: Indian Cotton Mills Federation Report, 2001-02.

TABLE 3

Cotton Consumption in India

Year	*In lakhs of Bales of 170 kg.*	*In Million kg.*
1996-97	119	2023
1997-98	135	2295
1998-99	122	2074
1999-2000	139	2363
2000-01	160	2720

Source: The Indian Cotton Mills Federation Report 2001-02.

TABLE 4

Sector-wise Exports of Textiles/Clothing

(Rs. Crores)

	1999-2000	*2000-01*	*2001-02*
Cotton	1960	2484	2438
Rayon/Synthetics	890	1020	1170
Woollen	2850	3204	3608
Non-Cotton Garments	69	68	68
Silk			
Total			

Source: Indian Cotton Mills Federation Report, 2001-02.

TABLE 5

Share of Exports of Cotton Textiles/Clothing in Total Exports of Goods

(In US $ Billions)

	Total Exports	*Exports of Cotton*	*% cotton to all commodities*
1998-1999	22.24	4.71	21.2
1999-2000	26.22	5.91	22.5
2000-01	31.80	6.26	19.7
2001-02	33.11	7.21	21.8

Source: Indian Cotton Mills Federation Report for (2001-02).

TABLE 6

Textile Exports in the Tenth Five Year Plan

(in Billion US $)

	Actual for 2000-01	*Projected Growth*	*Projections for (2006-07)*
Optimistic Scenario	10.7	16.6%	26.9
Pessimistic Scenario	10.7	11.2%	20.2

Source: Indian Cotton Mills Federation Report (2001-02).

cotton in the fibre state is small, 36 percent of the total production of cotton in India goes abroad, mostly in the form of yarn, cloth and garments (See Table 7).

Our garment industry was reserved for the SSI sector until 2001 knitting and knitwear industry is even now under SSI reservation. In knitting, wearing, processing and garmenting the decentralized nature of the industry and the small size of units have denied them scale economies, productivity and proper exploitation of technological advancements that have been taking place in the rest of the world. This has affected cost competitiveness in the international markets, both in fabrics and high volume clothing products. The importance of size in competitiveness is evident from the fact that as against 25 per cent share that we have in world trade for cotton yarn, our share in fabrics and clothing is around 3.44 per cent (See Table 8).

In 1999, Government established a Technology up gradation Fund Scheme (TUFS) for encouraging investments in benchmarked technology in the entire textile chain. In 2000, a Technology Mission on Cotton (TMC) was launched in order to improve production, productivity and quality of cotton. Investment of around Rs. 26,000 crore have taken place under TUFS so far, with a loan quotient of nearly Rs. 9500 crore. This has substantially improved the use of modern technology in the sector. Investment trends under the scheme show that process of rationalizing excise duty structure has substantially encouraged investments and with competition of the process, investments in recent year are likely to be more than double of last year (Table 9).

While welcoming and assisting the operating of TMC. Several industry organizations and individual mills have also been supplementing TMC through their own seed research and extension activities and efforts for establishing linkages with cotton farmers. As a result of all these efforts there have keen significant increase in production, productivity of cotton in recent years. While increased production has substantially bridged the gap between demand and supply of cotton and reduced cotton prices improvement in yield has provided reasonable profits to farmers (See Table 10).

As per the recently released Vision Statement of the

TABLE 7

Exports of Raw Cotton and Cotton Content in Exported Textile Products

(in Million Kg)

	Total Production	*,Raw Exports*	*Content of Textiles Exported*	*Total Exports*	*Exports/ production (%)*
1998-99	2066	66	663	729	35.3
1991-00	2355	18	774	792	33.6
2000-01	2720	136	842	978	36.0

Source: The Indian Cotton Mills Federation Report for (2001-02).

TABLE 8

Variety-wise Cotton Consumption by Textile Mills

No of Varieties	*1996-97*	*1997-98*	*1998-99*	*1999-00*	*2000-01*
Short Staple (Below 20 mm)	2	3.6	3.3	3.7	5.6
Medium Staple (20.5 mm to 25.5 mm)	24	48.4	44.7	42.1	37.8
Medium Long Staple (26.0 mm to 27.5 mm)	4	15.3	16.4	20.5	19.7
Long Staple (28.0 mm to 33.5 mm)	7	24.6	27.3	26.8	30.7
Extra Long Staple (34.0 mm and above)	4	15.3	16.4	20.5	19.7
Total	43	100.0	100.0	100.0	100.0

Source: Indian Cotton Mills Federation Report (2001-02).

TABLE 9

Export of Cotton Yarn—Count Group-wise

	2001	*10 months of 2002*
Total (Rs. Crores)	4772	5093
Share of Count Groups (%)		
1s to 40s	80.6	83.0
41s to 60s	9.5	9.0
61s to above	9.9	8.0

Source: Cotton Textiles Production Council, Mumbai.

TABLE 10

Installed Spinning Capacity and Production of Cotton: The Share of Leading States

	Installed/spinning Capacity (Millions of Spindles)	*Production in (1999-2000) (Millions Kg.)*
All India	32.9	2059
	Shares of the States (%)	
Tamil Nadu	34.2	4.9
Maharashtra	16.0	19.5
Gujarat	13.0	18.7
Andhra Pradesh	5.8	12.5
Karnataka	3.8	7.8
Madhya Prakesh	3.6	3.0
Rajasthan	3.4	7.2
Punjab	2.7	14.7
Haryana	1.5	11.3
Others	16.0	0.4
Total	100.0	100.

Source: Office of the Textile Commissioner.

TABLE 11

Growth of Exports of Cotton Yarn

Year	*Value (Rs. Crores)*	*Quantity (Million kg.)*	*Yarn Exports as % of yarn Production*
2000	3110	242	14.1
2001	4772	405	20.7
2002 (1st 10 months)	5093	436	22.0

Source: Cotton Textile Export Production Council, Mumbai.
*Estimated

TABLE 12

Membership Pattern of South India Cotton Association as on 30th June, (2001)

Mills	158
Traders	347
Brokers	42
Grower	1
Total	548

Source: South India Cotton Association, Coimbatore.

Indian Cotton Mills Federation for the Textile industry, the size of the Textile and Clothing (T&C) sector can grow from the current US $ 12 billion to US $ 85 billion and exports can growth from the current US$12 billion US$ 40 billion by 2010. This will generate 12 million additional jobs. Realizing this potential would entail from industry. The total addition investments required for modernizing the production facilities in all the segments of the industry has been estimated in the Vision Statement at Rs. 140,000 crore, of which Rs. 50,000 crore will be required in the processing sector alone.

The world consumption pattern of fibres shows that manmade fibre/filaments account for nearly 60 per cent and cotton for less than 39 per cent. In India the pattern is the reverse. Both in the domestic and international markets, there is substantial scope for our textile industry to diversify in to manmade fibre products. Rationalizing excise and customer duty for fibres and their intermediaries is an essential requirement for realizing this potential.

The Indian textile exports are expected to receive a big push once the trade quotas are dismantled. Top textile importing countries like USA and the EU are looking towards India for meeting their requirements. India, according to several recent studies is going to emerge as alternative source of supply to China. India's growth in exports will be driven by value added made ups and apparel as India has competitive advantages over its competitors in relation to: (i) availability of relatively inexpensive and skilled workforce,

(ii) design expertise, (iii) large production of basic raw materials like home grown cotton, yarn and fabrics, and (iv) availability of wide range of textile.

According to a recent study of CRISIL (Commissioned by ICMF) the Indian textiles and apparel industry can achieve a potential size of US $85 billion by 2010 of which, the domestic market potential would be US $ 45 billion and export potential would be US $ 40 billion. Nearly 60 percent of exports would comprise garments. This would create 12 million job opportunities, 5 million direct jobs in textile industry and 7 billion jobs in allied sectors.

Thus, cotton production and export has a large impact on the Indian economy. Therefore, there is need to hedge against fluctuations in production and price to mitigate the impact on economic performance and paved the way to increase to derivatives trading of cotton.

Cotton is a seasonal crop, so that cotton prices show great changes within a crop season. Monthly prices within a crop season have shown fluctuations between 7.5% in the last decade. One reason for this large variation is the crop output itself, with a variation of as much as 14% from year to the next. Added to this is inadequate information regarding output which causes panic buying or selling. Withholding stocks to manipulate prices is also not unknown. The resultant volatility is a strong justification for introducing cotton futures.

Recognising the importance of cotton in the economy, the Government of India is actively considering launching a Technology Mission on Cotton to improve the quality and quantity of cotton production in India to benefit the growers, and users of cotton. A part of the strategy to improve the cotton economy is the introduction of futures trading in cotton. GOI expects that cotton futures will assist in better price discovery, better hedging and smoother marketing operations. A number of agriculture economists have been urging the GOI to permit cotton futures for many years. In 1996, a team from World Bank and United Nations Conference on Trade and Development (UNCTAD) suggested that cotton futures be introduced for managing price risks in cotton.

HEDGING FOR FARMERS

How cotton futures can help cotton growers has been articulated often. Indeed, the ability to hedge price risk would be an additional motivation for farmers to take up cotton cultivation, with greater security of their income. Organised trading of cotton futures would bring about a transparency in the prices, to the advantage of growers. It is also expected that traders would reduce margins and pay a better price to the farmers, as they too will be able to hedge price risk on the stocks they hold.

HEDGING FOR MANUFACTURERS AND EXPORTERS

A part from helping the agricultural community, cotton futures have a big role to play in the exports of cotton textiles. We have seen the growing importance of cotton in industry and in export. Cotton futures can help producers and exporters of cotton textiles to manage the price risk associated with their purchases and inventories of cotton and cotton based products. It is expected that cotton futures would be welcome and immediately used by these cotton users, other than the cotton growers and ginners.

How would a futures contract be useful to a manufacturer/exporter of cotton textiles? Usually, most cotton textiles exports are done using forward contracts, which commit a producer in India to sell to a foreign buyer at futures dates at stated prices. The duration of the contracts could be six moths or even more. The duration of the contracts could be six months or even more. The buyers finalise their orders on the mills/exporters after the prices for a new cotton crop are known. Thereafter, the buyers place orders on firm prices, but deliveries are scheduled over a period of several months. Thus, the mills face a situation where its selling price is fixed and its raw material prices are variable, over the contract for purchase of cotton, so as to lock in the raw material prices.

Another example of hedging would be the mills, which have, brought a large stock at the cotton year. As soon as they acquire stocks, the mills can enter into future contracts to protect against loss of value of their inventory.

DESIGN OF FUTURES CONTRACT

In the earlier section, the issues of clearing and settlement assumed a given contract with defined quality and grades of cotton that could be delivered. The definition of the contracts are very important, because the use of the futures contract for hedging purposes and therefore, the king of trading it will attract, depend upon the contract definition. Some issues of contract definition are: (a) the grade of cotton that is to be delivered, (b) size of contract, and (c) the time to expiration of the contracts.

GRADES OF THE UNDERLYING

The grade of the underlying depend upon the varieties of cotton that are produced and their pattern of production and usage. India produces and consumes a large variety of cotton, covering the entire spectrum of staple. The data on the various ranges of staple length, the number of varieties in each range and the percentage of consumption in each range is given in Table 8.

The output and grade of the different varieties would depend on the weather conditions prevailing in the part of the country where it is grown. Consequently, the price of a variety depends on the output of that variety, which may not be synchronous with the prices of other cottons within a season. Even the prices of cotton varieties in the same staple length range may show a weak relationship. This would pose difficulties in the design of contracts.

Too many types of contracts, designed to reflect the price variations indifferent varieties, will result in liquidity for all of them. Too few may pose problems in delivery, and their effectiveness in providing a good hedging facility against price risk. Initially, one or two contracts may be introduced for the most popular varieties, as learning ground for contract definition. Subsequently, additional contracts will have to be introduced based on experience and need.

The first contract can be for cottons suitable for spinning yarns meant for export. This could be an easier task since bulks of the exports are in the (limited) count 0 to 40's. (see the Table 9)

SIZE OF THE CONTRACT

New York Cotton Exchange uses a defined size of 50,000 lbs (22,727 kg.), or approximately 133 Indian bales. Such a large sized contract in India, would deter individual speculators and liquidity will be limited. A smaller size of contract, say 8500 kg. (50 bales) would be more appropriate.

USERS OF COTTON FUTURES

Initially, when the markets have just begun, there is going to be a mismatch in the skill set available with the people who would find futures useful, compared to what they need to trade in the markets. This calls for a strong efforts on the part of the exchange to market the contracts. The marketing effort must aim at attracting both hedgers and speculators to the exchange. Without either in large numbers, an exchange will not be able to attract the king of liquidity that would make futures markets useful.

The marketing effort also must aim at removing the prejudice against speculation, based on socialist and/or moral ground. There is an apprehension that futures would result in lower prices to growers and higher prices to consumers. This has to be overcome.

SPECULATORS AND COMMODITY FUNDS

A futures exchange needs speculators who became counter parties to the hedgers. The extent to which speculators understand and appreciate commodity futures would depend on proper marketing being done. However, individual speculators alone cannot give sufficient liquidity to the futures. This market would benefit from having commodity funds, similar to mutual funds for financial securities. They have to be organised for increasing the liquidity of the futures contracts. Commodity funds have been profitable abroad, where many fund managers will find that commodities are more liquid than financial assets. There is no reason why they cannot be profitable in India.

One way to encourage speculators to enter futures trading would be to revoke Section 73, read with Section 46(5) of the Income Tax Act, 1961, which deals with the treatment of losses incurred in speculation. It prohibits the setting-off speculative losses against other income. This section must be suitably amended to remove this restriction for all these who participate in futures trading.

GEOGRAPHIC CENTERS OF COTTON USAGE

The Kabra Committee on Forward Markets constituted by the Ministry of Civil Supplies, Consumer Affairs and Public Distribution, Government of India in its report of September, 1994 had rightly recommended that "the futures trading may be introduced in Cotton and Kapas in the various producing and consuming centres where a functioning of a competitive market is possible..."

The Government has already permitted setting up a futures exchange at Mumbai. In so far as the location of the exchange can have a vital influence on its success, an exchange for cotton futures should be set-up at Coimbatore, which is the leading consuming centre of cotton.

The state-wise consumption of cotton can be estimated by the number of spindles installed in various states. Such an estimate is presented in Table 10.

For a comparison, the state-wise production of cotton is also given in the same table. Tamil Nadu accounts for more than one third of all the spinning capacity installed in India. Coimbatore, the centre of textile activity in Tamil Nadu, is the ideal place for an exchange.

Coimbatore is also a centre for export of cotton yarn. Cotton yarn exports are growing at a phenomenal rates, leading the entire exports of cotton textiles. The growth of cotton yarn exports are given in Table 11. As can be seen, 22% of all cotton yarn produced is now exported.

The producers and exporters of cotton yarn would be a large potential group of users of cotton futures. As a discussed earlier, this sector of cotton economy needs to hedge its requirement of cotton. This sector is familiar with the advantage of hedging and its will be an immediate user of the futures and would popularize it quickly. Therefore, an exchange at Coimbatore would be viable. The Coimbatore-based South India Cotton Association has members from all the major sections of cotton economy (Table 12) and can become an active market soon.

The volumes in the exchange are bound to be low initially. For a frame of reference, the New York Cotton Exchange had reported maximum volumes in India may take a long time. However, the exchange cannot remain viable with only one or two contracts. One way of increasing the viability of a new exchange is for the exchange to exploit the economies of scale that can come of using the infrastructure to trade several commodities. The physical infrastructure required to trade futures contracts, whether they are on cotton, gold, or sugar, is the same, irrespective of the underlying. Trading in other futures must be explored to spread the infrastructure costs on a wider volume of business. Apart from futures in cotton, the exchange may also trade in related products. Cotton yarn, kapas (seed cotton) and cottonseed oil are some of the possibilities.

The availability of a large body of information at the exchange should help the trader to develop expertise in these areas as well. Cotton yarn futures are actively traded in Tokyo, Osaka and Nagoya exchanges in Japan. Spinning mills, who produce the yarn, and fabric producers should find the cotton yarn futures attractive. Many of the issues which confront the design of cotton futures would also be present in the design of cotton yarn futures, but in a smaller measure

Along with different underlyings, the exchange can also allow for trading other types of derivatives. Options in cotton should be introduced as early as possible.

THE ROLE FOR THE REGULATOR

The goal of the Forward Markets Commission (FMC) should be to make a success of futures trading as early as possible in view of the enormous benefit it will bring to the

Cotton economy. A development approach is called for. The existing exchanges may not be able to assemble the expertise and resources for an early start of trading. FMC should help the exchange in these area.

FMC should help the exchanges in various matters relating to supervision, registration to traders, prevention and punishment of bad trading practices, registration and supervision of service providers like warehouses and assessers, coordination between exchanges, training exchange administrators and promoting legislations and institutions for the benefit of the futures trading.

FMC should encourage innovation by the exchanges including the introduction of new contracts for cotton and also related products.

CONCLUSION

1. Cotton is a very important agricultural crop, industrial raw material, and export input in the India economy.
2. Cotton futures would benefit the cotton economy by increasing the efficiency of price disovery by allowing for rapid dissemination of infomation on production and consumption into cottonprices, in addition to enabling the reduction of prce risk.
3. Cotton growers and users would benfit from futures trading on cotton.
4. Private initiative by the cotton economy an setup cotton futures. However, a pro-active Goernment can hasten things.
5. There is much knowledge and experiencethat can be transferred from the Indian securities ndustry to the cotton futures exchange. This transfer should enable cotton futures exchanges t evolve quickly to the level of sophistication and eficiency of such exchanges abroad, or even better.
6. A great deal of institution buildings awits the cotton futures market, like clearing corpration and methods for supervising trader and protecting the investors.

7. Multiple exchanges for cotton futures may be permitted and the cotton exchange should be given freedom to choose to deal in the related products.
8. A dynamic outlook should be adopted by the regulatory authorities to make cotton futures a success.

References

Agrawal, V.K., 2002, Derivatives: An Economic Perspective, *Indian Journal Commerce*, Vol. 16, No. 4, Jan.-March 2001, pp. 19-25.

Patil, R.H., 2003, Building a Derivative Market, Invest-India, Tata McGraw-Hill Service, pp. 72-82.

Gupta, Nitin and Jatna, Renu, 2002, Exchange Traded Funds: A Blend of Stock and Commodities Market.

Gupta, Amit, 2002, Interest, Risk Management: Invest-India, Tata McGraw-Hills Service, New Delhi.

Marithasan, Joseph, 2002, The Use and Abuse of Derivatives: Lessons for India, Tata McGraw-Hill Publishing Company Ltd., New Delhi.

Veena, 2005, India—A Player or A Winner, *Yojana*, Vol. 49, Feb.-March, pp. 12-18.

Business India, Feb. 2006.

Business line, 16.9.2003.

21

Land Reform Policy in Bihar: An Overview

TARIQUE A. SULTAN AND ARVIND KUMAR

Productivity in agriculture is mainly dependent on two sets of factors—technological and institutional. Among the technological factorsare the use of agricultural inputs and methods such as improved seeds, fertilisers, improved ploughs, tractors, harvesters, irrigation, etc. which helps to raise productivity. The institutional reforms include the redistribution of land ownership in favour of the cultivating classes so as to provide them a sense of participation in rural life, improving the size of farms, providing the security of tenure, regulation of rents, etc. It was thought that the institutional factors such as the existence of feudal relations, small and fragmented holdings, insecurity of tenancy rights, high rents, etc. act as disincentive to the peasantry to raise production. Thus with the coming of the independence, considerable emphasis was given to land reforms to reorganize the agrarian structure in order to achieve lasting improvement in agriculture.

The paper presents a brief overview of land reform policies in Bihar since independence.

ZAMINDARI ABOLITION

The Bihar Land Reforms Act, 1950 popularly called Zamindari Abolition Act, abolished the intermediary tenures. It did not, however, bring under raiyats the actual cultivators of land in contact with the state. The Zamindaris were abolished in three phases, the last one from 1.4.56. This state was charactrised by absentee landlordism. The Zamindari abolition Act allowed the exlandlords to retain land in their khas 'possession'. This meant that they were allowed to retain their homestead and private lands often by ejecting the tenants at will on these lands. The blanket provision was also not in consonance with the national guidelines which indicated that zamindar should be allowed to resume land upto three times the economic holding.

LAWS RELATING TO CEILING

Legislation for imposing ceiling on agricultural land was not simultaneously enacted. The bill proposing to impose ceiling on surplus land was introduced in Bihar Legislature in 1955. The bill was referred to a select committee of both the houses and their recommendations were received in 1957. The bill was then referred to Bihar Land Commission, set-up under section 34 of the Zamindary Abolition Act to advise the state Government on agrarian matter. The bill finally passed by the legislature in 1959 received President's assent in 1962. The intervening period was sufficient for intelligent landholders to transfer land during the intervening period.

The Act of 1961 imposed ceiling taking individual as a unit. It suggested a ceiling of 20, 30, 40, 50 and 60 acres of land on each individual. It also allowed exemptions to education, health, trust of other charitable institutions, public or private, plantations, etc. not much could have been expected out of this legislation. The later half of seventies also saw land grab movements launched by the left parties to focus attention. There was subsequently a Chief Minister's conference on land reforms. There was also the task force on land reforms. The ceiling Act was accordingly amended in 1973 with retrospective effect to give it bites. Some more time became available for transfer of land. It may incidentally be noted that the power to take cognizance was transferred from executive to judiciary with effect from 1.4.73. A brief discussion about the various amending acts and their salient provisions is being made in the succeeding paragraphs:

(a) Act 1 of 1973 introduced the definition of family. The due date was, however, not defined. It also introduced ceiling and classified the land into five categories. It also made a provision giving the collector the power to make enquiries in respect of transfers made after 22.10.59 and to annul such transfers. It also had a provision as to how the surplus lands should be settled. It also provided that land held by certain educational institutions, Universities, Research Council, hospitals, orphanages, public or charitable bodies or religious bodies of public nature is exempted till they were held as such. The sugar factories were allowed to hold sugarcane farm upto 100 acres. A unit could be held by religious institutions of public nature of performing religious functions.
(b) The amending Act 9 of 1973 introduced one more classification bringing total categories to six a classification, which is valid even till date. The new classification introduced was in respect of land irrigated or capable of being irrigated by works which provide or are capable of providing water for one season. This amendment also fixed the payable rates of compensation.
(c) The Bihar Act 12 to 1976 introduced a provision relation to voluntary surrender of surplus land. This pored a short-cut method for acquiring surplus land. This section was used to request the landholder to surrender their surplus land. It has been found that on account of improper verification lands, which were actually not in possession of the landholder, was also surrendered and accepted. This is one of the factors for the gap in distribution.

(d) Bihar Act 22 to 1976 clarified for the first time that the due date for determining majority shall be 9.9.70. Section 4 was also amended to make it clear that ceiling area has to be computed on 9.9.70. This had become necessary as a High Court judgment had held that the due date could not be a date earlier than the date of issue of notice asking the landholder to submit their returns. Another provision of this Act made it expressly clear that the proceeding decided under the 1962 Act shall be reopened. Certain provisions regarding tenancy were introduced to who could lease land and limit on rent. It also provided for Commissioner was taken away and vested in the Board of revenue. Two new sections 45A and 45B were also added. Section 45A gave the State Government the authority to give general or special directions. Section 45B empowered the State Government to call for and examine record and issue suitable directions.

(e) The amending Ordinance 219 of 1976 amended section 15(3) taking away the right of parties other than the landholder to file objection. It also contained provisions conferring the status of occupancy raiyat in the under-raiyat on such surplus land. These provisions were kept alive by successive Ordinance till the enactment in 1978. This enactment further provided a legislative basis to prevent abetment and to restore possession to allotters of surplus land.

A comprehensive amendment was made to the ceiling Act vide: Ordinance 66 of 1981 which was finally promulgated as Act 55 of 1982. The more important provisions of this amending Act as follows:

(a) The landholder had to necessarily retain land transferred in contravention of the Act, i.e. lands transferred after 9.9.70 without permission and lands transferred between 22.10.59 and 9.9.70, the transfers having been annulled.

(b) The collector was given the authority to examine transfers made after 22.10.59 by registered documents or otherwise not with standing anything to the contrary contained in any judgement, degree or order of any Court.

(c) The ceiling area shall be predetermined when the classification of land changes as a result of investment made in irrigation projects by the state Government.

(d) The most far reaching amendment was that the orders under section 5(1x3) regarding the transfer of land state even during the pungency of the appeal.

(e) Such of the surplus land in respect of which there was no claim or dispute could be acquired by the state even during the pendency of the appeal.

(f) All appeal, review, revisions, reference were to have abated and all proceedings in which lands have not been required shall be deemed to have begun afresh.

(g) A provision for substitution of legal heir was made.

There were obvious reasons for making many of these amendments. The death of a landholder was indirectly benefiting the family members as brothers one sisters do not come in the same family. It was but natural to ask landholder to retain land transferred in contravention of land. If a transferee, and there are a large number of transfers in each ceiling case, went up in appeal/revision after orders u/s 5(1) (3) the main proceedings were installed. The provisions relating to abatement, however, come for a fair deal of criticism. The rules were framed after quite some time and for want of modified forms the work could take-off after a lapse of time.

An up-to-date land record is an essential prerequisite for implementation of land reforms measures there is no legal or administrative practice for annual updating of land records. The State Government had enacted the maintenance of Land records Act, 1973 to provide a legal basis for updating of land records. This act has been notified for implementation in only 9 out of 587 Anchals of the state but does not appear to have been fully implemented. When the Janta Dal. Government led by Shri Karpoori Thakur came to power in 1977-78 the State Government had launched a project called Kosi Kranti. The basic philosophy of this progarmme was to first update the land records, including recording of the rights of share croppers under this act and only then implement the rural development programmes.

As has been indicated in the preceeding paragraphs a lot of time elapsed befor any leeth was put into the Ceiling Act. The landholders were able to make a lot of transfers including those permitled by law. The legal position as it obtained was that revenue officials are entitle to look into benami and farzi transfers made after 22.10.59 with a view to defeat the provisions of the Ceiling Act. The Patna High Court in one of the judgements has held that if a document created before 22.10.59 has not been acted upon the nevenue officials can look into these for determining the surplus land held by the landholder. The onus of proof initially is, however, on the State in such cases. The improper verifications created lot of problems. Earlier there was a provision under the Land Ceiling Act to issue notices and invite objections u/s 15(3). This section was deleted in 1976. After that till 1981 persons other than landholders were coming under various sections. Finally, after 1981 they have to file objections along with landholder.

The scheme of things under the pre-1981 situation envisaged that these cases of benami and farzi transactions are finally disposed-off before the main case can be taken up for hearing. This meant that even if a single transferee contested the case in appeal/revision or filed a writ petition in High Court the original case could not be heard u/s 10(2) of the land Ceiling Act. The same was actually the situation in case of majority of landholders. Similarly in case of trusts the question of exemption had to be first decided at the State level before the actual proceeding.

The distribution of surplus land also pose interesting problems. The act provides and rightly so that under tenants on the land should have the first right of settlement. There was an amendment to the Bihar Land Reforms Act set-up Land Reforms Tribunals. The Patna high Court has struck down the provision as unconstitutional not with standing the provisions of Article 323B of the constitution. The same is under appeal in Supreme/Court.

TENANCY REFORM

The Sen Committee on productivity of rice in Eastern India has identified tenancy reforms as one of the major constraints. Dr. C.H. Hanumanth Rao, the then member of Planning Commission, has mentioned that concealed tenancies to the extent of 50 to 60 is a reason for lack of investment. Sharecroppers, i.e. undertenants who share crops with tenants, are generally referred to as Bataidars in Bihar. Apart from the skewed landholding absentee landlordism and concealed tenancies are features of the Bihar land structure. Ladensky in his work Land Reforms—An unfinished Business refers to this question and has expressed the view that though tenancy reforms are more important the demand to implement the ceiling law is likely to be more pronounced.

Bihar achieved some sort of national fame in 1964 when instructions were issued to record sharecroppers during the course of settlement operations. Apart from the settlement operations and the provisions of Maintenance of land Records Act, 1973, the tenancies can be registered in accordance with section 48E of the B.T. Act. Though the Proceedings under section 48E of the B.T. Act care not kept in abeyance as per section 4C of the consolidation act, the Consolidation Act does not provide a forum for adjudicating such claims.

The scheme under the B.T. Act is that the bonafidse dispute has to be referred to a Board having panches of both the sides. The Patna High Court's decision implied that the dispute cannot be referred to the Board straightway. This is not with standing the fact that complaints are examined with the point of view of complainant, and injunctions are granted in civil matters. The other difficulty was transfer of land by landholder during the pendency of conciliation. The scheme of B.T. Act as it existed bill 1986 presumed that only landholders shall have a cause of disagreement and hence no appeal was provided against the order passed by LRDC rejecting the claim of Bataidar.

The National Development Council had recommended as early as in 1986 that all States should enact legislations conferring ownership rights on tenants. The second plan had recommended that personal cultivation should be precisely defined. Personal cultivation should have three elements—the risk of cultivation, personal supervision and personal labour. The tenant should bear the entire risk of cultivation and supervision should be by self or by his own family members. For effective supervision the owner or his own family member should reside in the village for greater part of agricultural season. The Revenue Minister's conference in 1985 also reiterated this position.

The Bihar Tenancy (Amendment) Act, 1986 provides a definition of personal cultivation. This has been defined as cultivation by one's labour, or his family's labour or by hired labour or by servants on wage payment in cash or in kind, but not in crop share under personal supervision of oneself or members of the family. The act also provides for acquisition of occupancy rights by under-raiyats but the amount paid has not been mentioned. The problem relating to transfer of land during the pendency of case and filing of appeal has been taken care of.

There is a need to study the West Bengal land Reforms (Amendement) Act, 1977 which raises a presumption in favour of sharecroppers and to implement the same after proper modifications, if necessary. The tasks force on land reforms in 1975 had expressed itself in favour of a law that persons not participating personally in operations should be allowed to hold land. The landholders in Bihar could be given an opportunity to start personal cultivation failing which the land may be resumed and settled either with the undertenants or with the landless persons. It is felt that effective implementation of tenancy reforms would go a long way in helping implementation of tenancy legislation also.

22

Agrigarian Crises in Bihar

VIJAY KUMAR YADAV

Bihar is an predominately an agricultural state but presently the state is facing many types of agricultural crises. Although agriculture is the backbone of Indian economic system. The importance of agriculture in the economic life of India of India can hardly be exaggerated. Infact, the prosperity of agriculture is synonymous with the prosperity of India. Being the largest sector in the country agriculture provides employment to around 57 per cent of total workforce in the country. Table 1 shows that (Insert Table 1) Data provided by the census of India reveals that in absolute terms, agriculture provided employment to 97 million person in 1951, the number of people working on land (Cultivation and agricultural labourers) increased to 235 million in 2001. In terms of percentage, however, people working an come down from 70 to 59 (57% according to Tenth Plan) during the five decades between 1951 to 2001.

Nearly one-fifth (24% of total national income) comes from agriculture even after 55 years of economics planning Indian agriculture has been the source of supply of raw material to our leading industries. Cotton and Jute textile industries, Sugar, Vanaspati and plantations all these depend on agriculture directly, agriculture also plays a great role.

TABLE 1

Employment of Main Workers in Agriculture

(In million)

	1951	*2001*
Total population	36.1	102.7
Rural population	289 (8.3)	142 (72)*
Cultivators	70 (50)	128 (32)
Agricultural labourers	27 (20)	107 (27)
Other workers	43 (30)	167 (41)
Total working population	40 (100)	402 (100)

In the field of international trade broadly speaking the proportion of agricultural goods which were exported, came to 50 percentages of our exports and manufactures with agricultural contents (such goods as manufacture Jute, Cloth and Sugar) contribute about 20 per cent or 50 and the total comes to 70 per cent of India's export. Bihar's principal crops are rice, paddy, wheat, Jute, maize and oil seeds. Cauliflowers, cabbage vegetables are grown in the state. Sugarcane, potato and barely are some of the non-cereal crops grown. Presently productivity of agriculture of Bihar is very low than other states. The average national productivity and the position of Bihar among the other states is shown in Table 2.

TABLE 2

Opportunities and Challenges

Crop	*National Best*	*Productivity in Bihar (Qtls./hect.)*	*Yield gap (Qtls./hect.)*
Rice	35.28 (Punjab)	14.93	20.35
Wheat	43.66 (Punjab)	21.05	22.61
Maize	31.15 (AP)	22.46	8.69
Sugarcane	1016.20 (TN)	245.93	770.27
Potato	261.00 (WB)	102.00	159.00
Banana	657 (Maharashtra)	200	457

Productivity in agriculture is mainly dependent on sets of factor: Technological and Institutional. Among the technical factors are the use of agricultural inputs and methods such as improved seeds, fertilizers harvesters, irrigation, etc. which help to raise productivity, even if no land reforms are introduced. The institutional reforms include the redistribution of land ownership in favour of the cultivating classes so as to provide them a sense of participation in rural life, improving the size of farms, providing the security of tenure, regulation of rent, etc. In other words the institutional factors, such as the existence of feudal relations, small size of farms, sub-division and fragmentations, insecurity of tenancy rights, high rents, etc...., act as disincentives to the peasantry to rise to production. Table 3 shows the productivity in Bihar is low. The agriculture productivity in Bihar is low because of technical and institutional factors.

TABLE 3

Land-use Profile

Category	*Area in lakh hect.*
Geographical Area	93.60
Net area sown	56.38
Area sown more than once	23.58
Gross Cropped Area	80.26
Forest	6.16
Other fallow (2 to 5 years)	1.41
Current fallow	5.95

Another factor that mainly affects the productivity in Bihar is poor facility of irrigations. Nearly one-third of the total sown areas have the benefit of assured irrigation, the rest has to depend on the vagaries of the monsoon. It is also well known that even when irrigation facilities are available, they are not fully utilized. Table 4 shows that average ground water exploitation in the state is 39 per cent, leaving a very large potential gap. The ultimate irrigation potential has assessed at 106 lakh hectares which far exceeds the gross sown area of 80 lakh hectares which is shown in Table 2 are sown area of 56 lakh hectares.

TABLE 4

Irrigation Profile

Source	*Net Irrigated area (Lakh Ha.)*
Canal	9.65
Pond	1.12
Tube well	22.38
Well	0.14
Other	1.33
Total	34.62

Another factor that mostly affected the productivity of agriculture is low level of fertilizer uses in Bihar. Although the per hectare consumption of fertilizers increased from 22 kgs in the early eighties to the level of 98 kg/hectare in 2003-04. The Table 5 indicates that the fertilizer consumption is much less than Punjab, Haryana, A.P. and U.P. Power generation and availability rate are the lowest in Bihar in the country compared to an all India average annual electricity consumption level of 334 kWh and 895 kWh of Punjab, the average per capita consumption of electricity in Bihar was only 55 kWh.

TABLE 5

Low Level of Fertilizer Use

State	*Fertilizer Consumption Kg./Hect. (2003-04)*
Punjab	173.38
Haryana	155.68
Andhra Pradesh	143.47
Uttar Pradesh	130.44
Bihar	98.39

An important factor that plays a vital role in the incensement of agricultural productivity is mechanization of farm. Even after the beginning of 58 year's of planning the Bihar has failed to mechanize its agriculture. In 2003-04 the availability of tractor per 1000 hectors in Punjab is 58 which is much more than the availability thousand per hectors 17 of Bihar.

Floods, water loggings and droughts affected the productivity and yield of crops every year in Bihar. Almost 41 per cent of the geographical area of the state is flood prone. On the other hand 40 per cent of the geographical area of the south Bihar is drought prone.

9.41 lakh hectors of land in Bihar are waterlogged of which around 7 lakh hectors can be drained after executive drainage works.

The institutional factor that lowers the production of agriculture in Bihar are landholding, land records and tenancy rights. The process of obtaining records of ownership right of land in cumbersome process and is reported to involve very high transaction costs. Unrecorded oral tenancy in Bihar overwhelming consists of leasing in by small and marginal farmers. The computerization of land records, protection of tenancy and fixation of rent are of prime importance for development of agriculture sector in Bihar. Table 6 indicates that landholdings in Bihar are predominantly marginal farms with a high level of fragmentation.

TABLE 6

Landholding Pattern: No. of Holdings

Category of farmers	*No. of Holdings (Lakh)*
Marginal (0-1 Ha.)	86.45 (82.9%)
Small (1-2 Ha.)	10.05 (9.6%)
Medium (2-10 Ha.)	7.68 (7.4%)
Large (10- above Ha.)	0.11 (0.1%)
Total (100%)	1,04.32

Indicates that landholding in Bihar ar predominantly marginal farms with a high level of fragmentation.

In this way technological and institutional factors like input crisis low level of fertilizer use, Low level of fertilizer use, low level of farm mechanization, low crop productivity, lack of irrigation facility, inequality landholding pattern, weak agricultural extension and research system, these are some issues behind low productivity of agriculture in Bihar.

The Prime Minister Dr. Man Mohan Singh on Oct. 16 2006 called for improving agricultural practices to effectively deal with agrigarian crises in many states like Bihar, Jharkhand, Orissa and Eastern States of the country. The Government of Bihar is also making strategies for facing the agrigarian crises by input management, strengthening of qualities control system, agriculture research transfer of technology system, Increasing in electricity production, shift in cropping pattern, improving agricultural marketing system, by providing financial facilities and lessening of natural calamities.

References

Economics Survey, 2003-04, p. 153, Govt. of India, New Delhi.

Directorate Statics and Evaluation, 2003-04, Govt. of Bihar, Patna.

NSSO, 59th round, 2003.

Dutta, Rudra and Sundram, p. 486, 2005.

Dewett, K.K., p. 680, 2006.

An approach to the 11th Five Year Plan p. 82, Govt. of India, New Delhi.

23

Winter Maize Revolution in Bihar: A Techno-Economic Appraisal

VINOD KUMAR, A.K. JHA, A.K. CHOUDHARY AND R.K.P. SINGH

INTRODUCTION

Despite the sluggish growth in Bihar agriculture, principal crops namely; Rice, Wheat and Winter Maize recorded annual production growth rates of 1.7 per cent, 4.2 per cent and 8.3 per cent respectively during 1981-2000. The slow growth in Rice production attributed to various technological reasons; the future of cereal production lies on two crops that are; Wheat and Winter Maize in Bihar. Wheat is also experiencing stagnation in area and productivity for the last 10 years, hence Winter Maize is considered most dependable crop for improving economic status of farm families at one hand and sustainable food security of poor households at another in Bihar. In Bihar, Maize is grown round the year which generates employment in even slack agricultural season, maintains continuous income flow and ensures regular food supply. Winter Maize is of recent origin of early sixties. The crop is grown only under irrigated condition. The duration of the crop is 160-165 days. The incidence of diseases and pests in this crop is very low. It is also worth-mentioning that the adoption of Winter Maize technology is not based to size of landholding, level of resources, cast and education level of farmers. It is adopted by all categories of farmers irrespective class, caste and social status.

RESEARCH EFFORTS

In Bihar also, attempts were made to grow Maize hybrids namely; Texis-26, Taxas-32 and Dixie-II of the hybrids of USA gave expected higher yields and crops did not perform well during Kharif season. Then State Government entrusted Dr. Rameshwar Singh, the then Maize and Millet specialist at Dholi-Pusa Centre (Bihar) with task of detailed check-up of crops grown, during kharif season and directed him to submit a report indicating reasons for poor performance of Maize hybrids of USA. After investigation, it was found that besides other small managerial factors the crop had greatly suffered due to heavy rainfall which is of usual occurrence in this season. Hence, it was decided to grow these Maize hybrids during Rabi (Winter) Season with the hope that these varieties may perform better in the milder winter condition of Bihar. Maize hybrids from the USA were grown in Rabi Season at Dholi-Pusa research centre which grew very well in winter season and produced disease free crops. In Bihar, an intensive Maize research with All India Co-ordinated Scheme was started in 1957 (RAU, 1987).

The important varieties developed for cultivation in Rabi Season are Hi-strarch, Deccan, Laxami, Hemant, Deoki, Rajendra Hybrid Makka-I, Rajendra Hybrid Makka-II, Saktiman-I, Saktiman-2 and Saktiman-3. The centre is also engaged in developing and standardizing varieties and packages of practices of intercrop of rabi maize and Potato since more than 20 per cent area under rabi maize is under maize + Potato inter-cropping system, particularly in Begusarai, Samastipur and Khagaria districts. Rajendra Private Seed companies namely; Pioneer, Pro-agro, Cargill, etc. have made significant dent in maize seed market of Bihar. Keeping in view the increasing importance of Winter

TABLE I

Zone-wise Production of Winter Maize in Bihar

(In lakh tonnes)

Year	Zone-I	Zone-II	Zone-IIIA	Zone-IIIB	Bihar
1980-81	1.52	0.29	0.09	0.07	1.97
	(77.16)	(14.72)	(4.57)	(3.55)	(100.00)
1985-86	1.75	0.28	0.30	0.10	2.48
	(72.02)	(11.52)	(12.36)	(4.11)	(100.00)
1990-91	3.36	0.60	0.68	0.09	4.73
	(71.04)	(12.68)	(14.38)	(1.90)	(100.00)
1995-96	2.66	2.05	1.03	0.08	5.82
	(45.70)	(35.22)	(17.70)	(1.38)	(100.00)
2000-01	2.86	2.20	1.11	0.09	6.26
	(45.69)	(35.14)	(17.73)	(1.44)	(100.00)
2003-04	2.53	2.51	0.71	0.25	6.00
	(42.17)	(41.83)	(11.83)	(4.17)	(100.00)

Note: Figures in parentheses indicate percentage to respective totals.

Maize, the Indian Council of Agricultural Research has also established a centre at Begusarai for conducting research on Maize. It is a common knowledge that the Maize is grown round the year in all the three crop seasons (Kharif, Rabi and Garma) in Biha.

Adoption of Winter Maize technology helped increasing total Maize production from 6.95 lakh tonnes in 1980-81 to 14.4 lakh tonnes in 2003-04. Whereas Winter Maize production increased by more than three-fold that is; from 1.97 lakh tonnes in 1980-81 to 6 lakh tonnes in 2003-04, contributing 28.34 per cent and 41.66 per cent of respective total Maize production (Govt. of Bihar, 2006). In 1980-81, Winter Maize contributes only 2.37 per cent to total foodgrain production in Bihar which increased to 5.34 per cent in the year 2003-04, indicating a substantial contribution of Winter Maize to food grain production in Bihar. There was a set back to Winter Maize production in Zone-I in mid-nineties, when Winter Maize production declined.

The main reason for decline in production has been the

declining trend in area under Winter Maize, which was attributed mainly due to decline in real price of Maize and distorted marketing arrangement. There was apparent shift of Winter Maize area to Wheat, Spices and Vegetables which had comparatively high price and better market.

Moreover, Zone-II is the late adapter of Winter Maize technology and farmers of this zone could not afford to shift their Winter Maize area to Spices and Vegetables since agro-climatic situation is not favourable for growing these crops.

Winter Maize showed an increasing trend in both the zones (Zone-IIIA and Zone-IIIB), the farmers might not face major problem of marketing due to low level of Winter Maize production. Hence, it may be inferred that the adoption of Winter Maize production contributed significantly to quantum of food grain production in Bihar, but could not sustain due to poor marketing arrangements and lack of local demand for Maize in Bihar.

EMPLOYMENT GENERATION

Employment is the main source of livelihood in rural area, particularly for weaker section of society. Lack of employment opportunity is considered to be the main reason for large scale poverty in rural Bihar. In this context labour-intensive agricultural activities should be preferred to provide employment opportunities to farm workers who constitute more than 77 per cent of working force in Bihar. Production of Winter Maize is known to be a labour-intensive enterprise. Despite mechanization labour employment in Winter Maize production is worked out to be 130 man-days that is; 88 males and 42 females. It has been estimated that the Winter Maize cultivation generates annual human labour employment of about 309 lakh man days in Bihar.

Out of 309 lakh man days of employment generation. 286 lakh man- days were generated for employment of hired agricultural labour whose livelihood is dependent on wage earning. Family labour of farm households could also find employment of 23.2 lakh man-days in cultivation of Winter Maize in Bihar. In addition to generation of employment Winter Maize is helping farming community for creating

TABLE 2

Farm Size-wise Generation of Human Labour Employment in Winter Maize Cultivation in Bihar

(lakh man-days)

Farm size	*Family labour*	*Hired labour*	*Total labour*
Marginal	2.5	13.1	15.6
	(16.0)	(84.0)	(100.00)
Small	2.1	13.5	15.6
	(13.5)	(86.5)	(100.00)
Medium	5.8	53.5	59.3
	(9.8)	(99.2)	(100.00)
Large	12.9	205.6	218.4
	(23.2)	(94.1)	(100.00)
Total	23.5	285.7	308.9
	(7.51)	(92.5)	(100.00)

Note: Figures in parentheses indicate percentage to respective totals.
Source: Estimate on the basis of thesis submitted by R.K. Singh (2005), entitled " A Study on Rationable of Resource Use Efficiency in Wheat and Winter Maize Production in Khagria District", Deptt. of Agril. Economics, R.A.U., Pusa.

employment is slack agricultural period, particularly in months of Oct., Feb., and May. When wages of these hired agricultural labour are computed @ Rs. 50/day, the total wage earnings of hired labours are worked out to be Rs. 142.85 crore. Hence, it may be said that the Winter Maize cultivation generates annual employment of 309 lakh man-days and increase income flow of Rs. 142.85 lakh in terms of wages to agricultural labour households in Bihar.

FARM INCOME

An effort has been made to estimate the farm income flow through adoption of Winter Maize technology in Bihar. Net cash in flow includes net value of Winter Maize production, value of by product and inputed value of family

human labour. Imputed value of land is not considered as cash in flow since these land could be used otherwise also in case of non-adoption of Winter Maize technology.

Analysis of data revealed that the total annual farm net income increased by Rs. 1960 million through cultivation of Winter Maize in Bihar. In Bihar, annual Winter Maize production at the triennium ending 2003-04 is estimated to be 6.0 lakh tonnes and its value on market price (Rs. 4450/ tonne) is worked out to be Rs. 2670 (Table 3) million.

TABLE 3

Total Farm Income in Winter-Maize Production in Bihar

Sl. No.	*Particulars*	*Maize production (in lakh tonnes)*	*By product (in lakh tonnes)*	*Family labour wages (in lakh days)*
1.	Quantity of production/employment	6.0	6.0	23.2
2.	Price/Rs. tonnes/per day	4450.0	300.00	50.0
3.	Total value (in Rs.)	2670	180	116
4.	Expenses/tonnes (Rs./tonnes)	3220	–	–
5.	Total expenses	1932	–	–
6.	Farm income (3-4)	730	180	116

But per tonne production cost of Winter Maize is Rs. 3220, hence net income through main product is worked out to be Rs. 730 million . When by product value of Rs. 180 million (6 million tonnes @ Rs. 300/tonnes) and imputed wage of family human labour (Rs. 116 million) are added, total annual income through Winter Maize production is estimated to be Rs. 1960 million.

The above estimate is worked out with average productivity of Winter Maize reported by the Government of Bihar. However, various studies indicated much high yield (75 quintals/ha). If farm income is estimated on the basis of productivity of 75 quintals/ha, annual farm income through Winter Maize production would be more than Rs. 85 thousand million in Bihar.

COST OF PRODUCTION

Adoption of Winter Maize technology helped increasing production and productivity of Maize in Bihar. An increase in productivity means higher output for each level in input. If the yield increases without increase in fixed costs per hectare, then the cost per quintal will fall, due to per quintal less fixed cost.

Per quintal cost of production of Winter Maize (at current price) increased from Rs. 261 in 1995-96 to Rs. 322 in 2003-04. But the real cost of production of Winter Maize declined from Rs. 209 (at 1993-94 prices) in 1995 to Rs. 174 in 2000-01 which marginally increased to Rs. 178 in 2003-04 (Table 4).

TABLE 4

Cost of Production of Winter Maize at Current Price and 1993-94 Prices

Year	*WPI at 1993-94 prices*	*Cost of production per quintal at current prices (in Rupees)*	*Cost of production prices per quintal at 1993-94 (in Rupees)*
1995-96	125	261	209
1997-98	136	277	203
2000-01	162	282	174
2003-04	181	322	178

Source: Economic Survey, 2005.

Hence, it may be said that per quintal real cost of production of Winter Maize declined by Rs. 31 per quintal during last eight years, indicating a nominal annual saving of Rs. 186 million (6 lakh tonnes production x Rs. 310) due to reduction in per quintal cost of Winter Maize production in Bihar.

FOOD AND NUTRITIONAL SECURITY

Rapid productivity increase in agriculture sector has led to gain the per capita production, reduced unit cost and price, and increased income and purchasing power, especially for weaker section of society. But State of Bihar failed to achieve required rate of growth in production of principal food grain crops namely; Rice and Wheat, but Winter Maize production has increased by more than three-fold during last two and half decades. Despite increase in population, per capita annual availability of Winter Maize production increased from 3.77 kgs in 1980-81 to 6.70 kgs in 2003-04. winter Maize is a surplus food grain in Bihar because per capita availability is about three times more than the actual consumption of maize in Bihar. (5.4 kgs/year/per capita-NSSO 1999). Hence, an increase in Winter Maize production has improved the physical and economics access to food, particularly to weaker section of society.

REDUCTION IN PRICE

An increase in supply of Winter Maize through adoption of modern technology is likely to have an impact on price of Winter Maize in Bihar, whereas Maize producers are adversely affected due to reduction in price. However, there is clear-cut evidence of reduction in per quintal cost of production of Winter Maize due to adoption of modern technology. It leads to substantial benefits for consumers of Winter Maize, particularly to weaker section of society and the livestock sector through cheap supply of feed.

As a result, the reduction in real price is likely to have beneficial impact on welfare of consumers of Winter Maize who could be able to have more access to food grain/feed on a given amount of money. However, the harvest price of Winter Maize picked-up during last 4-5 years (Table 5). It was mainly due to intervention of traders and industrialists of Gujarat, Maharastra and Delhi who started purchasing Winter Maize from farmers, particularly in Begusarai and Khagaria districts. But there is an urgent need to have public intervention in maize marketing to sustain its production in winter season in' Bihar.

TABLE 5

Real Price Index of Maize during 1993-2001-02 (at 1993 Price)

Year	*Price Index*
1993-94	100.00
1994-95	126.38
1995-96	126.65
1996-97	111.82
1997-98	109.74
1998-99	113.24
1999-2000	114.90
2000-01	106.32

Source: Report of the Commission for Agricultural Costs and Price, 2002-03), Deptt. of Agriculture and Co-operation, Ministry of Agriculture, Govt. of India, New Delhi (2003), p. 423.

PROCESS OF INDUSTRIALIZATION

Maize is used a staple food, animal feed and raw material for industrial products. In developed states, a larger proportion of Maize is used as livestock feed. In Bihar also, there is prospect of feed industry which is bound to be flourished due to various reasons. An increasing per capita income has taken upward trend which has been the main reason for changing consumption pattern towards protective and proteins food. This requires more animal product and consequently the demand for animal product and consequently the demand for animal feed may increase many fold. Maize is used extensively as the main source of calories in animal feeding and feed formulation as it gives the highest conversion of dry substance to meat, milk and eggs as compared to other cereal grains. About 10 lakh tonnes of Maize produced in Bihar is surplus to human consumption which could be used as raw material for the feed and other industries under the changed political-economic scenario of Bihar. Winter Maize production is likely to increase by 10 per cent annually, enhancing Maize production of 15.6 lakh tonnes by 2017 which will contribute significantly to demand

for maize industries in Country in general and Bihar, in particular.

MARKET ORIENTATION

Various studies revealed that the Winter Maize is grown for market purposes. A study conducted in the Department of Agril. Economics, Rajendra Agricultural University, Pusa (Bihar) found that 98 per cent of Winter Maize is sold and 2 per cent is kept for home consumption including feed. Proportion of sale to total production increases with the increase in size of landholdings. The study of maize marketing behaviour of farmers indicated that the itinerant traders still play an important role in Winter Maize marketing.

Winter Maize is produced for market purposes in Bihar, which increased the market orientation of farmers. But farmers are still mainly dependent on local traders for Winter Maize marketing who offer them low price and adopt mal-practices in purchase of Winter Maize. Farmers do not adopt any practice of grading of Winter Maize and devoid of any marketing information, particularly prices pertaining in different markets. Regulated markets do not provide any facility to farmers. In changed liberalized marketing scenario of Bihar; there is a need to initiate institutional efforts to motivate Winter Maize growing farmers through market-led extension activities for increasing the market orientation of farmers.

CONCLUSIONS

Winter Maize technology is a relatively new innovation which got perfection after the establishment of Rajendra Agricultural University, at Pusa, Bihar. Its adoption was concentrated mainly in North-West alluvial plains of Bihar (Zone-I) upto early nineties however it is now cultivated at large scale in Zone-II and Zone-IIIA also. In Bihar, adoption of Winter Maize cultivation increased the food grain production by 6 million tonnes annually and generates farm income of Rs. 1960 million and employment of 309 lakh man-days. Due to increased productivity per quintal real cost of production declined by Rs. 31 during last eight years which helped farmers in saving about Rs. 186 million. The adoption of Winter Maize improved the physical and economic access to food also, particularly of weaker section of society due to increase in production and decline in market and real prices of Maize in Bihar.

Maize production at lower cost results in cheap raw material for maize based industries hence it may help in accelerating process of industrialization in Bihar. There is a clear cut evidence that Winter Maize is produced for market purposes which leads to more market orientation to farmers in Bihar which is a sign of moving farm economic from subsistence to surplus economy. Due to higher productivity of Winter Maize, agriculture labour wage has increased in Maize growing districts and labour migration is also at low level in these districts. Hence, it reduces labour out migration from Maize growing districts due to higher wages and regular employment opportunities.

Finally, it may be concluded that the Winter Maize is generating net cash inflow of Rs. 3575 million annually. Besides it creates employment for family and agricultural labour, improves food security, particularly to weaker section of society, improves farmer's exposure to market and helps reducing labour out migration from Bihar.

References

Annual Report (1989). Maize Co-ordinated Project, Rajendra Agricultural University, Pusa, Samastipur, Bihar.

Govt. of Bihar, Statistical handbook, Govt. of Bihar (Various issues).

Govt. of India (2005), Economic Survey of India, Ministry of Finance, Govt. of India, New Delhi.

Singh, R.K. (2005), thesis submitted by entitled "A Study on Rationable of Resource Use Efficiency in Wheat and Winter Maize Production in Khagaria District", (Unpublished) Deptt. of Agril. Economics, R.A.U., Pusa, Bihar, Samastipur.

Report of the Commission for Agricultural Costs and Price (2002-03), Deptt. of Agriculture and Co-operation, Ministry of Agriculture, Govt. of India, New Delhi (2003), p. 423.

24

A Critical Analysis on Suicides of Farmers and Farm Loan Waivers

WISHWANATH KUMAR

Since globalization India is on the verge of take-off. During this period, industrial sectors have registered an impressive growth rate of about 7 to 9 per cent per annum, regarding agricultural sector there are several concerns, i.e. disguised unemployment, division of labour and land disputes, inadequate irrigation, lack of fertilizers and high breed seeds, water logging, land degradation, depletion of soil fertility land erosion, rate of surface irrigation has increased and ground water level have declined, etc. causes low rate of yield in farming. Its growth rate was less than 2 per cent in the last decade. While globalization policies and world trade organization agreements have created many international challenges to the farmers.

Obviously, the benefit of economic growth has not perlocated in right ways, resulting widening in the gap between the rich and poor. The basic problem is that there is some unethical in the system of government that does not value the lives of the poor farmers. Unfortunately, social support system (SSS) are disappearing leaving the farmers in isolation and hopelessness. This is the reason that 1.5 lakh farmers who taken their own lives between 1997-2005. About two-third did so in the state of Maharashtra, Andhra Pradesh, Karnataka and Madhya Pradesh. All four states shown an ascending trend in farmer's suicide. In 2005, these four states accounted for 43.9 per cent of all suicides and 64 per cent of all farmer suicides in the country. The following table presenting the study on farmer's suicides in India between 1997 and 2005. The study draw on data from the National Crime Records Bureau.

TABLE I

Year	*Total Suicides*	*Farmer Suicides*		*Pesticides Suicides*	
		Number of Suicides	*% of total Suicides*	*Number of Pesticide*	*% of Total Suicides*
1997	95829	13622	14.2	18311	19.1
1998	104713	16015	15.3	19075	15.3
1999	110587	16082	14.5	20251	18.3
2000	108593	16603	15.3	21801	20.1
2001	108506	16415	15.1	21530	19.8
2002	110417	17971	16.3	21414	19.5
2003	110851	17164	15.5	23001	20.8
2004	113697	18241	16.0	23311	20.5
2005	113914	17131	15.0	22316	19.6
Total Suicides 1997-2005	977107	149244		191010	

Source: The Hindu, November 12, 2007, p. 11.

The number of Indians committing suicides in each year rose from around 96,000 in 1997 to roughly 1.14 lakh in 2005. In the same period the number of farmers taking their own lives each year rapidly increased from 18 thousand in 1997 to 22 thousand in 2005.

FARM LOAN WAIVER

There have been several discussion within the government and outside, regarding policies for the revival of

the agriculture. Its development is an important component of inclusive growth. The government of India placed a National Policy for Farmers in Parliament. The document is based on the draft submitted by the National Commission of Farmers in October 2006. It is for the first time that this policy have recognized the need to focus on the economic well-being of the farmers. An expert group has identified the inadequacies and inappropriateness of several components in the packages introduced by the central and state governments that peek to stop the suicides. Some of the major conclusions are:

- The design of the relief measures is not based on the felt needs of households.
- There is a lack region and household specific flexibility build into the package.
- Implementation structures tend to be fragmented and there is little convergence and synergy among the different components.

The decision to waive farm loans on an unprecedented scale announced in the latest budget has attracted the people of the country. The budget speech has announced the decision to waire farm loans also estimated the cost Rs. 60,000 crore that government has to bear. It does not spell out the basis of the estimate nor of the institutions, loan categories and class of borrowers that will be covered by the scheme.

About 22 per cent of the farmers had taken loan from public institutions while others had borrowed from private moneylenders and relatives to repay institutional loans. The farmers had taken loans not only for farming but also for wedding and medical emergencies or to adopt high cost technology such as improvement in irrigation system, tractor or high breed seeds in the expectation of higher returns. Therefore, the resource less poor farmer is unable to face the shock of a crop failure. Between 70-90 per cent farmers with less than two hectares taken loan from moneylenders. In real terms, these farmers who need to be save from the clutches of moneylenders. Some people argue that the loan waiver scheme is discriminatory because government wants to check prices of food grains to safeguard the interests of consumers, it should subsidies them but this should not be happen at the cost of the poor farmers.

At present, it is accepted by all the people of the country, that the loan waiver is a best temporary decision to the problems facing rural India. Significant and sustained improvement in the welfare of the rural people is not possible without a faster pace of growth in the rural economy and improvement in education and other important awareness about health services.

References

A. Vaidyanathan: "Farm Loan Waiver: A Closure Look and Critique", *The Hindu*, 6th March, 2008, p. 11.

M.S. Swaminathan: "Farm Killing Fields to Smiling Fields", *The Hindu*, 17th October, 2007.

P. Sainath: "Farm Suicides rising, most Intense in 4 States", *The Hindu*, 12th November 2007, p. 11.

Index